CHICAGO PUBLIC LIBRARY

R03001 85641

# ALL ABOUT
# RETIREMENT FUNDS

D1522351

CHICAGO PUBLIC LIBRARY
WRIGHTWOOD ASHBURN BRANCH
8530 S. KEDZIE 60652

## OTHER TITLES IN THE "ALL ABOUT . . ." SERIES

# ALL ABOUT RETIREMENT FUNDS
## The Easy Way to Get Started

**ELLIE WILLIAMS**
**DIANE PEARL**

## McGraw-Hill

New York  Chicago  San Francisco  Lisbon  London  Madrid
Mexico City  Milan  New Delhi  San Juan  Seoul
Singapore  Sydney  Toronto

Copyright © 2004 by The McGraw-Hill Companies, Inc. All rights reserved. Printed in the United States of America. Except as permitted under the United States Copyright Act of 1976, no part of this publication may be reproduced or distributed in any form or by any means, or stored in a data base or retrieval system, without prior written permission of the publisher.

1 2 3 4 5 6 7 8 9 0   AGM/AGM   0 9 8 7 6 5 4 3

ISBN 0-07-138749-8

This publication is designed to provide accurate and authoritative information in regard to the subject matter covered. It is sold with the understanding that the publisher is not engaged in rendering legal, accounting or other professional service. If legal advice or other expert assistance is required, the services of a competent professional person should be sought.

*—From a Declaration of Principles Jointly Adopted by a Committee of the American Bar Association and a Committed of Publishers and Associations.*

McGraw-Hill books are available at special discounts to use as premiums and sales promotions, or for use in corporate training programs. For more information, please write to the Director of Special Sales, Professional Publishing, McGraw-Hill, Two Penn Plaza, New York, NY 10011-2298. Or contact your local bookstore.

This book is printed on recycled, acid-free paper containing a minimum of 50% recycled de-inked paper.

**Library of Congress Cataloging-in-Publication Data**

Williams, Ellie.
    All about retirement funds  /  by Ellie Williams and Diane Pearl.
       p.    cm.—(The All about series)
    ISBN 0-07-138749-8 (pbk. : alk. paper)
1. Finance, Personal.  2. Retirement—Planning.  3. Pension trusts.
4. Annuities.  5. Retirement income.  I. Pearl, Diane.  II Title.
III. "All about—" series (McGraw-Hill)
  HG179.W5339  2004
  332.024'01—dc21

                                       2003007729

*To Diane's children, Alexandra and Matthew Pearl, who are fighting a rare, deadly disease called Fanconi anemia. The only hope for children with Fanconi anemia is a bone marrow transplant, and a simple blood test is all it takes to find out whether you are a potential match. You can find out more at www.marrow.org, the National Marrow Donor Program's Web site, or by calling the Heart of America at (800) 366-6710. To follow Alex and Matthew's story, go to www.AlexandMatt.com.*

*Thank You*

*As always, special thanks goes to our families, Kip, Mark, and Nathan, and Mark, Austin, Alex, and Matthew.*

CHICAGO PUBLIC LIBRARY
WRIGHTWOOD ASHBURN BRANCH
8530 S. KEDZIE 60652

# CONTENTS

R07109 82023

**Appendix A**

**Appendix B**

**Appendix C**

You have probably been planning for your retirement for several years now, perhaps many years. If you have carefully worked out your plan, your retirement should be all set. But what if the Nasdaq plummets 50 percent the year before you retire, as it did in 2000? What if your company dissolves into bankruptcy in a matter of months, as did the once highly respected Enron, leaving your 401(k) account worthless? What if a recession puts your high-paying job or successful small business in jeopardy? What if Social Security goes bankrupt because our politicians can't agree on a way to save it? What if sending your children to college costs twice as much as you thought it would?

If you think your retirement is bulletproof, then sit back and wait to live the high life. But if you have even one question about retirement plans, if you want to maximize your returns and reduce your risk, read on. Learn how different retirement plans work, how to choose the best plan, and how to combine different plans for the biggest benefit. Find out how different investment strategies can make your nest egg grow and how to apply them at different stages of your life.

In this book we will address all the pieces of the retirement puzzle. We begin with finding out how much money you will need and how much you should be saving now. There are many variables you can't control, but there are many that you can. We will show you that there are several ways to reach the same answer; then you can choose what you want to change. The obvious choices are to save more now or spend less in retirement; however, there are several other effective strategies. Adjusting your retirement date by just a few years can make a big difference, as can changing your investment allocations.

The vehicles you use for investing can also have a profound influence on your retirement because many offer significant financial benefits. This means more money in your pocket. If your employer has a retirement plan, it may be called a 401(k), 457, or 403(b) plan. Don't be confused by all the numbers. With just a few exceptions, the only difference among these plans is the type of employer that offers them. Your employer plan should be your starting point for retirement saving. Why? Contributions to your plan are tax deductible, and annual contribution limits are high ($12,000 in 2003). Your money grows tax deferred, meaning that you won't pay taxes on any income or growth until you withdraw the funds. Perhaps the best part of investing in your employer plan is that you can do it without thinking. Having contributions taken out of your paycheck keeps you from spending your retirement savings now. We can't say it often enough: Always pay yourself first.

Most likely, you have some type of Individual Retirement Account (IRA), either a traditional IRA or a Roth IRA. If you are relatively young and qualify under the IRS income limits [$150,000 modified adjusted gross income (MAGI) for joint filers], you should learn more about Roth IRAs. While you won't receive a current tax deduction for contributions, all withdrawals during retirement are tax free if you follow the rules. That means your money grows for you from now until retirement and you never pay taxes on the income or gains. It may make sense for you to convert your traditional IRAs to Roth IRAs right now. You'll pay current income taxes on the money you convert, but the advantages in retirement can be significant. We'll talk about how to make that decision and who qualifies in Chapter 4.

You may be hearing a lot about insurance products, both life insurance and annuities, as vehicles for retirement saving. There are tax advantages to these products, but beware, there are disadvantages as well. We'll talk about the trade-offs in Chapter 5.

Knowing how much to save and which accounts to choose is a big step in the right direction. The next step is making investment decisions. For years, professionals have been preaching diversification. In a phrase, that means, "Don't keep all your eggs in one basket." Put some money in the stock market, some in bonds, some in cash, and maybe some in real estate. To take the concept further, you must diversify within your stock-based investments. Spread out your industries, and then buy some old, boring companies along with the small, new companies. Go for high growth in some places, and have a few with nice fat dividends too. In the 1990s, anyone who diversified was probably disappointed with their investment returns. The risk takers, whose plans were 100 percent invested in the technology fund of the day, were earning 30, 40, or even 50 percent in some years. But then the bear market came and wiped out all of those gains, and more. If you were one of those high-fliers, what should you do now? It isn't too late to diversify. Avoid the temptation to be aggressive to try to make those losses back quickly; dividing your money among different places makes it more likely that you'll catch the group that emerges as a market leader.

This book is for anyone who wants to get a better handle on investing for retirement. If you are just starting out and want to get on the right track fast, read here to learn about retirement plans and strategies in plain, ordinary English. If you are an old pro at retirement investing and are a bit shaken by the stock market of the last several years, it's time to get more involved with your investment decisions. Reevaluate your investing strategies, because "buy and hold" doesn't always work in this environment. Whatever your investor profile, learning to take advantage of the opportunities available and brushing up on your investing skills should yield a more comfortable retirement and a better night's sleep right now.

# CHAPTER 1

# How Much Money Will You Need?

**"R**etirement is coming! Retirement is coming!" You read about it in the newspaper, see it on television, and hear it on the radio. Does this cry echo the crazy panic of Chicken Little or the valuable warning of Paul Revere? The answer depends on how much you will need in retirement. If you are saving enough now, those chants may seem to be saying "The sky is falling" when it isn't. But, if you are like many people, your retirement needs may outweigh your current planning and saving, so you had better listen as if the voice were Paul Revere's.

The difficulty of retirement planning is its parameters—an undetermined amount of money, to last an unknown length of time, in a highly volatile financial environment including fluctuations in the stock market, the cost of living, medical care, taxes, and Social Security.

## THE VARIABLES

Is it possible to know just how much you will need in retirement? Unfortunately, it isn't. There are many variables, just some of which follow:

- Your lifestyle
- The age at which you retire

- When you begin retirement investing
- How long you will live
- Your Social Security benefits
- Your company pension benefits
- The total return on your retirement investments
- The rate of inflation
- Income tax rates
- Changes in retirement plan laws

Understanding these variables, especially those that you can control, is the first step in realizing a sensible savings plan for retirement. The old computer acronym GIGO, which stands for garbage in, garbage out, is very important to keep in mind when planning your retirement. Your estimate of how much you should save for retirement will be only as accurate as the variables you put into the formula.

## Your Lifestyle and Its Costs

Michelle and Steve have four children, all of whom live within 20 miles of their parents. They are devoted grandparents and prefer entertaining in their home to vacationing in exotic locales. Meg and Kurt have three children, two of whom are in graduate school on opposite coasts. Having worked, saved, and sacrificed during their children's growing years, they look forward to a retirement that includes travel and a winter home in a warmer climate. Will these two couples need the same amount of money to support their chosen lifestyle in retirement? Probably not. Decide now what your retirement lifestyle will be, so that your financial situation doesn't decide for you during retirement. Don't let a lack of planning dictate how you spend a much-deserved rest.

Most experts agree that, if your lifestyle in retirement is similar to your preretirement lifestyle, you will need less income. The rationale behind this comes from reduced costs in some or all of the following preretirement expense categories:

- Commuting, including gasoline, parking, and wear on your car

- Business wardrobe and supplies, such as suits and briefcases
- Business meals if they are not reimbursed
- Mortgage payments, which may be either completed or reduced by moving to a smaller home
- Retirement saving, which will no longer be necessary
- Income taxes, which will be lower if you are spending your savings rather than drawing an income

The last two cost categories are likely to be the most significant. Consider what percentage of your current income you are saving for retirement. The absence of this expense is an immediate saving during retirement. If you currently earn a high income but will not be working during retirement, you may see a substantial savings in income taxes. However, keep in mind that if you will be withdrawing from a qualified retirement plan, such as a 401(k) or an IRA, during retirement, you will be paying current income taxes on the funds that you withdraw. If the bulk of your retirement savings is in such plans, you may find that your income tax expense does not change greatly.

There are two ways to compute how much annual income you may need. The most common is to begin with your current income or expenses and multiply that number by a given percentage to estimate future income needs.

---

**Retirement Tip**   A general rule of thumb is to calculate retirement income needs at 75 percent of current income. If you expect your life to include extensive travel, financial help for your children or grandchildren, a retirement home in a more desirable climate, or expensive hobbies or activities, a figure nearer to 100 percent of your preretirement income may be more accurate.

---

Another method analyzes all current expenses and attempts to figure how each will change during retirement. When doing this, compute each of your current expenses just as you would when determining a budget. Deduct the items that you will no longer incur, make reductions in those that will exist to a lesser extent, add expenses that you expect but do not incur now, and estimate your necessary income from there. These two methods may or may not yield similar results. We recommend you try both. If you can't decide which method to work with, keep in mind that it is better to err on the conservative side and expect to need a higher income.

## Your Retirement Age

You may be 50 or you may be 70. You may wish you could retire tomorrow, or you may not want to retire at all. As you consider your options, keep in mind that the age at which you and/or your spouse leave your full-time jobs has a significant impact on your retirement planning. There are three things that happen if you choose to retire earlier rather than later:

1.  The sooner you begin drawing Social Security benefits, the smaller the amount you will receive annually. Under current (2003) law, full retirement age (the age at which you can receive full benefits) ranges from 65 for individuals born before 1938 to 67 for individuals born in 1960 or later. No matter what your full retirement age, you can begin drawing a reduced level of benefits as early as age 62. Details on full retirement ages and reductions for early withdrawal of benefits can be found in Chapter 6.

---

**Retirement Dilemma**  Greg is 60, earns $50,000 per year, and saves $4500 each year for retirement. He is trying to decide whether to retire this year or next. He estimates that his annual retirement expenses will be approximately $40,000. What will be the difference in his financial situation if he retires now?

| | |
|---|---|
| Annual living expenses withdrawn from savings | $40,000 |
| Savings not deposited to his retirement fund | 4,500 |
| Cost of retiring this year rather than next year | $44,500 |

Now consider what $44,500 could earn in his retirement account in the future. After 10 years, at 8 percent, that $44,500 would be worth $96,072. That makes an expensive year of early retirement.

2. For each year in which you do not earn an income, you cannot add to your retirement savings.

3. For each year in which you do not earn an income, you reduce your retirement savings by your living expenses for that year.

The second two items combined can really make a difference over just a few years.

## When You Begin Retirement Investing

It is never too early or too late to start building a retirement nest egg. Obviously, the earlier you can start saving, the more you will have later. Just looking at the numbers should convince you to get on the road to saving as soon as possible. (See Table 1-1.)

Table 1-1 shows how important it is to begin saving early. A 25-year-old can accumulate over $1 million for retirement by investing $3000 each year in a tax-deferred account that earns 10 percent. Even after taxes at 28 percent on investment growth, the retiree who began investing at age 25 would net nearly $990,000.

---

**Retirement Dilemma**   Megan and Brian work for the same company and are 25 years old. They are both eligible for their 401(k) plan, but they can't decide when they should start investing. Brian doesn't think he can afford 401(k) contributions right now, and he has decided to wait 10 years until age 35 and then begin investing $2000 each year until he retires at age 65. Megan wants to begin investing $2000 annually right away, but stop in 10 years. Considering the two scenarios, who will have accumulated the most money at age 65, assuming an 8 percent average return and identical tax situations?

**Solution**   If you said Megan, you were right. Due to the power of compounding, she would collect $291,547 on contributions of just $20,000. Starting later, Brian would only have $226,566 after contributing $60,000. You can see that your money works much harder when you give it more time to grow.

## TABLE 1-1

If You Invest $3000 Each Year, How Much Will You Have at 65?*

| Beginning Age | 5% Return | 10% Return | 15% Return |
|---|---|---|---|
| 25 | $362,399 | $1,327,778 | $5,337,271 |
| 35 | 199,317 | 493,482 | 1,304,235 |
| 45 | 99,198 | 171,825 | 307,331 |
| 55 | 37,734 | 47,812 | 60,911 |

*Before any taxes due at withdrawal.

## How Long You Will Live

None of us like to think about our own mortality, and in this exercise, it is better that you don't. People are living longer these days, and it isn't unlikely that you and/or your spouse will live past the age of 80 or 90, so plan for a long life and don't outlive your savings.

## Your Social Security Benefits

You don't have to look far for reports that Social Security, our taxpayer-funded retirement system, is on borrowed time. While you might think that the Social Security taxes you pay are deposited into a fund for your retirement, they are not. Social Security is a pass-through system, in which the payroll taxes of the working population are collected and then paid out to retirees. Funds are saved for later use only when more dollars are collected in taxes than are paid out in benefits. As the Baby Boomer population ages, experts predict that there will be only two tax-paying workers for every benefit-collecting retiree. Right now, that number is over three. Expectations are that many in this generation will pay much more into the system in the form of Social Security taxes than they will ever collect in benefits.

If you are 25 or older and working, you should receive a Social Security statement each year about 3 months before your birthday. This statement will include a record of your earnings history and, if you have worked and paid Social Security taxes for at least 10 years, an estimate of your retirement benefits. If your earnings record contains errors or you don't receive a statement, call the Social Security Administration at (800) 772-1213 or report it at *www.ssa.gov/mystatement*. Table 1-2 provides estimates of average Social Security benefits, and Chapter 6 discusses Social Security in more detail.

## Your Pension Plan

In years past, many working Americans depended on employer-funded pension plans to support them in retirement. These retirement plans, which often guarantee a certain percentage of your salary as a monthly retirement benefit (called a *defined benefit*), are tremendously expensive for the employer. Not only is it necessary for an employer to put away large sums of money to fund the plan, the funds can become an unexpected liability if the investments in the plan do not perform well enough to pay the benefits promised. As a result, many businesses have replaced pension plans with employee contribution plans such as 401(k), 403(b), or 457 plans. If you are lucky enough to work for a company that still offers a defined-benefit pension plan, periodically check your expected benefit level. If you are considering a new job, look at *vesting periods*—that is, the employment periods required to receive full benefits. Staying with your current employer for a few more years may provide a big financial benefit if you are not yet fully vested. If you are married and either you or your spouse has a pension plan, check into spousal benefits, should the primary beneficiary die.

**TABLE 1-2**

Estimated Average Monthly Social Security Benefits

| | |
|---|---|
| All retired workers | $ 895 |
| Aged couple, both receiving benefits | 1,483 |
| Widowed mother and two children | 1,838 |
| Aged widow(er) alone | 862 |
| Disabled worker, spouse, and children | 1,395 |
| All disabled workers | 833 |

*Source:* Social Security Administration, data as of January 2003.

## The Total Return on Your Investments

The amount of money you make on your investments can make a big difference in how much money you will have available at retirement. The sum of any dividends or interest you receive and changes in the principal value of your investment equal your total return. In an investment such as a money market account, your total return comes only from interest. In many growth stocks, your total return comes only from an increase in the value of each share. In other stocks or mutual funds, your total return may be derived from a combination of dividends or interest and an increase in share value.

When the stock market was roaring during the 1990s, it was not uncommon to see retirement models that called for annual total returns far in excess of the stock market's historical 10 percent total return. However, experts are now calling the 20 to 30 percent annual stock market returns of the last decade an aberration unlikely to be repeated in our lifetimes. Without these huge gains, small differences in return can become even more important. To see how just a few percentage points difference in total return can make a big difference in dollars earned, see Table 1-3.

**TABLE 1-3**

Total Return and Your Retirement Fund: How Much Will You Have at Age 65?

| Average Annual Total Return | Beginning Age / Investing $200 Each Month* | | | |
| --- | --- | --- | --- | --- |
| | 25 | 35 | 45 | 55 |
| 3% | $ 185,675 | $ 116,839 | $ 65,825 | $28,018 |
| 5 | 306,476 | 167,145 | 82,549 | 31,186 |
| 8 | 702,856 | 300,059 | 118,589 | 36,833 |
| 10 | 1,275,356 | 455,865 | 153,139 | 41,310 |
| 15 | 6,280,751 | 1,401,964 | 303,191 | 55,731 |

*Investments made at the beginning of the month.

## The Effects of Inflation

Your biggest enemy in long-range investment planning is inflation. Inflation can best be explained as a general increase in the prices of everyday goods and services. You may be saving for retirement with the idea that you can live comfortably on $75,000 per year. If you reach retirement and find that buying the same things you buy now costs $120,000, not $75,000, you could be in real trouble. In retirement, what you are really striving for is not a certain sum of money but a level of consumption, the ability to maintain a particular lifestyle. This is best described as *purchasing power*.

The fact that purchasing power and fixed dollars are not the same can be attributed to inflation (or in rare instances, deflation). In the past 10 years, we have experienced relatively low levels of inflation, ranging from 2 to 3 percent. With an annual inflation rate of 3 percent, it will take $1.03 next year to buy what $1.00 will buy today. That may not seem like much, but check Table 1-4 to see that, over 20 years, just 3 percent inflation can reduce the purchasing power of $1.00 to $0.55. That is a loss of nearly half your purchasing power. At a level of 6 percent, your purchasing power drops to only $0.31.

The argument for investing your long-term retirement funds in growth investments has much to do with inflation and the concept of *real returns*. The real return on an investment is its total return less the rate of inflation.

---

**Retirement Tip**  Total return – inflation rate = real return.

---

For example, if you have an investment whose total return (dividends or interest plus price change) is 10 percent, such as a growth or balanced mutual fund, while the rate of inflation is 4 percent, its real return is 6 percent (10 percent – 4 percent = 6 percent). If you have another investment, such as a money market

## TABLE 1-4

The Purchasing Power of $1 Over Time at Various Rates of Inflation

| | Inflation Rate | | | | | |
|---|---|---|---|---|---|---|
| Years | 2% | 3% | 4% | 6% | 8% | 10% |
| 5 | $0.91 | $0.86 | $0.82 | $0.75 | $0.68 | $0.62 |
| 6 | 0.88 | 0.84 | 0.79 | 0.70 | 0.63 | 0.56 |
| 7 | 0.87 | 0.81 | 0.76 | 0.65 | 0.58 | 0.51 |
| 8 | 0.85 | 0.79 | 0.73 | 0.63 | 0.54 | 0.47 |
| 9 | 0.84 | 0.77 | 0.70 | 0.59 | 0.50 | 0.42 |
| 10 | 0.82 | 0.74 | 0.68 | 0.56 | 0.46 | 0.39 |
| 15 | 0.74 | 0.64 | 0.56 | 0.42 | 0.32 | 0.24 |
| 20 | 0.67 | 0.55 | 0.46 | 0.31 | 0.21 | 0.15 |
| 25 | 0.61 | 0.48 | 0.38 | 0.23 | 0.15 | 0.09 |
| 30 | 0.55 | 0.41 | 0.31 | 0.17 | 0.10 | 0.06 |
| 35 | 0.50 | 0.36 | 0.25 | 0.13 | 0.07 | 0.04 |
| 40 | 0.45 | 0.31 | 0.21 | 0.10 | 0.05 | 0.02 |
| 45 | 0.41 | 0.26 | 0.17 | 0.07 | 0.03 | 0.01 |
| 50 | 0.37 | 0.23 | 0.14 | 0.05 | 0.02 | 0.01 |

account, whose total return is 3 percent, its real return is −1 percent (3 percent − 4 percent = −1 percent). The argument for growth investments follows the concept that many low-return, fixed-income investments, while considered *safe*, can have negative real returns. After inflation, you lose purchasing power.

## Changes in Income Tax Rates

• Changes in income tax rates could have a significant effect on your retirement if you are currently investing in tax-deferred plans such as 401(k), 403(b), or 457 plans and/or traditional IRAs. Because you do not pay current income taxes on the funds invested in a 401(k), 403(b), or 457 plan (and in some instances, traditional IRAs) and you do not pay current income taxes on capital gains and income earned by those funds, you must pay the taxes due during retirement, when you withdraw your money.

If you are just a few years from retirement and are older than 59½, you can make adjustments for changes in tax law, as they are generally not sprung upon us. Consider withdrawing funds from retirement plans before an increase in income tax rates to avoid paying additional income taxes. If you are 20 or more years from retirement, you may want to consider converting traditional IRAs into Roth IRAs. You will have to pay income taxes now on the amounts converted, but you will avoid paying taxes on funds you withdraw during retirement. For more discussion on the pros and cons of converting a traditional IRA to a Roth IRA, see Chapter 3.

---

**Retirement Tip**   Check to see whether a withdrawal will bump you into a higher tax bracket. If it does, it will cost you more in taxes.

---

## Changes in Retirement Plan Laws

Without a doubt, tax laws will change over time. Fortunately, the current trend is toward helping the retirement investor with increases in maximum IRA and 401(k) contributions and the creation of Roth IRAs. Remember that the tide can change. Take advantage of the favorable current laws by maximizing your contributions to retirement plans and evaluating the benefits of converting traditional IRAs to Roth IRAs.

To keep abreast of tax law changes, check the IRS Web site, *www.irs.gov*. If the tax lingo is less than clear, look to consumer-friendly financial Web sites, such as *www.smartmoney.com*, *www.moneycentral.msn.com*, or *www.cbsmarketwatch.com*.

Don't let the uncertain nature of all these variables discourage you. It doesn't mean that you can't devise a reasonable plan to save for a comfortable retirement. What it does mean is that you can't figure it out once and then stay on autopilot. Each year, you should check to make sure you are on track.

# USING WORKSHEETS TO CALCULATE WHAT YOU WILL NEED

Now that you have a handle on some of the different components necessary to calculate your retirement needs, you are ready to crunch the numbers. One of the easiest ways is to try several of the retirement calculators available from investment firms. Many are available online.

Try Fidelity Investments' calculator at *www.fidelity.com* for a comprehensive look. Click on the explanations for each question to reveal many helpful tips on making estimates. Putnam Investments' Web site at *www.putnaminv.com* provides your results in both numeric and graphic form and gives you the opportunity to change several variables in order to meet your goal. The calculator at *www.quicken.com* considers taxes paid on the funds coming from retirement accounts, which can be a big issue if the bulk of your retirement assets are in 401(k)s, ordinary IRAs, and annuities. Quicken's results page features a stoplight to tell you whether your current plan will meet your needs; then it lets you solve for certain variables, such as a realistic retirement age, given the other information you have entered. Be aware that most calculators have fields with default values in them. You may or may not want to change these values.

The problem with retirement calculators, as so many people in the late 1990s found out, is GIGO. Most retirement calculators allow you to enter your own estimate of investment returns. In a decade when returns of higher than 20 percent were the norm, it was easy to be too optimistic about how quickly your investments would grow. If you want to be more accurate, consider the *Portfolio Survival Simulator*, a program developed by chartered financial analyst Bill Swerbenski. The program offers three techniques to analyze your portfolio survival. In each of the simulations, you input your cash flows (current assets, preretirement savings, postretirement withdrawals), tax rates, your asset allocation, and time frames.

The simulations, called *Monte Carlo, Bootstrap Resampling*, and *Rolling Historical simulation*, use historic rates of return for different asset classes and inflation to determine the change in your portfolio over a given time frame. The program runs random simulations (the default number is 100, but you can increase it) and averages the results. *Portfolio survivability* refers to whether your portfolio can survive the withdrawals you plan to take without falling below zero. Once you input the variables, you can change components, such as preretirement saving levels, asset allocations, or postretirement withdrawals, until you get an optimum survivability. You can see examples at Swerbenski's Web site, *www.portfoliosurvival.com,* and you can download the program for a reasonable fee ($14.95 in May 2003). The following section provides an example.

## A Financial Calculator Example Using the *Portfolio Survival Simulator*

Financial calculators can be helpful in retirement planning, but as we have already discussed, there are numerous variables, many of which are out of your control. For this reason, the benefit of the calculator may not be in the absolute answer you receive, but in the ability to change variables that you can control and see how these changes affect the outcome. Let's look at an example of this, in which we can get to a desired result in several different ways.

### Entering the Data

Tomea is 45 and wants to see how well her plan for retirement is working. She'll begin by entering her cash flows. (See Table 1-5.) Tomea has $200,000 in her Roth 401(k), Roth IRAs, and other savings earmarked for retirement. She enters this amount as her initial balance. She plans to save $2500 after taxes each month until retirement at the age of 65. She enters this amount with a starting year of 1 and an ending year of 20. As she doesn't expect to increase the amount with inflation, she enters "Subject to inflation." She makes no adjustment for income taxes, as this is the amount she expects to save, not her gross income available for savings. During retirement, in years 21 through 40, she expects to receive $2000 per month in Social Security income and $2000 per month from her pension plan. She estimates that she won't have to pay income taxes on the Social Security, but she will have to pay taxes on the pension. Social Security payments will be adjusted for inflation, but her pension will not. Finally, she expects that she'll need $8000 per month to spend in retirement. She wants to index this to inflation, so that her purchasing power will remain the same throughout retirement. She doesn't adjust it for income taxes because she will be spending capital, not income.

Next, Tomea must decide how she will invest her funds. (See Table 1-6.) From years 0 to 21, she has decided to be fairly aggressive, with 10 percent allocated to cash, 10 percent allocated to bonds, and 80 percent allocated to stocks. Then, in early retirement, from years 21 to 30, she adjusts her allocation to 25 percent cash, 25 percent bonds, and 50 percent stocks. After year 30, she moves to 50 percent cash, 25 percent bonds, and 25 percent stocks.

**TABLE 1-5**

*The Portfolio Survival Simulator:*
Data for Simulating Cash Flow from Saving $2500 a Month until Retirement, Then Spending $8000 a Month throughout Retirement

| Starting Year # | Ending Year # | Cash Flow Amount | Cash Flow Recurrence | Relationship to Inflation | Income Tax Adjustment | Optional Line Item Notes |
|---|---|---|---|---|---|---|
| 0 | 0 | $200,000 | One-time | Not applicable | Not applicable | Initial balance |
| 1 | 20 | 2,500 | Monthly | Subject to inflation | No adjustment | Savings |
| 21 | 40 | 2,000 | Monthly | Indexed to inflation | No adjustment | Social Security income |
| 21 | 40 | 2,000 | Monthly | Subject to inflation | Adjust for income tax | Pension income |
| 21 | 40 | (8,000) | Monthly | Indexed to inflation | No adjustment | Retirement expenses |

**TABLE 1-6**

*The Portfolio Survival Simulator:*
Data for Simulating Investment Asset Allocations

| Starting Year # | Optional Line Item Notes | Rebalancing Periodicity | Cash Allocation (%) | Bonds Allocation (%) | Stocks Allocation (%) |
|---|---|---|---|---|---|
| 0 | Initial allocation | Annually | 10 | 10 | 80 |
| 21 | Early retirement | Annually | 25 | 25 | 50 |
| 30 | Late retirement | Annually | 50 | 25 | 25 |

## The Results

Tomea's results, after running a Bootstrap simulation 250 times (it takes less than 10 seconds), is a 62.8 percent* probability that her portfolio will survive for 40 years. In other words, there is a 62.8 percent probability that she won't run out of money. (See Figure 1-1.) Though the median result of all 250 iterations shows that she'll have $382,400 left at the end of 40 years, Tomea would like a higher probability that she won't run out of money before she's 85. Let's see what changes she can make.

**FIGURE 1-1**

*The Portfolio Survival Simulator:* Simulation Results of Saving $2500 a Month until Retirement, Then Spending $8000 a Month throughout Retirement

### 40-Year / 250-Iteration / Bootstrap Simulation

| Stats | Terminal Value ($) | Nominal Annual Avg. Returns (%) | Survived Years |
|---|---|---|---|
| Median | $382,400 | 8.71% | 40.00 |
| Average | $770,939 | 8.81% | 37.91 |
| Std. Dev. | $1,621,045 | 1.85% | 3.64 |
| Minimum | −$1,203,640 | 3.63% | 24.50 |
| **Probability of Surviving 40 Years:** | | | **62.80%** |

### Survived Years Histogram & Cumulative Survival Rates

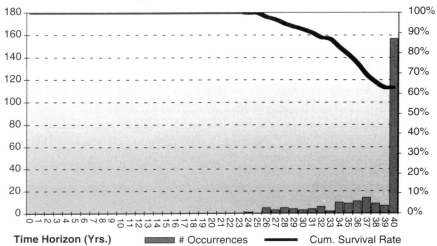

Time Horizon (Yrs.)    ▬ # Occurrences    ▬▬ Cum. Survival Rate

---

* Because the results are a composite of 250 random simulations, the same set of variables will never yield the exact same results.

## FIGURE 1-1 (Continued)

*The Portfolio Survival Simulator:* Simulation Results of Saving $2500 a Month until Retirement, Then Spending $8000 a Month throughout Retirement

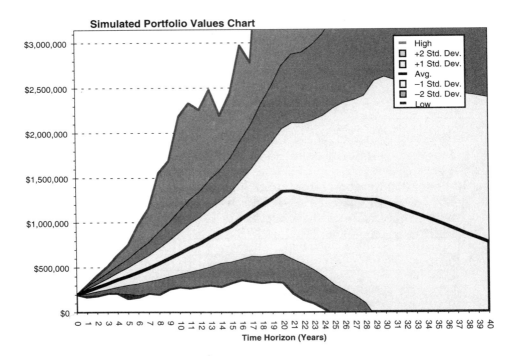

### Live on Less in Retirement

Obviously, if Tomea spends less in retirement, her money will last longer. She decides that she can live on $7000 per month and enters this into her cash flows. (See Table 1-7.) Her results look much better, with a 74.8 percent probability that her money will last 40 years. (See Figure 1-2.)

**TABLE 1-7**

*The Portfolio Survival Simulator:*
Data for Simulating Cash Flow from Saving $2500 a Month until
Retirement, Then Spending $7000 a Month throughout Retirement

| Starting Year # | Ending Year # | Cash Flow Amount | Cash Flow Recurrence | Relationship to Inflation | Income Tax Adjustment | Optional Line Item Notes |
|---|---|---|---|---|---|---|
| 0 | 0 | $200,000 | One-time | Not applicable | Not applicable | Initial balance |
| 1 | 20 | $2,500 | Monthly | Subject to inflation | No adjustment | Savings |
| 21 | 40 | $2,000 | Monthly | Indexed to inflation | No adjustment | Social Security income |
| 21 | 40 | $2,000 | Monthly | Subject to inflation | Adjust for income tax | Pension income |
| 21 | 40 | ($7,000) | Monthly | Indexed to inflation | No adjustment | Retirement expenses |

**FIGURE 1-2**

*The Portfolio Survival Simulator:* Simulation Results of Saving
$2500 a Month until Retirement, Then Spending $7000 a
Month throughout Retirement

## 40-Year / 250-Iteration / Bootstrap Simulation

| Stats | Terminal Value ($) | Nominal Annual Avg. Returns (%) | Survived Years |
|---|---|---|---|
| Median | $577,783 | 8.64% | 40.00 |
| Average | $843,346 | 8.58% | 38.64 |
| Std. Dev. | $1,250,700 | 1.71% | 2.98 |
| Minimum | −$888,627 | 3.53% | 25.68 |
| **Probability of Surviving 40 Years:** | | | **74.80%** |

## Survived Years Histogram & Cumulative Survival Rates

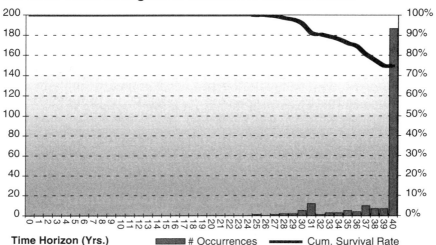

Time Horizon (Yrs.)          ▬▬ # Occurrences          ▬▬▬ Cum. Survival Rate

## FIGURE 1-2 (Continued)

*The Portfolio Survival Simulator:* Simulation Results of Saving $2500 a Month until Retirement, Then Spending $7000 a Month throughout Retirement

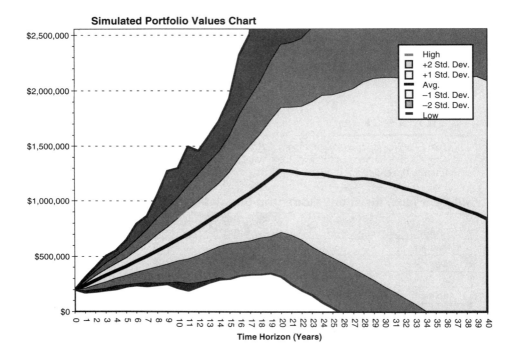

Simulated Portfolio Values Chart

### Live on Less Now

In a different way to tackle the problem, Tomea decides to save more now, so that she can spend more later. If she saves $3000 per month instead of $2500 (see Table 1-8), her results look better, with a 73.2 percent chance that her portfolio will survive. (See Figure 1-3.)

**TABLE 1 - 8**

*The Portfolio Survival Simulator:*
Data for Simulating Cash Flow from Saving $3000 a Month until
Retirement, Then Spending $8000 a Month throughout Retirement

| Starting Year # | Ending Year # | Cash Flow Amount | Cash Flow Recurrence | Relationship to Inflation | Income Tax Adjustment | Optional Line Item Notes |
|---|---|---|---|---|---|---|
| 0 | 0 | $200,000 | One-time | Not applicable | Not applicable | Initial balance |
| 1 | 20 | $3,000 | Monthly | Subject to inflation | No adjustment | Savings |
| 21 | 40 | $2,000 | Monthly | Indexed to inflation | No adjustment | Social Security income |
| 21 | 40 | $2,000 | Monthly | Subject to inflation | Adjust for income tax | Pension income |
| 21 | 40 | ($8,000) | Monthly | Indexed to inflation | No adjustment | Retirement expenses |

**FIGURE 1 - 3**

*The Portfolio Survival Simulator:* Simulation Results of Saving
$3000 a Month until Retirement, Then Spending $8000 a
Month throughout Retirement

## 40-Year / 250-Iteration / Bootstrap Simulation

| Stats | Terminal Value ($) | Nominal Annual Avg. Returns (%) | Survived Years |
|---|---|---|---|
| Median | $613,978 | 8.72% | 40.00 |
| Average | $1,062,280 | 8.81% | 38.57 |
| Std. Dev. | $1,792,106 | 1.85% | 3.17 |
| Minimum | −$1,085,119 | 3.59% | 25.16 |
| **Probability of Surviving 40 Years:** | | | **73.20%** |

## Survived Years Histogram & Cumulative Survival Rates

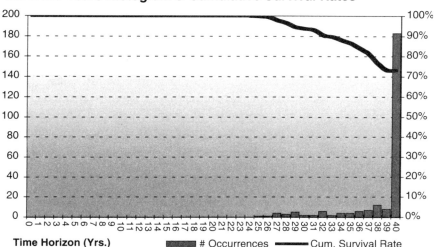

Time Horizon (Yrs.)       # Occurrences       Cum. Survival Rate

**FIGURE 1-3 (Continued)**

---

*The Portfolio Survival Simulator:* Simulation Results of Saving $3000 a Month until Retirement, Then Spending $8000 a Month throughout Retirement

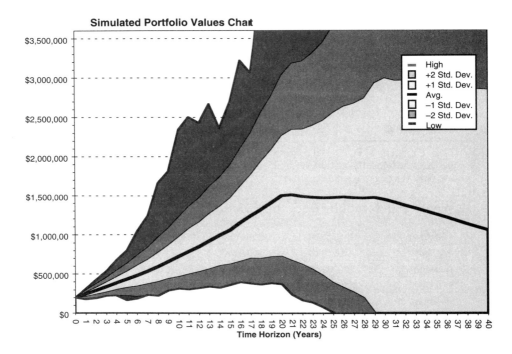

## Invest Better

If Tomea doesn't think she can live on less now or later, she'd better make her money work harder. By historical standards, this means investing more aggressively, with higher allocations of funds in the stock market. By changing her investment allocations to 20 percent cash, 20 percent bonds, and 60 percent stocks in early retirement and 30 percent cash, 30 percent bonds, and 40 percent stocks in late retirement, her portfolio survival rate rises to 74.8 percent. (See Table 1-9 and Figure 1-4.)

## TABLE 1 - 9

*The Portfolio Survival Simulator:*
Revised Data for Simulating Investment Asset Allocations

| Starting Year # | Optional Line Item Notes | Rebalancing Periodicity | Cash Allocation (%) | Bonds Allocation (%) | Stocks Allocation (%) |
|---|---|---|---|---|---|
| 0 | Initial allocation | Annually | 10 | 10 | 80 |
| 21 | Early retirement | Annually | 20 | 20 | 60 |
| 30 | Late retirement | Annually | 30 | 30 | 40 |

## FIGURE 1 - 4

*The Portfolio Survival Simulator:* Simulation Results of Saving $2500 a Month until Retirement Using Revised Asset Allocations, Then Spending $8000 a Month throughout Retirement

### 40-Year / 250-Iteration / Bootstrap Simulation

| Stats | Terminal Value ($) | Nominal Annual Avg. Returns (%) | Survived Years |
|---|---|---|---|
| Median | $546,240 | 9.37% | 40.00 |
| Average | $1,073,554 | 9.43% | 38.51 |
| Std. Dev. | $1,727,421 | 1.83% | 3.13 |
| Minimum | –$1,033,738 | 4.50% | 26.85 |
| | Probability of Surviving 40 years: | | 74.80% |

### Survived Years Histogram & Cumulative Survival Rates

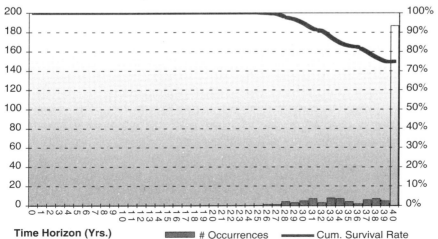

Time Horizon (Yrs.)        # Occurrences        Cum. Survival Rate

**FIGURE 1-4 (Continued)**

*The Portfolio Survival Simulator:* Simulation Results of Saving $2500 a Month until Retirement Using Revised Asset Allocations, Then Spending $8000 a Month throughout Retirement

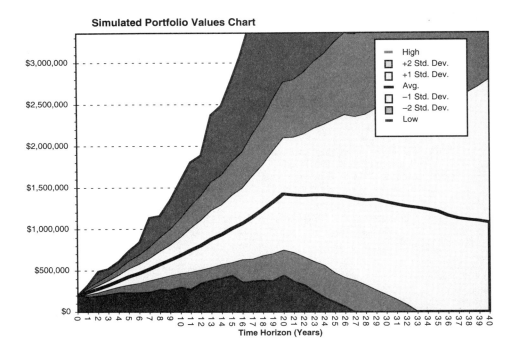

Simulated Portfolio Values Chart

## THE BOTTOM LINE

There are many ways to arrive at your desired result, and choosing the path is up to you. Some courses are inherently riskier than others, though it may not be apparent on a chart. The most conservative course is to save more now, thus leaving the other options open if they are needed as well. Relying on an aggressive investment policy may work *on average*, but remember that your retirement is an individual occurrence, not an average.

## SUMMARY

The old saying that "nothing is certain except death and taxes" is certainly true in retirement planning. And even death isn't certain—if we each knew how long we would live, we could better prepare for retirement. However, try not to worry about all the unknowns, and control what you can—how much you save, the vehicles you use to save, how you invest, and when you retire.

Use retirement worksheets as a starting point, not as the final word on how much you should save, since there is no foolproof method to calculate exactly how much is enough. Understand the variables and make changes accordingly, and then read the rest of this book so that you can do the most with the money that you save. You'll be well on your way to a comfortable retirement.

# CHAPTER 2

# Retirement Plan Basics

If you are confused about all the different retirement plans available, you are not alone. It reminds us, a couple of nontechies, of the daunting prospect of buying a new computer. The configurations and new technology can be overwhelming if you begin with the differences rather than the similarities. Retirement plans can pose the same problem. Luckily, while a few rules for different retirement plans may get complicated, all of them—including IRAs, Roth IRAs, 401(k) plans, 403(b) plans, SEPs, and annuities—operate with some common characteristics. In the next few chapters we will detail the specific rules for each type of plan, but in this chapter, we'll begin with the common features of retirement plans and some terminology that you can use later.

## RETIREMENT PLAN CHARACTERISTICS

### Tax Deferral on Investment Growth

With ordinary investments that are not part of a retirement plan, capital gains and interest or dividends are taxed in the year in which they are earned. (Capital gains are incurred when you sell an investment for more than your purchase price. Interest and dividends are the periodic earnings of your investment.) In a retirement plan, you do not pay any income tax on the growth or earnings on your investments until you withdraw your money. This allows you to use money that you would have paid to the IRS in taxes to earn more money for you.

The tax plan passed in 2003 made changes to the rules on taxation of dividends and capital gains. Dividends on most stock investments* are now taxed at a 15 percent rate rather than at ordinary income tax rates. Capital gains on securities held for more than 1 year are now taxed at a 15 percent rate rather than a 20 percent rate. This change can lessen the advantage of tax deferral for investors in the highest income tax brackets, because current taxes on dividends and capital gains are less onerous and withdrawals of growth from tax-deferred accounts are still taxed at ordinary income tax rates.

---

**Retirement Tip**

|  | Tax Rate under 2003 Law | Tax Rate under Previous Law |
|---|---|---|
| Dividends | 15% | Ordinary income tax rate, up to 38.6% |
| Capital gains* | 15% | 20% |

*Investments held for over 1 year.

---

For the investor in Table 2-1, there is still a slight advantage to tax deferral. The $3000 investment in a tax-deferred account (perhaps a tax-deferred annuity or nondeductible IRA) is worth $14,780 after 20 years. After ordinary income taxes due at withdrawal, the account is worth $11,835. The same $3000 invested in a taxable account, in which dividends and capital gains are taxed annually, is worth $11,729. If the investor's investment income in the taxable account is interest, such as the return from a certificate of deposit or a bond, the advantage to the tax-deferred account is more pronounced. This is because interest is still taxable at ordinary income tax rates. In this case, the taxable account is worth $10,038.

Table 2-2 shows the taxable account at a slight advantage after 20 years of annual contributions of $3000. If the growth in the taxable account was all dividends and long-term capital gains, it would be worth $135,456 after 20 years, while the tax-deferred account would

---

* Dividends on real estate investment trusts are excluded from the favorable treatment.

## TABLE 2-1

A Single Contribution of $3000: Tax-Deferred versus Taxable Accounts

|  | Tax-Deferred Investment | Taxable Investment | |
|---|---|---|---|
|  |  | Dividends and Capital Gains Income | Interest Income |
| Amount invested | $ 3,000 | $ 3,000 | $ 3,000 |
| Value after 20 years earning 8%* | 14,780 | 11,729† | 10,038‡ |
| Taxable growth at withdrawal | 11,780 | 0 | 0 |
| Taxes due on withdrawal at 25% | 2,945 | 0 | 0 |
| **Money you keep after 20 years** | **11,835** | **11,729** | **10,038** |

*Returns compounded monthly.

†Dividends and capital gains taxed at 15% annually.

‡Interest taxed at 25% annually.

## TABLE 2-2

Contributions of $3000 for 20 Years: Tax-Deferred versus Taxable Accounts

|  | Tax-Deferred Investment | Taxable Investment | |
|---|---|---|---|
|  |  | Dividends and Capital Gains Income | Interest Income |
| Amount invested **annually** | $ 3,000 | $ 3,000 | $ 3,000 |
| Value after 20 years earning 8%* | 156,714 | 135,456† | 123,101‡ |
| Taxable growth at withdrawal | 93,714 | 0 | 0 |
| Taxes due on withdrawal at 25% | 23,428 | 0 | 0 |
| **Money you keep after 20 years** | **133,286** | **135,456** | **123,101** |

*Returns compounded monthly.

†Dividends and capital gains taxed at 15% annually.

‡Interest taxed at 25% annually.

be worth $133,286. If the returns in the taxable account were interest, the account would be worth $123,101.

In Tables 2-1 and 2-2, the results for taxable accounts are divided into those whose income is all dividends and capital gains and those whose income is all interest. However, it is possible that investment returns in a well-diversified account will be a combination of the two. In this case, the results fall somewhere between the two figures. For future examples, all taxable investments will be illustrated as if the returns were dividends and capital gains. In Chapter 10, we will discuss allocating types of investments between taxable and tax-deferred accounts in order to take advantage of the tax treatment of different investment returns.

## Making Tax-Deductible Contributions

You may be able to deduct your retirement plan contributions from your gross income before computing your federal and state income taxes. This means you do not pay any current income tax on the amount contributed. For example, if you earn $50,000 per year and elect to contribute 10 percent ($5000) of your salary to your 401(k) plan, you declare only $45,000 ($50,000 minus $5000) of taxable income for the year. In a 25 percent tax bracket, this saves you $1250 in taxes. Table 2-3 shows how a single tax-deductible investment compares to an ordinary investment after 20 years. In the end, the tax-deductible account has $2288 more than the taxable account.

**TABLE 2-3**

A Single Contribution of $3000: Tax-Deductib● Retirement Account versus Taxable Account

| | Tax-Deductible, Tax-Deferred Investment | Taxable Investment |
|---|---|---|
| Investible income | $ 3,000 | $3,000 |
| Current income tax | 0 | 750 |
| Amount invested | 3,000 | 2,250 |
| Value after 20 years earning 8%* | 14,780 | 8,797† |
| Taxable amount at withdrawal | 14,780‡ | 0 |
| Taxes due on withdrawal at 25% | 3,695 | 0 |
| **Money you keep after 20 years** | **11,085** | **8,797** |

*Returns compounded monthly.

†Dividends and capital gains taxed at 15% annually.

‡Because the contribution was tax deductible, the entire amount of the account is taxable at withdrawal.

---

**Retirement Tip**   State income taxes, if they apply to you, make the differences even more striking because your state taxes are also reduced by tax-deductible contributions.

---

## Income Taxes on Withdrawals

When you retire and begin taking money out of your retirement accounts (or if you withdraw from them before retirement age), your withdrawals may be taxable:

- *Contributions.*   Withdrawals of any *pretax* (tax-deductible) contributions will be taxable as ordinary income. These are contributions you made to an IRA or employer's retirement plan that reduced your taxable income in the year they were made. Withdrawals of contributions made *after tax* that did not reduce your taxable income are not taxable. Examples of after-tax contributions include contributions to a nondeductible IRA, a Roth IRA, an annuity, or the after-tax options in your employer's retirement plan.

- *Investment Growth.*   Capital gains and income on your investment contributions are always taxable except under certain circumstances in a Roth IRA or qualified Roth contribution program. Your investment growth is calculated as the value of your account less the sum of your contributions.

If your retirement account is a Roth IRA or a qualified Roth contribution program, no income taxes will be due on withdrawal after age 59½. Look at the tax-deferred investments in Tables 2-1 and 2-2 again and omit taxes on withdrawal to see how much money you would keep in a Roth IRA. You can find out more about Roth IRAs and their tax treatment in Chapter 3.

## No Access to Your Money before Retirement

The benefits of retirement plans do not come without a price. In return for the tax breaks you receive, you must agree to leave your funds in the accounts until after you reach the age of 59½. Except under certain circumstances, if you withdraw from a traditional IRA before reaching retirement age, you can expect to pay a 10 percent penalty to the IRS, in addition to ordinary income taxes. Roth IRAs offer more flexibility, giving you access to the funds you have contributed.

Employer plans are often the strictest. Most will not allow distributions from the plan unless you are terminated, become disabled, die, or are separated from service (leave your job). A hardship distribution may be the only way to take money out of your plan if you do not meet any of those criteria. For a distribution to qualify as a hardship distribution, it must satisfy two requirements:

- It must be due to the employee's immediate and heavy financial need.
- It must be necessary to satisfy that need.

If you take a hardship distribution, you may still pay IRS penalties and taxes. See Chapter 12 for specific rules regarding plan withdrawals and check your plan document to see whether you may take a loan from your account if you need money before retirement.

While you might consider it a disadvantage that you can't spend your money before retirement, it can be good for those who have trouble saving. If ordinary savings accounts are just too tempting, you may find that retirement accounts are the best way to save.

## Portability

You can move your IRA from one financial institution to another at any time through a transfer or rollover. You might choose to do this if you aren't happy with your investment choices and performance or if you want to consolidate separate accounts into one.

---

**Retirement Tip**  A *transfer*, sometimes called a *direct rollover*, occurs when the current retirement plan custodian sends assets to a new retirement plan custodian. The plan participant never takes control of the assets. (In some cases, the sending custodian will send a check or securities to the participant, made out as follows: XYZ Bank, custodian for the IRA of Joe Zero.) A *rollover* occurs when the current custodian sends a check or securities to the plan participant. If the participant deposits them with a new custodian in fewer than 60 days, it is a rollover.

If you plan to change jobs and are concerned about the money in your employer's retirement plan, don't be. The money you have contributed is yours, and you can take it with you through a rollover or a transfer. If your employer has made contributions, you may have to wait several years before those contributions belong to you and may be moved. This is called *vesting*. Check your plan document for any vesting schedules that apply.

Recent (2001) changes in the law allow transfers or rollovers between a former and current employer's plan even if the plan types differ. Now you can make a direct transfer between 401(k), 403(b), or 457 retirement plans as long as the plan documents allow it. You have always been able to transfer or roll over these plans into IRAs, but the previous law restricted transfers and rollovers into employer plans from IRAs. You could roll an IRA into an employer plan only if it had originally been transferred from an employer plan and you had not made any IRA contributions to the account, called *comingling*. Now you can roll pretax contributory IRAs into your employer plan if your plan document allows it. See Chapter 12 for more details on rollovers and transfers. When making transfers or rollovers into your plan, always check your plan document. Your plan document governs when its rules are stricter than the law.

## Credits for Low-Income Taxpayers

The 2001 tax law changes include a provision to encourage low-income individuals to save for retirement. Under the law, if your adjusted gross income is low enough, you will receive a tax credit of up to 50 percent of your contribution to an IRA or other qualified retirement plan. The credit is in addition to any tax deduction on the contribution and is limited to $1000 per person per year. For example, if you file a joint return with adjusted gross income of $30,000 or less and contribute $2000 to an IRA, you will receive a $1000 tax credit, making the true cost of your contribution just $1000, not to mention any income tax saved on a tax-deductible contribution. Maximum incomes differ depending on your filing status, and within each status the credit percentage phases out as income rises. The credit is not available to students and dependents. See Table 2-4 for details.

## TABLE 2-4

Saver's Credits

| If Your Filing Status Is: | And Your Adjusted Gross Income Is: | Then Your Credit Rate Is: |
|---|---|---|
| Married filing jointly | Not over $30,000 | 50% |
| | $30,001–$32,500 | 20% |
| | $32,501–$50,000 | 10% |
| | Over $50,000 | You do not qualify. |
| Head of household | Not over $22,500 | 50% |
| | $22,501–$24,375 | 20% |
| | $24,376–$37,500 | 10% |
| | Over $37,500 | You do not qualify. |
| Single, qualifying widow(er), or married filing separately | Not over $15,000 | 50% |
| | $15,001–$16,250 | 20% |
| | $16,251–$25,000 | 10% |
| | Over $25,000 | You do not qualify. |

**Retirement Tip**  While the tax credit for retirement plan contributions may not apply to you, it may apply to your children or grandchildren. For example, if you have a son who is not a dependent or full-time student, who earns $15,000 or less, the rule applies to him. If he cannot afford it, consider giving him $3000 for a Roth IRA contribution. He will get the benefit of a $3000 Roth IRA, plus a tax credit of $1000 (even though his credit rate is 50 percent, the maximum credit is $1000) to spend or save now. That is a $4000 gift that costs you only $3000.

## Important Terms

Before you read on, take note of different relevant terms and definitions that are helpful in understanding the language of retirement plans.

   **401(k) plan**  An employer-sponsored retirement plan that allows employees to make contributions through payroll deductions. Contributions are tax deductible unless designated as "after tax" by the employee. Investments grow tax deferred and are subject to current income taxes when withdrawn during retirement.

**403(b) plan**   An employer-sponsored retirement plan, similar to a 401(k) plan, offered by public schools and tax-exempt organizations.

**457 plan**   An employer-sponsored retirement plan, similar to a 401(k) plan, offered by government entities and some tax-exempt organizations.

**after-tax contribution**   A contribution that is not deducted from your gross income when computing taxes.

**capital gain**   If you sell an investment for more than its purchase price, the difference is a capital gain. If you held the investment for over 1 year, the gain is taxed at 15 percent.

**custodian**   The bank, brokerage firm, or trust company that houses your retirement plan investments.

**dividend**   The income, generally paid quarterly, from common or preferred stock. Under 2003 tax law, dividends are taxed at 15 percent.

**elective contribution**   An employer plan contribution that is withheld from your paycheck per your instructions. In some plan documents, the term *elective contribution* is synonymous with *pretax contribution*.

**hardship distribution**   If you need money from your employer plan before retirement and do not meet the standard criteria of being terminated, disabled, dead, or separated from service, you may be able to take a hardship distribution. While it doesn't free you from paying taxes or penalties, it does allow you access to your funds. For a distribution to qualify as a hardship distribution, it must satisfy two requirements:

- It must be due to the employee's immediate and heavy financial need.
- It must be necessary to satisfy that need.

**Individual Retirement Account (IRA)**   A retirement plan set up by an individual. Contributions may be tax deductible, depending on income levels. Investments in an IRA grow tax deferred until they are withdrawn during retirement. In most cases, funds withdrawn before age 59½ are subject to a 10 percent IRS penalty.

**interest**  The income from a bond, certificate of deposit, or other fixed-income investment. Interest income is taxed at ordinary income tax rates.

**investment option**  The investment choice or choices in which you direct your money to be invested.

**loans**  You may not borrow from an IRA or use it as collateral for a loan. However, many employer plans allow you to borrow a portion of your retirement plan account and pay yourself back, with interest.

**matching**  The amount contributed by an employer to your retirement plan, expressed as a percentage of your contribution.

**premature distribution**  Generally defined as a withdrawal taken from a retirement plan before the account owner dies, reaches age 59½, is disabled, or retires after reaching age 55.

**pretax contribution**  A tax-deductible retirement plan contribution.

**qualified retirement plan**  A retirement investment that qualifies for special tax treatment under the law.

**required withdrawals**  The IRS requirement that you begin taking withdrawals from your retirement plans by April 1 of the year after you reach the age 70½. Traditional IRAs (not Roth IRAs) are subject to required withdrawals, as are most employer plans, unless you are still employed.

**rollover**  A method of moving funds from one retirement plan to another, in which you receive the funds and must reinvest them within 60 days in order to avoid taxes and possible penalties.

**Roth IRA**  An IRA with key differences from the traditional IRA. Contributions to a Roth IRA are never tax deductible, and as long as certain conditions are met, withdrawals from a Roth IRA are not taxable. In order to be eligible to contribute to a Roth IRA, you may not have income above certain limits.

**tax-deferred annuity (TDA)**  A type of 403(b) plan for employees of public schools and some charities. These plans offer annuity contracts from an insurance company as investment choices.

**transfer**   Also called a *direct transfer, custodian-to-custodian transfer*, or *direct rollover*. A method of moving funds between retirement plans in which the funds are sent directly to a new custodian, never to the participant.

**vesting**   An employer's method of rewarding length of employment by creating a schedule in which matching funds do not belong to participants until they have been employed for a certain number of years.

## SUMMARY

Before you know it, you will be facing retirement. How much will you have if you begin investing in your twenties in a retirement plan? Maybe millions. Even if your twenties are long gone, you can still make a difference in your retirement with every year of tax deferral and compound interest.

It is easy to feel intimidated by the financial jargon and perplexing literature written to define employer retirement plans, and changes in the tax law every few years can add to your frustration. However, don't be deterred from taking that important first step to save something from each paycheck for your retirement. After reading this chapter, you should have a better understanding of the mechanics of retirement plans and the definitions for terms commonly used. The following chapters will break down the complexities of each type of retirement account. They will show you how to best save for retirement. Take time NOW to think about retirement because it is just around the corner.

# CHAPTER 3

# Individual Retirement Accounts (IRAs)

**N**early everyone has heard of Individual Retirement Accounts (IRAs) and nearly everyone can have one. No matter who your employer is, even if you are self-employed, you can have a retirement plan in the form of an IRA if you or your spouse has earned income. Investment growth in an IRA is tax deferred, and in some cases, contributions are tax deductible. In this chapter, we will discuss the two primary types of IRAs: the traditional IRA and the Roth IRA. Simplified Employee Pension IRA (SEP-IRA) and Savings Incentive Match Plan IRA (SIMPLE-IRA) will be covered in Chapter 4 with other employer-based retirement plans.

## TRADITIONAL IRAs

If you opened an IRA when they were first created, that account is now referred to as a *traditional IRA*, or sometimes an *ordinary IRA*, to differentiate it from the more recently created Roth IRA. In this book, an IRA not specifically designated as a Roth IRA is a traditional IRA.

### Eligibility and Contribution Limits

If you are under age 70½, you can contribute a maximum of $3000 per year (2002 to 2004 rules) to your IRA. You cannot contribute more than you have in earned income except in cases of spouses filing jointly in which a nonearning spouse may contribute up to $3000 as long as the combined contributions of both spouses do not exceed the earnings of the working spouse. This limit of $3000 is an increase over the previous $2000 limit, and it will continue to increase according to Table 3-1. After 2008, the maximum contributions will be adjusted for inflation in increments of $500.

## Contribution Deadlines

You may make an IRA contribution at any time during the taxable year and up until April 15 of the following year.

## Catch-Up Contributions

The 2001 law that established increased contribution limits also provided help for those nearing retirement. If you reach the age of 50 before the close of the taxable year, you can increase your contribution as shown in Table 3-2.

### TABLE 3-1

IRA Contribution Limits

| For Taxable Years Beginning in: | The Contribution Limit Is: |
| --- | --- |
| 2002 through 2004 | $3000 |
| 2005 through 2007 | 4000 |
| 2008 and thereafter | 5000 |

### TABLE 3-2

Catch-Up Contributions

| For Taxable Years Beginning in: | Additional Contribution Allowed: |
| --- | --- |
| 2002 through 2005 | $ 500 |
| 2006 and thereafter | 1000 |

## Deductible Contributions

For traditional and spousal (the nonearning spouse's) IRAs, you can deduct the full amount of your IRA contribution from your taxable income if neither you nor your spouse was an active participant in a company-sponsored retirement plan, such as a 401(k) plan, in the same year. By IRS definition, you are considered an active participant if *either* you or your employer makes contributions to the plan. Therefore, it is possible to be an active participant in an employer plan, such as a profit-sharing plan, without being fully aware of it. Check with your human resources department if you are unsure.

If you or your spouse contributed to an employer plan, you can fully deduct your contribution if you are

- Single and earned less than $40,000 in 2003
- Married, filing jointly, and earned less than $60,000 in 2003

If you are married and filing jointly and only one spouse is covered by a retirement plan at work, a higher income limit applies for the spouse without an employer-sponsored plan. For 2003, the spouse without an employer plan can fully deduct an IRA contribution as long as joint income is less than $150,000.

Contribution deductibility is subject to phase-outs for certain levels of income. This means that as you move from the lower level to the upper level of the range, less of your contribution will be deductible. If you or your spouse contributed to an employer plan, your contribution will be partially deductible if you are

- Single and earned between $40,000 and $50,000 in 2003
- Married, filing jointly, with joint income between $60,000 and $70,000 in 2003

Higher income limits apply for a spouse not covered by an employer plan when married and filing jointly. For 2003, the spouse without a plan receives partial deductibility for contributions when joint income is between $150,000 and $160,000. IRS Publication 590 contains a worksheet for calculating how much of your contribution is deductible.

## Nondeductible Contributions

You cannot deduct your contribution from taxable income if you contributed to an employer-sponsored plan and you are

- Single and earned over $50,000 in 2003
- Married, filing jointly, with joint income over $70,000 in 2003

For couples in which only one spouse is covered by an employer retirement plan, the spouse not covered cannot deduct an IRA contribution in 2003 if joint income is over $160,000.

The investment earnings in a nondeductible IRA are not taxed until withdrawal. Your contributions are not taxable at withdrawal because they were already taxed as part of your current income in the year earned and contributed. It is very important to keep track of the amounts you have contributed to a nondeductible IRA, so that you do not mistakenly pay taxes on contributions during retirement. Be especially careful if you are subject to the phase-outs, in which a portion of your contribution is deductible and a portion is not.

Never invest in a traditional, nondeductible IRA if you are eligible for a Roth IRA. Neither provides a tax deduction for contributions, but retirement withdrawals of investment growth from a traditional, nondeductible IRA are taxable, and qualifying withdrawals from a Roth IRA are tax exempt.

## Withdrawing from a Traditional IRA

All withdrawals from a tax-deductible IRA are subject to ordinary income taxes. Withdrawals from nondeductible IRAs are taxable only to the extent that they exceed the amount contributed. In other words, only the investment earnings are taxed.

In order to encourage you to use your IRAs for retirement purposes, the law restricts withdrawals. Unless you meet certain exceptions, any money withdrawn from a traditional IRA before you reach the age of 59½ is subject to a 10 percent IRS penalty. The exceptions to this rule follow:

- You as the taxpayer are making the withdrawal to pay for qualified higher education expenses for yourself, your spouse, or your or your spouse's child (or stepchild) or grandchild. It is not required that the child be a dependent. See Internal Revenue Code (IRC) 151(c)(3) for a full definition. Eligible expenses include tuition, fees, books, supplies, and other necessary equipment required to attend an eligible postsecondary educational institution. The expenses must be net of any tax-free benefits such as scholarships and grants. IRC 529(e)(3) and IRC 529(e)(5) provide exact IRS definitions of eligible expenses and institutions.

- You are making the withdrawal, up to a lifetime limit of $10,000, for a first-time home purchase. A first-time home buyer is defined as anyone who has not had an ownership interest in a principal residence during the 2-year period ending on the date of acquisition. If married, the home buyer's spouse must also meet this condition.
- You become disabled as defined by the IRS.
- You die.
- You set up a schedule, based on your life expectancy, to take out substantially equal payments every year for the rest of your life. If you stop before taking payments for 5 years and before the age of 59½, you will owe back penalties plus interest.
- Your unreimbursed medical expenses exceed 7.5 percent of your adjusted gross income.
- You use the withdrawal to pay for medical insurance while you are unemployed.
- You reinvest (roll over) the money into an IRA or other qualified plan within 60 days.

## Rollovers and Transfers

Once you have chosen an IRA custodian, such as a bank, brokerage firm, or mutual fund, you are not locked into that decision for life. You may have an IRA with a bank that offers only certificates of deposit and decide you would like to invest in something different. Opening an account with a mutual fund gives you access to any of the funds that the firm offers. An account with a brokerage firm, often called a *self-directed IRA*, is generally the most flexible. With this type of account, you can usually invest in any combination of stocks, mutual funds, bonds, CDs, or money market accounts.

To move your account, you may make a *custodian-to-custodian transfer*, sometimes called a *direct rollover*, in which the funds are sent from your existing custodian to a new custodian and you are never in possession of the funds. There is no limit to the number of transfers allowed and no IRS penalty or tax for a transfer. However, there may be fees and commissions charged by the sending or receiving custodian.

In an IRA *rollover*, you withdraw funds from an IRA or other qualified retirement plan, take possession of the money, and deposit it into the same or a different IRA. If you accomplish this within the 60-day time limit set by the IRS, you will not incur any taxes or penalties. The same money can only be rolled over once per year.

## Required Withdrawals

You must begin withdrawing from your traditional IRA by April 1 of the year following the year you turn 70½. If you do not, the IRS will assess a penalty of 50 percent on the amount you should have withdrawn. The amount that you should withdraw is called your *required minimum distribution*, or RMD. The RMD is applied to the aggregate amount of your IRAs and is based on the joint life expectancy of you and your beneficiary as outlined in the IRS Uniform Withdrawal Factor Table. All beneficiaries are assumed to be 10 years younger, regardless of their actual age or life expectancy. In an exception to this rule, you may use actual joint life expectancies if your beneficiary is your spouse and is more than 10 years younger than you are. See Chapter 12 for more discussion of required distributions and factors for computing your RMD.

## ROTH IRAs

The Roth IRA, named for Senator William Roth of Delaware, is a relatively new (since 1998) wrinkle on retirement investing. There are key differences between traditional IRAs and Roth IRAs. In some circumstances, contributions to a traditional IRA are tax deductible and withdrawals are taxed as ordinary income. In contrast, contributions to a Roth IRA are never tax deductible; however, withdrawals from a Roth IRA are not taxable if certain conditions are met.

## Eligibility Requirements for Contributing to a Roth IRA

Similar to an ordinary IRA, in order to be eligible to make a Roth IRA contribution, you must have earned income equal to or greater than the amount of your contribution, which cannot exceed $3000 per year for the years 2002 through 2004, less the amount of any contribution to a traditional IRA. (See Table 3-1 for future limits.) If you are married and filing jointly, either or both spouses can contribute, as long as one spouse has earned income equal to or greater than the combined total contribution. This allows a nonworking spouse to plan for retirement.

There is a limit to the amount of income you may earn and still be eligible to contribute to a Roth IRA. For single taxpayers, you may contribute $3000 (2002 to 2004 rules) to a Roth IRA if your modified adjusted gross income (MAGI) is less than or equal to $95,000. Eligibility begins to phase out at MAGI of $95,000 and ends at $110,000. To phase out, reduce the allowable Roth IRA contribution by $15 for each $75 in income over $95,000. For example, if you are single and earn $96,500, your income is $1500 over $95,000. Dividing $1500 by $75 equals 20. Multiply 20 by $15 to arrive at $300, and that is the amount by which you must reduce your allowable contribution. In this instance you can contribute $2700.

If you are married and filing jointly, you are eligible for a full $3000 contribution with income of $150,000 or less. The phase-out begins at $150,000 with a $15 reduction in the allowable contribution for each additional $50 in income. You are completely ineligible at $160,000. For married taxpayers filing separately, the phase-out begins at $0 and ends at $10,000.

## Withdrawing from a Roth IRA

You can withdraw your contributions to a Roth IRA at any time without tax consequences or penalty, but the earnings withdrawn from the account are considered taxable income and may be subject to a 10 percent penalty if withdrawal requirements are not met. The requirements for tax-free, penalty-free withdrawals are the following:

1. The Roth IRA has existed for more than 5 years, *and* either
   - you are over age 59½ or
   - it is for a qualified first-time home purchase (up to a lifetime limit of $10,000).

OR

2. The withdrawal is made due to death or disability.

> **Retirement Tip**   The mandatory distribution requirement that applies to ordinary IRAs at age 70½ does not apply to Roth IRAs.

Withdrawals for qualified higher education expenses (tuition, books, fees, and supplies, net of tax-free assistance such as grants and scholarships) can be made without penalty, but earnings withdrawn are taxable as income. For tax purposes, such withdrawals are treated as if all contributions are withdrawn first. If you have multiple Roth IRAs but withdraw from just one, contributions to all accounts will be aggregated to determine whether any of the withdrawal is taxable.

> **Retirement Dilemma**   Holly has two Roth IRAs, the first of which has contributions of $4000 and a market value of $7500 and the second of which has contributions of $2000 and a market value of $2500. How much can she withdraw for college costs without paying taxes?
>
> **Solution**   She can withdraw up to $6000 (the total of her contributions) before incurring any taxes. Even if she withdrew the entire $6000 from the first Roth IRA, $2000 more than she contributed to it, she would not owe any income taxes because the limit applies to the aggregate amount of contributions and is not calculated per account.

# OPENING AND CONVERTING IRAs
## Opening an IRA

You can open an IRA with most financial institutions, including banks, mutual fund companies, or brokerage firms. Banks generally offer accounts invested in certificates of deposit or money market funds. These offer safety of principal but low investment growth. If you open an account with a mutual fund company, you can invest in any of the funds offered within the "family," or group of funds, from the very conservative to the very aggressive. You may or may not have to pay a commission to invest and to move your account to different funds within the family. If you open a self-directed IRA with a brokerage firm, you generally have access to a very wide array of investment choices, including money market accounts, stocks, bonds, and mutual funds. Commissions will vary depending on the investments that you choose.

You may have multiple IRAs, as long as the sum of the deposits you make to them does not exceed your annual contribution limit. The contribution limit applies to traditional and Roth IRAs or any combination of the two. While you can have as many IRAs as you like, it makes sense to consolidate your accounts because many firms charge an annual fee in the range of $35 to $50.

Because there are limits to the amount you can contribute to an IRA each year, you must designate the tax year for each deposit that you make and you must make all deposits by April 15 of the following year. It is your responsibility, not the financial institution's responsibility, to ensure that you are eligible and to keep track of the amount you have contributed for the year.

## Converting Traditional IRAs to Roth IRAs

You may be able to convert a traditional IRA to a Roth IRA if your MAGI is less than or equal to $100,000. This applies to both single and joint filers. If you are married, you must file jointly in order to be eligible for conversion. Income taxes apply on the amounts converted, just as if they had been withdrawn from ordinary IRAs (no taxes are due on the contribution amounts from nondeductible IRAs), but the 10 percent IRS penalty for those under the age of 59½ is waived. The amount of the converted IRAs, though it is included in income for tax purposes, is not counted toward the $100,000 income limit for conversion eligibility.

If you establish the Roth IRA with an amount less than you withdrew from the traditional IRA, the difference is considered a distribution, and taxes and penalties will apply. Be careful. If you plan to use some of the money withdrawn from your traditional IRA to pay taxes and don't convert the entire amount, you may end up paying penalties.

Why convert your ordinary IRA to a Roth IRA? Consider Deidre's dilemma for an answer.

---

**Retirement Dilemma**   Deidre has a traditional, tax-deductible IRA worth $50,000, which will be taxable as ordinary income upon withdrawal. She is interested in converting it to a Roth IRA so that her retirement withdrawals will be tax free. She is 40 years old, has an MAGI less than $100,000, and her combined federal and state taxes are 30 percent. If she converts this year, she will owe $15,000 ($50,000 times 30 percent) in income taxes. If she can pay the income taxes from other sources, she will have a Roth IRA worth $50,000 but $15,000 less in other assets that would have grown for her.

**Solution**   If, over the next 20 years, her investments grow at an average rate of 8 percent, the value of her Roth IRA will be $246,340, tax free. The $15,000 paid in taxes would have grown to $58,644, given the same nominal return of 8 percent in a taxable account on which dividends and capital gains are taxed annually at 15 percent. If she converts, she would net $187,696, which is the total value of the Roth IRA, less the investment gain lost by using $15,000 to pay taxes on the conversion ($246,340 − $58,644 = $187,696).

She can compare this to leaving the $50,000 in the traditional IRA, which, growing at 8 percent, would also be worth $246,340 after 20 years. Upon withdrawal, she would owe 30 percent in taxes, or $73,902, making her net $172,438 ($246,340 − $73,902 = $172,438). The advantage to converting is $15,258 ($187,696 − $172,438 = $15,258).

The key in this example is the ability to pay income taxes with outside funds. This increases the amount deposited in the Roth IRA for tax-free growth and avoids the 10 percent penalty that would be assessed if you had to use IRA funds to pay the taxes. (Depositing less in the Roth IRA than you withdrew from the ordinary IRA would constitute a withdrawal.)

Consider converting your traditional IRAs if:

- You do not plan to withdraw any IRA funds in the next 5 years (otherwise you will owe income taxes and possibly penalties).
- You can pay the income taxes with outside funds.
- You expect your tax rate in retirement to be the same as or higher than it is now.
- You have estate tax problems. Paying taxes on large IRAs now is a benefit in that it can reduce your taxable estate.
- Your heirs will be in the same or higher tax brackets.
- You would like to avoid mandatory distributions at age 70½.

To find out whether converting makes sense for you, try one of the Roth IRA calculators at any of the following Web sites:

*www.fidelity.com*
*www.strong-funds.com*
*www.vanguard.com*
*www.troweprice.com*

Not all calculators are the same, so try a few before making your decision, and read the fine print about the variables included. Make sure that the model includes the opportunity cost of outside funds used to pay taxes (what that money could have earned if you hadn't used it to pay taxes) or the taxes and possible penalty for using IRA funds to pay taxes. Some calculators consider the fact that you are required to take minimum distributions from an ordinary IRA after age 70½ but are not required to take distributions from a Roth IRA. Make sure the calculator you use includes this fact if you would prefer not to take IRA distributions (that is, you have enough in other assets to support yourself). It is a significant advantage of the Roth IRA. If, however, you expect to take distributions in excess of the minimum, make sure the software allows you to input that. If it uses only the minimum, the Roth will look better than it actually is.

## SUMMARY

The key differences between traditional and Roth IRAs are detailed in Table 3-3.

**TABLE 3-3**

Comparing the Roth IRA to an Ordinary IRA

|  | Traditional IRA | Roth IRA |
| --- | --- | --- |
| Who is eligible? | Anyone under age 70½ with earned income or whose spouse has earned income. No limit on income amount. | Anyone, regardless of age, whose earned income (MAGI) is below $110,000 for single filers and $160,000 for joint filers. Allowable contributions begin phase-out at $95,000 single and $150,000 joint. |
| Is the contribution tax deductible? | Yes, if neither spouse has an employer-sponsored retirement plan. Income limits apply if you also contribute to an employer-sponsored plan. | No. |
| Other tax benefits | Tax-deferred growth of investments. Taxes on investment growth are not due until withdrawal. | Tax-free growth of investments if the account is open over 5 years and the owner is over 59½ at withdrawal. |
| Penalties | Most withdrawals made prior to age 59½ are subject to a 10% penalty, in addition to income taxes. Exceptions include first-time home purchases and the expenses of higher education. | Contributions may be withdrawn penalty free at any time. Most withdrawals of investment growth prior to age 59½ (except first-time home purchases and higher education expenses) are subject to a 10% penalty. |
| Mandatory distributions | Distributions must begin by age 70½. Amounts are mandated by the IRS based on life expectancy. Noncompliance results in stiff penalties. | No minimum age or distribution amount. |

Once you have a clear picture of how they work, you can make an educated decision on which IRA to choose and whether to convert existing traditional IRAs to Roth IRAs.

If you are eligible for an employer's plan and your income is between $50,000 and $95,000 in 2003 for single filers or between

$70,000 and $150,000 for joint filers, you are fully eligible to contribute to either a traditional IRA or a Roth IRA. However, due to your income level, traditional IRA contributions will not be tax deductible. In this case, always choose the Roth IRA over a traditional nondeductible IRA. While neither provides a tax deduction for contributions, you will pay income taxes on investment growth when you withdraw it from a traditional nondeductible IRA, and you will not owe any taxes on investment growth in the Roth.

If your income level and the availability of an employer retirement plan mean you are eligible for either a Roth IRA or a traditional *deductible* IRA, the answer is less clear cut. It depends upon how many years you have until retirement, your expected investment return, and your tax bracket both now and in retirement. In general, the Roth will be more appealing if you have many years until retirement, a high expected investment return, and a retirement tax bracket that is equal to or greater than your preretirement tax bracket. These three factors make the tax exemption on investment growth in a Roth IRA more valuable. If you have relatively few years until retirement, a fairly low expected rate of return on your investments, and expect to be in a lower tax bracket when you withdraw from the IRA, the current tax deduction on contributions to a traditional deductible IRA may prove more valuable than a tax exemption on investment growth in the Roth IRA.

The Web sites listed previously to help with the decision to convert all have calculators that compare traditional and Roth IRAs. Enter your years until retirement, expected rate of investment return, and current and retirement tax brackets. The calculator will crunch the numbers to decide which retirement account is better.

# CHAPTER 4

# Employer-Sponsored Plans

Today, fewer and fewer employers can shoulder the financial risks and responsibilities of traditional pension plans. However, those that provide an alternative contributory retirement plan allow you, the employee, the opportunity to control your financial future. Willing or not, you become your own pension manager.

Suddenly, you are thrown into a world dominated by lingo that is often derived from sections of the IRS code, a document not known for its user-friendly wording. Fortunately, understanding it is easier than it sounds. The main differences among 401(k), 403(b), and 457 plans, SEP-IRAs, and SIMPLE-IRAs are not the plan characteristics but the characteristics of the employers offering the plans. In the following section, we will outline the common features of employer-sponsored retirement plans. Then we will step into the specifics of who offers each plan and any features specific to that plan type. Our discussion here builds on the basics explained in Chapter 2, so refer back for explanations of *tax deferral*, *tax deductibility*, and other terms and concepts if necessary.

## EMPLOYER-SPONSORED RETIREMENT PLANS: HOW THEY WORK

Employer retirement plans allow your employer to deduct money from your paycheck to be invested in an account for your retirement.

You choose the percentage of your gross income to be deducted each pay period and whether you want it invested before or after you pay taxes on it. Generally, your plan will allow you to change that percentage periodically. After it is deducted, your employer transmits your money to a custodian (a bank or trust company) who deposits it into an account in your name. All amounts that have been deducted from your salary legally belong to you, and changes in your employer's retirement plan or in the status of your employment cannot affect the ownership of the money that you have deposited.

Once the money reaches your account, it is invested in the manner you choose. You may invest your money in any of the options offered through the plan, and you may even split your investments, for example, 50 percent in one choice and 50 percent in another. Just as you can change the amount you deduct, you can also change your investment choices periodically. It is as easy as a phone call or a computer click. See Chapter 9 for a complete discussion about choosing among the investments offered.

Different employer retirement plans share the features described in the following paragraphs.

## Tax-Deductible Contributions, Tax-Deferred Growth

You can deduct employer plan contributions from your taxable income, subject to IRS limits and the limits of your plan. This savings in current income taxes makes retirement saving much easier. If you are in a 28 percent tax bracket, contributing $10,000 to your plan will save $2800 in federal income taxes, so you are "out of pocket" only $7200. If your state income taxes are 6 percent, you'll save another $600, so it will only cost you $6600 to invest $10,000.

In addition to deductibility of contributions, employer plans offer tax deferral on investment growth, meaning that you will not pay any income taxes on interest, dividends, or capital gains on your investments until you withdraw funds from your account. Both tax treatments allow you to invest money that would otherwise be paid to the IRS in taxes. Table 4-1 is an illustration of the benefit of tax-deductible contributions with tax-deferred growth.

In Table 4-1, the money invested is ordinary income, derived from a salary or other business earnings. In the taxable account, it is

## TABLE 4-1

Annual Contributions of $10,000:
Taxable Investment versus Tax-Deductible Retirement
Account

|  | Taxable Investment | Tax-Deductible Plan |
|---|---|---|
| Investible income | $ 10,000 | $ 10,000 |
| Current income tax | 2,800 | 0 |
| Amount invested | 7,200 | 10,000 |
| Value after 20 years earning 8%* | 296,945† | 473,112 |
| Taxable amount at withdrawal | 0 | 473,112 |
| Taxes due on withdrawal at 28% | 0 | 132,471 |
| **Money you keep after 20 years** | **296,945** | **340,641** |

*Returns compounded monthly.

†Dividends and capital gains taxed at 15% annually.

taxed at 28 percent. After paying $2800 to the IRS, $7200 is available to invest each year. Growth on investments held in the taxable account is in dividends and capital gains, taxed at 15 percent annually. Funds invested in the employer plan are tax deductible, so the entire $10,000 can be invested each year. Withdrawals from the employer plan are taxed as ordinary income at 28 percent. In this example, you have a total of $200,000 to invest in both accounts, but the employer plan is worth $43,696 more at the end of 20 years.

## Investing After-Tax Funds in Your Employer Retirement Plan

Most plans give you the option of investing through the traditional pretax method or of investing income that has already been taxed. After-tax investment accounts are often called employee savings accounts or savings plans, rather than retirement accounts. While most participants choose the pretax option, some take advantage of after-tax investing, reasoning that their funds are readily available, without penalty or additional taxes. They forgo the tax advantages in favor of liquidity. If you are trying to decide whether to invest in pre- or after-tax accounts, consider the following rules:

- Always take full advantage of tax deductibility and tax deferral on savings earmarked for retirement.
- Company matching funds often apply only to pretax contributions. Contribute at least the full amount that will be matched by your employer.
- Avoid investing funds that you will need *before* retirement in pretax retirement accounts with penalties for early withdrawal.

So, consider the use of the money you are investing. Choose *pretax* for retirement funds and *after tax* for home and auto savings. If the convenience and investment performance of your employer plan make it an appealing investment vehicle, consider the after-tax method for your *nonretirement savings*.

## Convenience

Your retirement savings contribution is deducted directly from your paycheck, before you get a chance to spend it. Do you ever have those months where you just don't know where the money went? Or have you created a budget that shows plenty left over after expenses, but real life just doesn't seem to work the same way? Having your contributions deducted from your paycheck makes saving for retirement easy and relatively painless. Don't wait until you can "afford" it. Do it now!

---

**Retirement Tip**   Always pay yourself first, in your retirement plan and in additional savings. Then you can be assured that you get paid. Let the other bills fight for what's left over.

---

## High Contribution Limits

You can save much more in an employer-sponsored retirement plan than you can in an IRA. In 2003, the maximum you can legally contribute to a 401(k), 403(b), or 457 plan is $12,000 or 100 percent of compensation, whichever is lower, compared to $3000 for an

IRA. (Keep in mind that you may be able to do both.) The maximum combined employee and employer contribution in 2003 is the lesser of $40,000 or 100 percent of your annual compensation. Future limits will be adjusted for inflation. Table 4-2 outlines maximum contributions for different retirement plans.

**Retirement Dilemma** Daniele's salary is $50,000, and she wants to contribute the maximum allowed under IRS law to her 401(k). She knows that the limit for 2003 is $12,000, but the employee benefits officer at her company says she can't contribute more than $7500. How can that be?

**Solution** She may reach her maximum well before the IRS limit, due to her plan limits. If her plan allows her to contribute a maximum of 15 percent of her $50,000 salary, the most she can contribute each year is $7500, not $12,000. If her employer matches 50 percent ($3750) of her contributions, the upper limit to combined deposits is $11,250, not $40,000. She shouldn't get discouraged though; as her income grows, so will the amounts she can contribute.

## High Catch-Up Contributions

The Economic Growth and Tax Relief Reconciliation Act of 2001 (EGTRRA) allows workers over age 50 to make larger contributions as they near retirement. This new law favors employer plans. Catch-up contributions on IRAs and Roth IRAs are $500 over the standard limit until 2006, when the extra contribution allowed rises to $1000. For 401(k), 403(b), and 457 plans, the catch-up amount is $2000 in 2003 and increases by $1000 per year until it reaches $5000 in 2006. After 2006, the catch-up contribution will be adjusted for inflation. See Table 4-2 for the 50+ catch-up contributions. In addition to the new 50+ catch-up provision available for participants in any of these plans, participants in 403(b) and 457 plans may utilize the catch-up provisions previously in existence for their particular plan types. See the discussions on 403(b) and 457 plans for more details.

## TABLE 4-2

Maximum Employee Contributions to Retirement Plans

| Retirement Plan | Age | 2002 | 2003 | 2004 | 2005 | 2006 | 2007 | 2008 |
|---|---|---|---|---|---|---|---|---|
| IRA | Under 50 | $ 3,000 | $ 3,000 | $ 3,000 | $ 4,000 | $ 4,000 | $ 4,000 | $ 5,000* |
| | 50+ | 3,500 | 3,500 | 3,500 | 4,500 | 5,000 | 5,000 | 6,000 |
| SIMPLE | Under 50 | 7,000 | 8,000 | 9,000 | 10,000 | 10,000* | 10,000* | 10,000* |
| | 50+ | 7,500 | 9,000 | 10,500 | 12,500 | 12,500 | 12,500 | 12,500 |
| 401(k), 403(b), 457 | Under 50 | 11,000 | 12,000 | 13,000 | 14,000 | 15,000* | 15,000* | 15,000* |
| | 50+ | 12,000 | 14,000 | 16,000 | 18,000 | 20,000 | 20,000 | 20,000 |
| Roth 401(k) | Under 50 | N/A | N/A | N/A | N/A | 15,000 | 15,000* | 15,000* |
| | 50 + | N/A | N/A | N/A | N/A | 20,000 | 20,000 | 20,000 |

*Plus inflation adjustment in $500 increments.

*Note:* SEP-IRA and Keogh plans are not included because they are generally funded through employer contributions. For 2003, the maximum employer contribution in a SEP-IRA or defined contribution Keogh is the lesser of 100% of compensation or $40,000.

## Matching

Many employer plans contain matching provisions in which your employer contributes to your account each time you contribute. Matching is generally described in percentage terms, such as "25 percent matching." In a plan with 25 percent matching, your employer deposits $0.25 in either company stock or cash for every $1 you contribute. This is an immediate 25 percent return on your money. Table 4-3 shows the same investment options illustrated in Table 4-1, except that the tax-deductible employer plan provides a 25 percent match. In this example, the retirement plan account is worth more than twice the $200,000 invested, and it surpasses the taxable account by $128,855.

---

**Retirement Tip**  Matching funds are free money. Take it! Where else can you get an immediate 25 percent return on your investment?

To see how your plan stacks up, check the Web site for the Profit Sharing Council of America (PSCA) at *www.401k.org* for statistics on employer plans. According to the PSCA, 94 percent of 401(k) plans currently offer a matching program. The most common match offered is 50 percent.

---

**TABLE 4-3**

Annual Contributions of $10,000:
Taxable Investment versus Tax-Deductible Retirement
Account with 25% Matching

|  | Taxable Investment | Tax-Deductible Plan |
|---|---|---|
| Investible income | $ 10,000 | $ 10,000 |
| Current income tax | 2,800 | 0 |
| Employer matching | 0 | 2,500 |
| Amount invested | 7,200 | 12,500 |
| Value after 20 years earning 8%* | 296,945† | 591,389 |
| Taxable amount at withdrawal | 0 | 591,389 |
| Taxes due on withdrawal | 0 | 165,589 |
| **Money you keep after 20 years** | **296,945** | **425,800** |

*Returns compounded monthly.

†Dividends and capital gains taxed at 15% annually.

## Vesting

While your contributions to a retirement plan always belong to you, your employer has the option of rewarding employee loyalty by creating a schedule in which matching funds do not belong to you until you have worked there for a certain number of years. This is called *vesting*. Matching funds (employer contributions) are considered vested once they have passed the time test. Once vested, funds are yours and may be withdrawn subject to the same restrictions as contributed funds. Funds that are not yet vested cannot be withdrawn. In *cliff vesting*, the entire employer contribution vests after a certain number of years. By law, the vesting period cannot be more than 3 years. In *graded vesting*, a certain amount of the employer contribution vests each year. The maximum period for graded vesting is 6 years.

For example, a 3- to 6-year graded vesting schedule might look like this:

| | |
|---|---|
| 40% | After 3 years |
| 60% | After 4 years |
| 80% | After 5 years |
| 100% | After 6 or more years |

If you contributed $1000 and received matching funds of $250, then left your employer after 3 years, you would be entitled to withdraw, transfer, or roll over your $1000 contribution plus 40 percent of the $250 matching funds, or $100. The total available to you would be $1100.

## Dollar Cost Averaging

Investing a regular amount at periodic intervals takes the emotion out of investing. With a consistent plan, you continue to buy shares when markets are low (probably the best time to invest, but psychologically the most difficult), and you do not jump in headfirst when sentiments are high (and markets may be ripe for a fall). By investing a constant dollar amount, you will buy more shares when individual share prices are low and fewer shares when prices are high, resulting in a low average cost per share. See Table 4-4 for a numerical example of how dollar cost averaging works.

**TABLE 4-4**

Dollar Cost Averaging

| Month | Regular Investment | Share Price | Shares Purchased* |
|-------|-------------------|-------------|-------------------|
| January | $ 200 | $ 10 | 20.00 |
| February | 200 | 10 | 20.00 |
| March | 200 | 9 | 22.22 |
| April | 200 | 8 | 25.00 |
| May | 200 | 8 | 25.00 |
| June | 200 | 8 | 25.00 |
| July | 200 | 9 | 22.22 |
| August | 200 | 9 | 22.22 |
| September | 200 | 10 | 20.00 |
| October | 200 | 11 | 18.18 |
| November | 200 | 10 | 20.00 |
| December | 200 | 11 | 18.18 |
| Total | $2,400 | $113 | 258.02 |

Average share price over time period = $113/12 = $9.42

Average cost of shares purchased = $2400/285.02 = $8.42

*Assumes fractional mutual fund share purchases.

## Transfers and Rollovers

If you leave your job, you have several options that will allow you to maintain your retirement account. Many employers will allow you maintain your retirement account of $5000 or more as it is, minus any contributions or matching. If you are happy with your investment choices and plan fees, there is no reason to move your account unless you want to consolidate it with other accounts to minimize paperwork. If your account balance is between $1000 and $4999, your employer is required to transfer your account into an IRA unless you request a cash distribution.

In a *transfer*, your plan custodian sends your funds directly to another retirement account. If your new employer has a retirement plan and will allow you to transfer deposits from your previous plan into it, you may request that your current custodian send your funds directly to the custodian of your new plan. Under the law enacted in 2001, funds from 401(k), 403(b), and 457 plans may be transferred into each other. If you would prefer to have control of the funds, you may open a self-directed IRA with a bank, brokerage firm, or mutual fund company and have your retirement funds transferred directly to your new investment company. In either case, the transfer will provide your funds with continuous custodial care, preventing any tax liability.

If your current custodian sends the funds to you, you have 60 days to reinvest the money in an IRA or another retirement plan in order to avoid current income taxes (and a penalty if you are under 59½ and do not meet one of the exceptions). This is called a *rollover*. Under IRS law, your employer is required to withhold 20 percent of any distribution sent to you, even if you intend to roll it over. This can get sticky because now you are short 20 percent of the money you need to reinvest. If you roll over the entire predistribution value of the account, making up the 20 percent from other sources, you can avoid taxes and penalties, and the IRS will refund the withheld 20 percent when you file your taxes the following year. If you can't come up with the missing 20 percent, it will be considered a distribution, and you will owe current income taxes and possibly penalties on that amount. For an example of this law in action, see the following dilemma.

---

**Retirement Dilemma**   Anna, age 42, is leaving the law firm where she has worked for 15 years to go into private practice. A diligent saver and smart investor, she has accumulated a 401(k) balance of $200,000. While concentrating on her new business, she let the letter from her benefits department work its way to the bottom of a pile on her desk. With no instruction, they simply sent her a check for $160,000, the balance of her account less 20 percent withholding. Anna had intended to keep the money in a retirement plan. What should she do?

**Solution**   To avoid paying current income taxes and penalties, she must come up with the missing $40,000 to add to the $160,000 they sent her so that she can roll over the full $200,000. If she doesn't have the money, she should consider borrowing it, especially if it is near the end of the year and she can file for a refund soon. A small amount of interest paid is worth avoiding taxes and a 10 percent penalty on $40,000.

## Loans

You may not borrow from an IRA or use it as collateral for a loan. However, many employers allow you to borrow a portion of your retirement plan account and pay yourself back, with interest. While it is not advisable to use your account for current expenses, in the case of financial emergency, it is better to borrow and repay than to withdraw and pay penalties and taxes.

By law, a retirement plan loan cannot exceed the lesser of $50,000 or one-half of the present value of the employee's vested interest in the plan. An exception is provided for accounts whose value is less than $20,000. The loan maximum in those cases is $10,000. Loans must be repaid within 5 years unless they are used to acquire a principal residence. In those cases, the loan may be amortized in equal payments, made not less than quarterly.

Before taking a loan from your plan, read about the hidden costs of retirement plan loans in Chapter 12.

## Premature Distributions

Because retirement plans are designed to support us in our old age, the IRS makes it hard to get your money out before retirement. Do not invest every available dollar into your plan without creating separate investment accounts for emergencies (we recommend 3 to 6 months' living expenses) or for other nonretirement needs.

To get your money out of your retirement plan, you must do one of the following:

- Die
- Separate from service (that is, leave your job)
- Reach age 59½
- Become disabled
- Encounter financial hardship

### Hardship Distributions

For a withdrawal to qualify as a hardship distribution, it must satisfy two requirements:

- It must be due to the employee's immediate and heavy financial need.
- It must be necessary to satisfy that need.

Hardship distributions are subject to ordinary income tax and to the 10 percent IRS penalty for withdrawals before age 59½. The following are examples of what is considered immediate and heavy need:

- Medical expenses previously incurred by the employee or his or her spouse or dependents; or the amounts necessary for any of these persons to obtain medical care
- Costs incurred in purchasing a principal residence (not including mortgage payments)
- Tuition and related educational expenses for the next year of postsecondary education for the employee or his or her spouse or dependents
- Payments to prevent eviction from or foreclosure on a principal residence

**Retirement Tip**   Many plans that allow hardship distributions will not allow an employee to participate in the plan for 1 year following such a distribution.

## Credit for Start-Up Costs

Many small businesses cite start-up costs as a reason for not having a retirement plan. If you are employed by a small business that doesn't have a retirement plan, make sure your employer knows about tax credits available to cover plan start-up costs. Beginning in 2002, small businesses (100 or fewer employees) may be able to take a tax credit for the costs involved in establishing a SEP, SIMPLE, or other qualified plan. The credit equals 50 percent of the cost to set up, administer, and educate employees about the plan. The maximum deduction is $500 per year for each of the first 3 years of the plan.

# 401(k) PLANS

The 401(k) plan is the most common type of contributory retirement plan offered by private-sector employers. For the basic characteristics of your 401(k) plan, see the preceding discussion of employer-sponsored retirement plans. Following are a few notable characteristics that set 401(k) plans apart.

## Employer Stock

The ability or requirement to invest your retirement funds in the common stock of your employer has come under great scrutiny with the collapse of Enron, in which employees lost $1 billion in their retirement plans due to the falling stock price of their employer. While most 401(k) plans offer a variety of mutual funds as investment choices, many publicly held companies offer the option of investing in their stock and may also use stock for matching contributions. [This is not an issue for 403(b) and 457 plans because they are not offered by publicly held companies.]

Using company stock for its matching program benefits your employer in two ways: There is no cash cost to the match, and employees who own stock often take their jobs more seriously when the bottom line affects their own investments. As an employee, you benefit by being able to directly contribute to the success of your investment through your job performance. Keep in mind, though, that there is danger in having too much of your financial well-being tied up in one place. For more discussion on the relative merits of investing in your employer's stock, see Chapters 8 and 11. If your matching contributions are in company stock, direct your own contributions to be invested in a diversified portfolio of unrelated securities.

---

**Retirement Tip**   When deciding how much of your plan to have invested in your employer's stock, remember the Rule of Five, which says that for every five stocks you buy, one will perform wonderfully, three will move with the stock market, and one will be your worst nightmare. Consider the effect on your retirement if your employer's stock falls into the last category.

---

## Contribution Limits

Table 4-2 outlined annual employee contribution limits for different employer plans. In addition to those limits, there is a cap on combined employer and employee contributions that applies to 401(k) and 403(b) plans. The employer contribution includes both matching contributions within the plan and other employer contributions, such as those made to a separate pension or profit-sharing plan. The maximum dollar amount of combined contributions for 2003 is $40,000. You may hear your benefits coordinator refer to this limit as the "Section 415 limit." The EGTRRA increased the maximum percentage of pay that the employee can contribute to 100 percent of pay, from 25 percent. This is a big benefit for some two-income families, in which a second salary can go entirely to retirement savings.

**Retirement Dilemma**  Kim and Johnny are financially comfortable and can easily live on Johnny's salary. Kim would like to take a part-time job at her favorite clothing store. She would enjoy the work and would get a nice discount to boot. Johnny says that due to their high tax bracket, they would pay so much in taxes on her income that she'd end up spending far more than she'd earn. Can they make this work?

**Solution**  If her potential employer has a good 401(k) plan, they might. If she earns $12,000 and the plan allows her to contribute all of it, they won't pay any income taxes on her salary. In addition, if the plan has a 50 percent match, they would end up with a retirement account worth $18,000 at the end of the year. Surely she can't spend that much!

In another cap on retirement saving, the law provides for a maximum amount of compensation that can be used as a basis for 401(k) contributions. The 2001 changes increase the maximum compensation to $200,000 from $170,000. Going forward, this amount will be adjusted for inflation in $5000 increments.

Another IRS regulation attempts to prevent those with high salaries from benefiting more from a 401(k) plan than those with low salaries. It can limit the amount that "highly compensated employees" may contribute. You fall in this category in 2003 if you earned more than $90,000 in 2002 or owned more than 5 percent of your company. Limits can apply after IRS discrimination testing that compares relative amounts that employees of different salary levels contribute. Small businesses in which a higher percentage of the workforce is highly compensated are more often affected than businesses with the same number of executives and many additional employees. In 401(k) plans, employee and employer contributions are combined for testing, while in 403(b) plans only employer contributions are considered.

## 403(b) PLANS

When we talk to a group about 401(k) plans, invariably the question is asked, "I have a 403(b); does this apply to me?" The answer is, "Generally, yes, with a few differences." While the 403(b) plan may sound like a unique beast, it is similar to other employer-sponsored retirement plans as outlined earlier in our general discussion. The main difference between a 403(b) and a 401(k) plan is the type of employer that offers each.

Your employer can offer a 403(b) plan if it is a public school or a tax-exempt organization. A *public school* is defined as an educational organization of a state or local government or any of its agencies or instrumentalities. You are eligible as an employee of a public school if you perform either direct or indirect services. *Direct services* include those provided by teachers, principals, custodial employees, and administrative employees. *Indirect services* include jobs that are not performed in the schools but that are involved in the operation or direction of educational programs for the public schools. Department of Education employees and those elected or appointed to office in the field of education are also eligible.

Tax-exempt organizations, defined by Section 501(c)(3) of the Internal Revenue Code, such as religious, charitable, or educational groups, are eligible providers of 403(b) plans, as are hospital service organizations or the separate, tax-exempt entities of a government instrumentality.

## 403(b)(7) Plans and Tax-Sheltered Annuities

Another factor that may differentiate a 403(b) plan from other employer plans is the type of investments offered. While 401(k) plans generally offer a variety of mutual funds, guaranteed investment contracts, and possibly employer stock as investment options, many 403(b) plans only offer tax-sheltered annuities as investment choices. In this case the plan may be called a *tax-sheltered annuity* (TSA). Your 403(b) plan is technically called a 403(b)(7) if it can invest in regulated investment company stock, the IRS name for mutual funds.

In Chapter 5, we discuss annuities in depth from the point of view of investing outside a retirement plan. It is commonly accepted in the investment community that the high annual expenses, surrender charges, the tax treatment of withdrawals, and the generally lackluster performance of annuities make them poor investments. Yet the benefit of tax deferral can outweigh these disadvantages for some.

In a 403(b) plan, you have tax deferral automatically; you don't need the annuity to get it. If your 403(b) provider offers only annuities as investment choices, compare their annual expenses and performance against mutual funds with similar investment objectives. If you find that the annuities in your plan don't stack up well, you are not necessarily out of luck. First, talk to your coworkers to see if you can make a group effort to convince your plan administrator or provider to offer a wider array of investment choices. A lack of investment alternatives may simply be due to the fact that no one has asked for more. Remember, the squeaky wheel gets the grease!

If your provider isn't willing to offer more choices, you still have an option, called a *90-24 transfer*, available to you if your employer doesn't make contributions to your account. In this type of transfer, you can move your 403(b) account funds to the financial institution of your choice. The financial institution may be a low-fee mutual fund company and need not be on your employer's approved list. The transfer must take place between the two trustees; in order to avoid a penalty, you may not take possession of the funds.

Before you begin a 90-24 transfer, find out whether the investments you currently have are subject to surrender fees. Many annuities have declining surrender fees that begin as high as 7 percent and last as long as 7 years. If you have been in the plan a long time, some of your contributions may have been invested long enough that surrender charges no longer apply. Consider moving these funds, while waiting until the end of the surrender period on your newer funds.

---

**Retirement Tip**  If your 403(b) invests in annuities with stiff surrender fees and you would like to perform a 90-24 transfer without paying fees, invest new contributions into money market accounts. Generally money market funds do not impose a surrender charge, so you can transfer without paying a penalty. Check with your provider to make sure yours doesn't impose any fees.

---

## Cost of Insurance

If your 403(b) plan invests in annuity contracts that provide you with incidental life insurance protection, you must include the cost of the insurance in your taxable wages for the year. To compute the amount of your life insurance protection, use the following formula:

$$\text{Amount payable upon your death} - \text{Cash value of the contract at year end} = \text{Amount of current life insurance protection}$$

The 1-year cost of term life insurance protection can be figured from the table provided in IRS Publication 571 or from current published life insurance premium rates of your annuity company. You may use whichever is lower.

## Special Catch-Up Provisions

In addition to the recently introduced 50+ catch-up contribution provision that applies to the three major employer plans, 403(b) plan participants may take advantage of a special catch-up rule. To qualify, you must have 15 years of service (not necessarily consecutive) with the same employer and you must not have contributed the maximum contributions in previous years. Then you may contribute up to an additional $3000 per year, up to a lifetime limit of $15,000.

### Tax-Exempt 501(c)3 Organization 403(b) Plans

If you work for a church or other tax-exempt 501(c)3 organization, your 403(b) plan may not follow the rules of the Employee Retirement Income Security Act (ERISA) that govern other 403(b) plans. In general, non-ERISA church 403(b) plans are simpler and easier to set up, but they may provide less legal protection for participants. These plans are not subject to minimum participation requirements, and they are not required to have a plan document or to provide participants with a summary plan description. Distribution requirements are less stringent, and investment opportunities may be wider. If you work for a church or related organization, check with your plan administrator to find out whether your plan follows standard ERISA rules for 403(b) plans. If not, ask the administrator or plan trustee for the special rules involved.

For more information about 403(b) plans, consult your tax advisor, plan document, and IRS Publication 571, *Tax-Sheltered Annuity Programs for Employees of Public Schools and Certain Tax-Exempt Organizations.*

## 457 PLANS

A 457 plan is another form of employer-sponsored retirement plan. Employers that can offer 457 plans include state and local government entities and some tax-exempt organizations. Those offered by government entities are called *public-sector plans,* and they generally allow employee salary deferrals but not employer contributions. A different kind of 457 plan is offered by some nonprofit institutions to their top executives and allows employer contributions but not employee contributions.

### Exceptions to Maximum Contribution Limits

In our general discussion of retirement plans earlier in this chapter, we outlined contribution limits for 401(k), 403(b), and 457 plans. In an interesting twist of the law, workers with two jobs during a year may be able to contribute more than the stated maximums if one employer sponsors a 401(k) or 403(b) plan and the other sponsors a 457 plan. The same may be true if your employer offers a 457 plan in conjunction with a 401(k) or 403(b) plan. While annual deferral limits refer to combined deferrals of 401(k) and 403(b) plans, 457 plan contributions are considered separately.

---

**Retirement Dilemma**   Janet has already contributed the maximum allowable $12,000 to her 403(b) plan in 2003. When she changes jobs midyear, her new employer has a 457 plan that she is immediately eligible to enroll in. Is she maxed out for the year?

**Solution**   No, she can contribute up to another $12,000 to her new 457 plan.

---

Another way that 457 plans are set apart from 403(b) and 401(k) plans is that participating in a 457 plan doesn't affect whether an IRA contribution is deductible.

---

**Retirement Dilemma**   Nathan's employer offers a choice between a 403(b) and a 457 plan, each funded with employee salary deferrals. Nathan's income is high enough that he can deduct an IRA contribution only if he isn't an "active participant" in a workplace retirement plan.

**Solution**   He should participate in the 457 plan if he intends to contribute to an IRA as well. Then he can deduct his IRA contribution. If he chooses the 403(b) plan, he cannot.

---

## Special Catch-Up Provisions

In the 3 years preceding retirement, 457 plan participants can make catch-up contributions to compensate for amounts they didn't save earlier. In 2003, the special catch-up limit is $12,000, and it increases by $1000 per year until 2006, effectively doubling the amount you can contribute each year. These catch-up contributions are limited to the amounts that could have been contributed in prior years but weren't. If your plan allows the special catch-up contribution, you can't take advantage of the 50+ catch-up provision at the same time. For example, this means that the maximum you could contribute in 2008 under catch-up provisions is $30,000, or a $15,000 regular contribution plus a $15,000 special 3-year catch-up contribution. You cannot add in the extra $5000 allowed under the 50+ provision.

## ROTH 401(k) AND 403(b) PLANS

The tax law passed in 2001 allowed for the creation of *qualified Roth contribution programs*, legalese for Roth 401(k) and 403(b) plans. These plans will be available in 2006, and they may be offered as part of new or existing 401(k) and 403(b) retirement plans. As with Roth IRAs, contributions will not be tax deductible, and withdrawals, subject to some limitations, will be tax exempt. If Roth accounts are offered in your employer's plan, you will be given the option to direct your contributions into a deductible account or a Roth account, or split them between the two. Your employer will be required to keep separate accounts for deductible and Roth contributions. Contribution limits will apply to the sum of deductible and Roth contributions to the plan.

## PLANS FOR SMALL BUSINESSES AND THE SELF-EMPLOYED

### SEP-IRA

The SEP-IRA is the Simplified Employee Pension IRA for small businesses and sole proprietors. Contributions to SEP-IRAs are made pretax by your employer (or you, if you are self-employed), and they must be made at the same percentage of compensation for all eligible employees. Employer contributions do not reduce your taxable income unless you are a sole proprietor. The rules surrounding SEP-IRAs are the same as those for ordinary IRAs except that the contribution limit is significantly higher. The maximum contribution is the lesser of 25 percent of total compensation or $40,000 for each employee.

## SIMPLE-IRA

The Savings Incentive Match Plan for Employees–IRA, or SIMPLE-IRA, is a tax-deferred retirement plan for sole proprietors and businesses with fewer than 100 employees who earned $5000 or more in the previous year. The SIMPLE-IRA replaced the SARSEP-IRA (Salary Reduction SEP-IRA) for plans established on or after January 1, 1997, and it similarly allows employee contributions to the retirement plan. (SEP-IRAs do not, unless you are self-employed.)

Employee contributions are made pretax, up to a maximum of $8000 in 2003; this limit increases by $1000 per year until it reaches $10,000 in 2005, and it is adjusted for inflation thereafter in multiples of $500. Employers can contribute either

- a 100 percent match for all employees, up to 3 percent of each employee's total compensation

or

- 2 percent of each employee's compensation, regardless of employee contribution, up to a maximum of $3200 per employee

## SIMPLE 401(k)

Similar to the SIMPLE-IRA, the SIMPLE 401(k) is designed for employers with 100 or fewer employees who earned $5000 or more in the previous year. The plans are similar in other ways, including contribution limits and withdrawal rules. An advantage of the SIMPLE 401(k) is that participants can take loans from their accounts. A disadvantage is the additional paperwork required for IRS reporting.

## Solo 401(k)

The solo 401(k) is a retirement plan that works well for small businesses in which the owners or the owners and their spouses are the only employees of the business. The attractive feature of the plan is its high contribution limits due to a slight change in the 2001 wording of contribution limits for 401(k) plans. As previously noted, the maximum employee contribution to a 401(k) plan is 100 percent of compensation or $40,000. The maximum employer contribution is 25 percent of compensation. Previously, combined employer and employee contributions were subject to a 15 percent limit. Presently, as a self-employed person, you can contribute the 25 percent maximum employer contribution *and* the $12,000 maximum employee contribution allowed in 2003. Given this quirk, those whose incomes are under $160,000 and who can afford to contribute a large amount of their current income can contribute more with a solo 401(k) than with a SIMPLE-IRA or SEP-IRA. At an income of $160,000 or above, participants in both the SEP-IRA and the solo 401(k) reach the maximum contribution of $40,000.

In addition to higher contribution limits, the solo 401(k) has several other benefits:

- Less paperwork required than for a standard 401(k) plan
- Lower costs than are generally incurred in a standard 401(k) plan
- The ability to offer loans from retirement accounts (not available with SIMPLE-IRAs or SEP-IRAs)

Table 4-5 outlines the differences in allowed contributions for different income levels. As you look at the table, keep in mind the formulas for maximum contributions on each type of plan.

- Solo 401(k): $12,000 + 25 percent of compensation, maximum $40,000
- SIMPLE-IRA or 401(k): $8000 + 3 percent of compensation
- SEP-IRA: 25 percent of compensation, maximum $40,000

## Keoghs

Keoghs are retirement plans for self-employed individuals or partners, including those who are incorporated. Keoghs are employer-contribution plans. The maximum contribution allowed is the lesser of $40,000 or 25 percent of compensation. The maximum wage base upon which you may make a contribution is $200,000 for 2002.

There are two types of Keogh plans, and they may be used independently or together. They differ primarily in their requirement to contribute every year.

**TABLE 4-5**

Comparison of Contribution Limits for Solo 401(k), SIMPLE-IRA, and SEP-IRA

|  | Annual Contribution Limits for 2003 | | |
| Compensation* | Solo 401(k)† | SIMPLE-IRA† | SEP-IRA |
| --- | --- | --- | --- |
| $200,000 | $40,000 | $14,000 | $40,000 |
| 160,000 | 40,000 | 12,800 | 40,000 |
| 150,000 | 40,000 | 12,500 | 37,500 |
| 125,000 | 40,000 | 11,750 | 31,250 |
| 100,000 | 37,000 | 11,000 | 25,000 |
| 75,000 | 30,750 | 10,250 | 18,750 |
| 50,000 | 24,500 | 9,500 | 12,500 |
| 25,000 | 18,250 | 8,750 | 6,250 |
| 10,000 | 10,000 | 8,300 | 2,500 |

*Compensation is defined as earned income for self-employed individuals and unincorporated businesses. Earned income is generally net earnings from self-employment, reduced by plan contributions and one-half of the self-employment tax.

†Those who are age 50 or older may make additional catch-up contributions.

## Profit-Sharing Plans

The profit-sharing plan is the most flexible Keogh because it allows you to vary the percentage of income that you contribute each year. You may also choose not to contribute in a given year. Consider a profit-sharing plan if your income varies significantly from year to year and you don't want to be committed to an annual contribution.

## Money Purchase Plans

Money purchase plans offer the same contribution limits but less flexibility. The percentage of each eligible employee's compensation to be contributed is set when the plan is established and cannot be changed each year. Consider a money purchase plan if your income is stable enough that you don't mind committing to an annual contribution.

Table 4-6 provides a summary of characteristics of retirement plans available to small businesses.

## TABLE 4-6

### Comparison of Retirement Plans Available to Small Businesses

|  | SEP-IRA | SIMPLE-IRA or 401(k) | Solo 401(k) |
|---|---|---|---|
| Key advantage | Easy to set up and maintain; high contribution limits. | Salary reduction plan with little paperwork. | Highest contribution limits of small business plans. |
| Employer eligibility | Any employer with one or more employees. | Any employer with 100 or fewer employees. | Best where owners and spouses are the only employees. |
| Set up | Complete IRS Form 5305-SEP. No annual filing requirements. | Complete IRS Form 5304-SIMPLE or IRS Form 5305-SIMPLE. No annual filing requirements for IRA; required for 401(k) plan. | Need a plan document and a trustee to hold plan assets. Annual filing of Form 5500 when assets exceed $100,000. |
| Who contributes | Employer contributions only. | Employee and employer contributions. | Employee and employer contributions. |
| Maximum annual contributions | Up to 25% of compensation, maximum $40,000.* | Employee: Up to $8000 + catch-up contributions for over age 50. Employer: 2% of each eligible employee's compensation or 100% match of first 3% of compensation for participating employees. | Employee: Up to $12,000 + catch-up contributions for over age 50. Employer: Up to 25% of compensation, maximum $40,000. |
| Contributor's options | Employer can decide whether to make contributions each year. | Employee can decide how much to contribute. Employer must either match or contribute. | Employee and employer (generally the same person) decide how much to contribute. |

| 401(k) | Profit Sharing | Money Purchase | Defined-Benefit Pension |
|---|---|---|---|
| Salary reduction plan. | High contribution limits with discretionary contribution amounts. | High contribution limits. | Provides a fixed, preestablished retirement benefit. |
| Any employer with one or more employees. | Any employer with one or more employees. | Any employer with one or more employees. | Any employer with one or more employees. |
| Need a plan document and a trustee to hold plan assets. Annual filing of Form 5500 and nondiscrimination testing required. | No IRS model form; annual filing of Form 5500 required. | No IRS model form; annual filing of Form 5500 required. | No IRS model form; annual filing of Form 5500 required. |
| Employee salary reduction and/or employer contributions. | Discretionary annual employer contributions. | Fixed annual employer contributions. | Employer contributions. |
| Employee: $12,000 + catch-up contributions for over age 50. Employer/employee combined: lesser of 100% of compensation or $40,000. | Lesser of 100% of compensation or $40,000. Employer can deduct amounts that do not exceed 25% of aggregate compensation for all participants. | Lesser of 100% of compensation or $40,000. Employer can deduct amounts that do not exceed 25% of aggregate compensation for all participants. | |
| Employee can choose how much salary to contribute. Employer can contribute per plan document. | Contributions set by plan terms. | Contributions set by plan terms. | |

**TABLE 4-6 (CONTINUED)**

Comparison of Retirement Plans Available to Small
Businesses

| | SEP-IRA | SIMPLE-IRA or 401(k) | Solo 401(k) |
|---|---|---|---|
| Employee coverage requirements | All employees who are 21, have been employed 3 of the last 5 years, and have had earned income of $450. | All employees who earned $5000 or more in one of the last 2 years. | All owner/employees are covered. |
| Withdrawals, loans, and payments | Withdrawals permitted subject to federal income tax; early withdrawals subject to IRS penalty; loans are not permitted. | Withdrawals permitted subject to federal income tax; early withdrawals subject to IRS penalty; loans permitted only in 401(k) plan. | Withdrawals permitted after a specified event (e.g., retirement or termination). May permit loans and hardship withdrawals; early withdrawal subject to penalty. |
| Vesting | Contributions are 100% vested immediately. | Employee and employer contributions are 100% vested immediately. | Employee and employer contributions are 100% vested immediately. |

*Maximum compensation on which 2003 contributions can be based is $200,000.

# SUMMARY

Employer-sponsored retirement plans can be the best thing going when it comes to saving for retirement. The combination of tax-deductible contributions, tax deferral on investment growth, high contribution limits, convenience, and employer matching contributions should put your employer plan at the top of your list for saving. Pay yourself first and you won't even notice what you never have a chance to spend.

| 401(k) | Profit Sharing | Money Purchase | Defined-Benefit Pension |
|---|---|---|---|
| All employees over 21 who worked 1000 hours in the previous year. | All employees over 21 who worked 1000 hours in the previous year. | All employees over 21 who worked 1000 hours in the previous year. | All employees over 21 who worked 1000 hours in the previous year. |
| Withdrawals permitted after a specified event (e.g., retirement or termination). May permit loans and hardship withdrawals; early withdrawal subject to penalty. | Withdrawals permitted after a specified event (e.g., retirement or termination). May permit loans; early withdrawal subject to penalty. | Payment of benefits after a specified event (e.g., retirement or termination). May permit loans; early withdrawal subject to penalty. | Payment of benefits after a specified event (e.g., retirement or termination). May permit loans; early withdrawal subject to penalty. |
| Employee contributions are 100% vested immediately. Employer contributions may vest over time. | Employer contributions may vest over time. Employee contributions, if any, are 100% vested immediately. | Employer contributions may vest over time. Employee contributions, if any, are 100% vested immediately. | Employer contributions may vest over time. Employee contributions, if any, are 100% vested immediately. |

Take some time to read further about your personal investment pyramid in Chapter 7, investment risk in Chapter 8, and danger signs in Chapter 11. Having a good plan is part of the equation; knowing how best to use it is the rest.

# CHAPTER 5

# Annuities and Life Insurance

**T**here is much disagreement in the financial community about whether life insurance should be used as an investment and whether the advantages of annuities outweigh the disadvantages. Because there isn't a definitive right answer, you should learn why these products are sold as retirement saving vehicles, what the advantages and disadvantages are, and whether or not they can be a valuable part of your plan.

## ANNUITIES

An *annuity* is a tax-deferred investment product that you buy from an insurance company. Each annuity has two distinct phases, accumulation and distribution. During the *accumulation phase*, you contribute funds to the annuity, and the money invested grows tax deferred. During the *distribution phase*, you withdraw money either in one lump-sum payment or in a stream of payments, called an *annuity*. These payments can come either over a specified time period or over the rest of your life.

### Types of Annuities: Fixed or Variable, Deferred or Immediate

If you purchase an annuity, you will be able to choose whether you prefer a fixed or variable investment style. A *fixed annuity* offers a set return, much the way a certificate of deposit does. Periodically, the annuity comes up for renewal, with a new rate of return, based on current interest rates. You can choose to lock in your rate for different time periods, such as 6 months, 1 year, or 2 years.

A *variable annuity* allows you to choose among subaccounts, similar to mutual funds, to invest your money. Investment objectives range from money market accounts to aggressive stock funds. Generally, you can choose a combination of different accounts and switch between accounts at least four times per year.

You can also choose when you will begin receiving annuity payments. Most annuities are deferred annuities. In a *deferred annuity* there is an extended accumulation phase in which contributions are made to the annuity before payouts begin. An *immediate annuity* begins payments right away. This type of annuity is often used to pay out retirement accounts.

**Retirement Dilemma**   Alice is retiring this year and has several choices for the payout of her retirement plan. One choice offers her a series of payments for the rest of her life, no matter how long she lives. This appeals to her because the stock market is uncertain and the rest of her retirement savings are invested there. How can her retirement plan offer guaranteed payments for life?

**Solution**   The plan administrator will take the balance of her account and buy a *single-premium, immediate annuity* (SPIA) from an insurance company. Her account balance pays the single premium. The insurance company compiles information such as the amount invested, her life expectancy, and the estimated return on their investments to compute a monthly payment for her, which they will begin to pay immediately.

## Advantages of Annuities as a Retirement Investment

Annuities can be appealing as retirement investments for the reasons outlined here. Before making up your mind, read the disadvantages as well.

## Tax Deferral of Investment Growth

Contributions to an annuity are not tax deductible, but the earnings in the investment account are not subject to income taxes until they are withdrawn. As noted in Chapter 2, deferring income taxes on investment gains allows you to invest and earn with money that would otherwise have been paid in taxes. If the investments allocated to this portion of your portfolio earn interest, which is taxed at ordinary income tax rates, tax deferral can provide a significant benefit.

## The Option of Annuitizing

Ask anyone who is saving for retirement what the worst possible retirement scenario is and you likely will be told, "Outliving my retirement savings." In a time when many of us live into our nineties and beyond, this can be a legitimate concern, even for the best prepared. One of the benefits of an annuity is the many distribution choices available, including payments for the rest of your life, no matter how long that may be.

Your payment options are generally variations of payments over your lifetime or payments over a certain time period. For example, you might have the following choices:

- *Life Income or Straight Life.*   Annuity payments are made as long as the owner lives. They cease when the owner dies.

  *Advantage.*   You will never outlive your payments.

  *Disadvantage.*   If you die shortly after beginning payments, you might receive much less than you paid into the policy.

- *Temporary Annuity Certain.*   The annuity is payable for a fixed dollar amount or fixed time period whether the owner lives or dies. If the annuitant dies, payments are made to a beneficiary.

  *Advantage.*   You (or your beneficiary) will be certain to receive either a certain amount or a particular number of payments.

  *Disadvantage.*   You can outlive your payments.

- *Life Income, Period Certain.*   The annuity is payable over the owner's life, with a minimum period. For example, "life income, 10 years certain," means that if the owner dies after 5 years, a beneficiary will continue to receive payments until the tenth year. If the owner lives past 10 years, payments will continue throughout but will not exceed his or her lifetime.

*Advantage.* You (or your beneficiary) will be certain to receive a certain number of payments *and* you will not outlive your payments.

*Disadvantage.* Due to the life insurance company's guarantee to pay for at least the specified time period, the monthly payment will be lower than it would be with a simple life income option.

- *Life Income with Refund.* The annuity is payable over the owner's lifetime. If the owner dies before receiving an amount equal to payments made into the plan, a beneficiary will receive the balance.

  *Advantage.* You (or your beneficiary) will be certain to receive a specific dollar amount in payments, *and* you will not outlive your payments.

  *Disadvantage.* Due to the life insurance company's guarantee to pay out at least the specified amount, the monthly payment will be lower than it would be with a simple life income option.

- *Life Income Joint and Survivor.* The annuity is payable to two or more people while either is living. Upon the death of the first, payments will continue, sometimes at a reduced rate.

  *Advantage.* The spouse of a married annuitant will continue to receive payments after the annuitant's death.

  *Disadvantage.* There is a chance that the annuitant's spouse will outlive the annuitant, requiring more payments by the insurance company. For this reason, monthly payments will be lower than they would be with options based on just one life.

- *Joint Life.* The annuity is payable to two or more annuitants while both are living. Payments stop upon the death of either annuitant.

  *Advantage.* Monthly payments are higher than they would be with an annuity based on just one life since there is an additional chance of death, which stops payments. If both parties have significant life insurance policies and will not need the annuity after the other's death, this can increase current income.

*Disadvantage.* An early death could mean a very small amount paid out as compared to amount in premiums paid in.

If you are deciding among payment choices such as those just given, keep in mind that the dollar amount paid per month will not be the same under different options. Higher payment guarantees generally mean lower monthly payments.

## No Contribution Limits
There are legal limits to the amount that you can invest in tax-deferred retirement plans, such as IRA, 401(k), or 403(b) plans. If you have reached those contribution limits, you can still take advantage of tax-deferred growth through annuities. If you are in a high tax bracket and anticipate being in a lower bracket during retirement, this may make sense. The strategy of investing in annuities or life insurance only after exhausting other tax-deferred options is part of the hierarchy discussed more fully in Chapter 10.

## Disadvantages of Annuities as a Retirement Investment

There are quite a few arguments against using annuities for retirement investing, some of which are listed here.

## Penalties for Early Withdrawal
Similar to other qualified retirement accounts, there are penalties for withdrawing the funds invested in an annuity before retirement age. If you make a partial or full withdrawal before reaching the age of 59½, the IRS charges a 10 percent penalty on growth in the annuity's value (excess of value over premiums paid in). This penalty does not apply if:

- The contract owner has died.
- The recipient has become disabled, as defined by federal law.

- The withdrawal is part of the annuitization process.
- The annuity was purchased by an employer for an employee and held by the employer until the employee separated from service.

---

**Retirement Tip**  If you are not pleased with the performance of an annuity, you don't have to make a withdrawal in order to invest differently. There is an IRS provision, called a *1035 exchange*, which allows you to liquidate an annuity without paying taxes or penalties as long as you immediately exchange it for another annuity. This is similar in concept to an IRA transfer.

---

## Fees

In many cases, the high fees charged by annuity providers outweigh the benefits of tax deferral. Some fees to note are:

- *Sales Commissions.*  Commissions, which often run as high as 7 percent of the amount contributed, are not explicitly charged to the account. However, the money has to come from somewhere. Often it is taken out in the form of higher asset charges.
- *Mortality and Expense/Asset Charges.*  Similar to the cost of insurance in a cash value life insurance policy, this is the cost of providing guaranteed death benefits and guaranteed lifetime payments to those who outlive their life expectancy. This fee may also include some general expenses, such as the cost of paying an agent's commissions. According to the National Association of Variable Annuities (NAVA), the industry average is 1.15 percent.
- *Management Fees.*  The cost of managing each subaccount, management fees are also charged by mutual funds and differ depending on the particular subaccount chosen. According to the NAVA, the industry average is 0.82 percent. This figure is dependent on the type of securities held in the account. Just as with mutual funds, expect lower management fees on index and bond funds, higher fees on actively managed stock funds.

- *Annual Contract Charge.*  A maintenance fee ranging from $30 to $40 per account is typically charged.
- *Surrender Charges.*  Substantial penalties apply on many annuities if you cash out in the first few years. Most surrender charges work the same way that a contingent deferred sales charge (CDSC) applies to a mutual fund, typically beginning at 7 percent and declining by 1 percent each year.

---

**Retirement Tip**   Fees are generally charged as a percentage of the amount invested, but they are often quoted in basis points. To convert a basis point to a percentage, place a decimal in front of the last two numbers. For example, 125 basis points equals 1.25 percent, and 60 basis points equals 0.60 percent.

---

## Inheritance Tax Laws

Annuities do not receive favorable tax treatment upon the owner's death. The growth in the annuity account is taxed as ordinary income to heirs. In contrast, the appreciation of a taxable investment account escapes income and capital gains taxes at death because heirs receive a *stepped-up* basis, meaning that their cost basis is the value of the account at the time of death rather than the previous owner's original cost basis.

## Ordinary Income Tax versus Dividend and Capital Gains Tax

Gains in the value of an annuity are considered ordinary income and are taxed at ordinary income tax rates, which range as high as 35 percent. This is in contrast to dividends and capital gains on a mutual fund or stock investment, which are taxed at 15 percent. (Capital gains must be the result of increases in the share price of a security held for more than 1 year, to receive favorable treatment.)

When money is withdrawn or paid out of an annuity, the amount of premiums paid in is treated as a return of capital and is not taxable. The gain in the account (difference between the account value and premiums paid) is taxable as ordinary income.

During *annuitization* (the distribution phase), a pro rata portion of each payment is considered ordinary income, based on the ratio of the growth in the account (computed as the account value less total premiums paid) to the entire account value. For lump-sum distributions, in which you take the entire account value at once, all growth in the account is taxable as ordinary income.

Partial withdrawals taken before the distribution phase are treated as if all interest or growth is being withdrawn first. For example, if you took a $10,000 partial withdrawal from an annuity with a cost basis (premiums paid in) of $100,000 and a current value of $120,000, the full $10,000 would be taxable as ordinary income. If you took a $30,000 withdrawal from the same annuity, $20,000 would be taxable as ordinary income and $10,000 would be considered a return of capital and would not be taxable.

In a full surrender (withdrawal), the entire amount of the gain in the account would be taxable as ordinary income. In both cases, the withdrawals might also be subject to surrender charges and a 10 percent penalty tax, depending on the contract and your age.

**Retirement Dilemma**   Trevor and Sue want to invest $50,000 of the money they have saved for retirement in several stocks that do not pay dividends. They expect all of their return to come from increases in the stocks' prices. A friend is suggesting they buy a variable annuity instead. If both the stocks and the annuity double in value over the next 6 years (a 12 percent annualized return) and they are in a 30 percent tax bracket, where will they be better off?

**Solution**   They would be better off in the taxable stock account. In a 30 percent tax bracket, they would pay $15,000 in ordinary income taxes on the $50,000 in annuity growth, versus $7500 in capital gains taxes (at 15 percent) on a $50,000 increase in value for stocks held in a taxable account.

## Should You Invest in Annuities?

The overwhelming opinion of the investment community (excluding those in the business of selling annuities) is that the additional fees, tax treatment of proceeds, and lack of liquidity outweigh the benefit of tax deferral. That said, annuities may make sense under the following conditions:

- You have contributed the maximum allowable to your IRA and employer retirement plans. Both of these avenues of retirement saving provide tax deferral without the additional expenses of annuities. Take maximum advantage of these before investing in annuities. *Note:* Do not buy an annuity in your IRA. There is no reason to pay the extra fees when the IRA provides tax deferral already.
- Your time horizon is at least 15 and preferably 20 years, during which time you will gain significant benefit from tax deferral and will not be subject to high surrender charges.
- You expect your tax bracket to be lower in retirement.
- Your preferred investments pay interest income, which would result in a stiff annual income tax bill at ordinary income tax rates for taxable investment accounts.
- You are willing to search out no-load, low-expense annuities. Consider annuities without a death benefit. Unless you make terrible investment choices, this is an expense without much value.
- You are not terribly concerned with leaving assets to your heirs, as they will have to pay income taxes on the growth of the account if they inherit it.
- You would like the peace of mind of knowing that lifetime annuitization means you will not outlive your payments.

## LIFE INSURANCE

Life insurance can be an important part of planning for your family's financial security. In its simplest application, you need life insurance if there is anyone who depends on your income. Additionally, if you have debts, such as a mortgage that would be a burden to those left behind, you need life insurance. Other applications of life insurance include its use for estate tax payment, the buyout of a closely held business, and charitable contributions.

Lastly, life insurance is often used as an investment for retirement planning, which is what we will concentrate on here.

Life insurance can be divided into two categories, term and cash value, depending on whether the policy is pure insurance (*term*) or insurance plus an investment (*cash value*). (See Table 5-1.) When you buy term insurance, you pay premiums in exchange for a death benefit over a specified term. It is the cheapest way to obtain the most in death benefits. Because the death benefit is all you get with term insurance, it is never sold as an investment.

*Cash value life insurance*, also called *permanent life insurance*, promises to protect you for your entire life, not just a stated number of years. Initially, the premiums are higher than term life premiums, but later in life they are more comparable, even lower. With the excess premium paid over the actual cost of insurance, the insurance company sets up an investment, called an *accumulation account*.

The appeal of cash value life insurance as a retirement investment is its tax treatment. The accumulation account of a cash value policy grows tax deferred, meaning that taxes are not due on income and capital gains as they would be on an ordinary investment. The argument over whether cash value insurance is a good investment centers on the question of whether you would be better off buying an inexpensive term policy and separately investing the additional amount that the cash value policy would cost.

The cash value of a policy can be withdrawn tax free until the withdrawals exceed the amount of premiums that have been

## TABLE 5-1

Features of Life Insurance Policies

| Type of Policy | Flexible Premium | Flexible Death Benefit | Choice of Investment Accounts | Guaranteed Minimum Return |
|---|---|---|---|---|
| Term life | No | No | N/A | N/A |
| Whole life | No | No | No | Yes |
| Variable life | No | No | Yes | No |
| Universal life | Yes | Yes | No | Yes |
| Universal variable life | Yes | Yes | Yes | No |

paid into the policy. Note, however, that these withdrawals reduce the policy death benefit by the amount of cash withdrawn. The death benefit on life insurance is not subject to income taxes for the beneficiary.

There are four primary categories of cash value insurance, each discussed below.

## Types of Cash Value Life Insurance

*Whole life insurance* offers permanent protection while building cash value in an accumulation account managed by the insurance company. There are several different types of whole life insurance, all of which have fixed premiums but differ in the timing and amount of premiums paid.

*Variable life insurance,* designed for the more risk-oriented policyholder, allows cash in the accumulation account to be invested in mutual fund–like investments at the direction of the policyholder. Returns on the accumulation account vary with the returns of the funds chosen.

*Universal life policies* offer the policyholder some flexibility in both premiums and the policy's face amount or death benefit. Within limits, the policy owner can decide how much to pay in premiums. The premiums on universal life policies are not guaranteed as in whole life and term policies, but they are projected based on assumptions of the returns on the policy's accumulation account and the ability of those returns to subsidize premium payments. Actual premiums required may be higher or lower depending on the returns of investments in the accumulation account. Subject to insurability, the death benefit may be increased or decreased as the owner chooses. The accumulation account earns market rates of interest in investments managed by the insurance company, subject to a guaranteed minimum. Market returns can vary greatly over the life of a policy, making universal life policies more risky than whole life and term life due to the possibility that premiums may be higher than initially projected.

*Variable universal life policies* combine the features of variable life and universal life policies. Like variable life policies, they earn interest based on investment choices similar to individual mutual funds. Like universal life policies, they have flexibility in premiums and death benefits. What makes them riskier is the lack of a guarantee of premiums or minimum investment returns.

## Evaluating Insurance Companies

The promise of a death benefit or return of your cash value is only as good as the financial solvency of the company standing behind it. There are several well-known services that evaluate the insurer's ability to pay future claims to policyholders and publish ratings for the consumer. Check ratings by consulting any of the following firms' ratings:

### A.M. Best
(908) 439-2200
*www.ambest.com*
Top ratings: A++, A+, A

### Standard & Poor's Insurance Rating Services
(212) 208-8000
*www.standardandpoors.com*
Top ratings: AAA, AA+, AA

### Moody's Investor's Service
(212) 553-0300
*www.moodys.com*
Top ratings: Aaa, Aa1, Aa2

### Weiss Ratings Hotline
(800) 289-9222
*www.weissratings.com*
Top ratings: A, B

Consider only those insurers that have been rated by at least two rating companies and that consistently receive ratings in the top three categories. Check your insurer's ratings annually.

## Insurance as an Investment

The main argument for using insurance as an investment hinges upon the tax deferral of growth in the accumulation account.

Another key factor is the ability of the policyholder to borrow or withdraw cash value should the need arise. These arguments can be rationally considered only in the case that you need life insurance. Due to the cost of the insurance, it will never make sense to purchase insurance purely as an investment. The cost of insurance, also called *mortality cost*, is the cost to the insurance company of providing a death benefit. This cost is passed on to the policyholder as a fee or as a reduction in the rate of return on assets in the account.

If you need life insurance, should you buy term insurance, which is much cheaper than cash value insurance, and invest the difference? In making that decision, there are several issues to consider:

- *Your Ability to Pay Premiums.*   First, determine how much insurance you need. Then check the premium cost for both term and cash value policies. If you can afford only the term policy, go with that policy. Never skimp on the amount of the death benefit.
- *Your Tax Bracket, Both Federal and State.*   The benefit of tax deferral is only as valuable as the amount of taxes you would be deferring. The higher your tax bracket the more valuable it is.
- *The Possibility That You Might Not Be Able to Qualify for Insurance Later.*   Some people use this argument to insure children, who should never be insured. As an adult with potential health issues, it may be more of a concern. If it is, compare guaranteed renewable term with permanent cash value policies.
- *Your Willingness to Shop for No-Load (That Is, No Commission) Insurance Policies.*   Unless you buy no- or low-load insurance policies, the costs of cash value policies drag down returns so much that it almost always makes more sense to buy term and invest the difference.

### Shopping the Internet for Insurance

If you have decided to buy life insurance, the Internet is a great place to comparison shop. There are two types of sites available, aggregators and online insurance companies. The *aggregators* provide one-stop shopping for insurance quotes. They promise to shop for the best-priced policy within your chosen parameters.

In the *online insurance company* category, there are two types of firms. One is the *agent-driven company*, like State Farm or Travelers. These companies use Web sites as an alternative distribution channel or to generate leads for their agents. The other type is the *direct company*, such as Progressive or GEICO, which previously operated by telephone, using 800 numbers. Gomez Advisors, a market research and analysis firm in Lincoln, Massachusetts, ranks online insurance sites at its Web site, *www.Gomez.com*.

## SUMMARY

As we mentioned in the introduction to this chapter, there isn't a one-size-fits-all answer when it comes to using life insurance and annuities as investments. A clear benefit to investing in insurance products is the tax deferral on investment growth. The higher your tax bracket and the longer you have until retirement, the more valuable the tax-deferred treatment of investment earnings is. However, recent changes in the tax law have diluted this benefit by reducing taxes on capital gains and dividends for investments held in taxable accounts.

The disadvantages of investing in insurance products include high fees and expenses, which make it difficult for them to compete with the returns of an ordinary investment like a mutual fund. Even more objectionable is the tax treatment of annuities, in which dividends and capital gains are taxed as ordinary income when paid out and heirs pay ordinary income tax on growth rather than the stepped-up basis that the heirs of a taxable investment would receive.

You must weigh the pros and cons to decide whether insurance and annuities have a place in your retirement plan. If they do, shop wisely, choosing low-load products after doing your homework, then read Chapter 10 about allocating investments in order to take maximum advantage of the tax law.

# CHAPTER 6

# Should You Count on Social Security?

$A$sk people under the age of 50 whether they expect to receive Social Security benefits and the answer will likely be a resounding "No!" Not surprising, given doomsday reports that the agency is nearly bankrupt. In reality, Social Security trust funds contain about $900 billion and are projected to exceed $6 trillion in the next 25 years (see Figure 6-1).* However, this may not be enough.

Social Security was established in 1935 as a "pay-as-you-go" system in which the working population funds retiree benefits through payroll taxes. When Social Security takes in more in taxes than it pays out in benefits, the excess is credited to the Social Security trust funds, which are invested in interest-bearing U.S. government securities. These assets are expected to fund future situations in which benefits paid out exceed payroll taxes collected. In the 1930s, when a 65-year-old had a life expectancy of 12.5 additional years, the system worked. Nearly 70 years later, a 65-year-old can expect to live and collect benefits for 17.5 additional years. So, not only will retirees live longer and collect more, there will be more of them alive at any given time. In 2010, the Baby Boom generation will begin to retire, doubling the present number of American retirees by 2030. The result will be a decrease in tax-paying workers for each benefit-drawing retiree from 3.4 to 2.1. The Social Security

---

*Social Security Administration, Publication No. 05-100055, August 2000, ICN462560.

**FIGURE  6-1**

Social Security Trust Fund

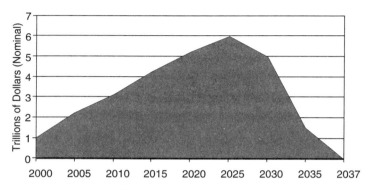

*Source:* Social Security Administration.

Administration estimates that benefit payments will begin to exceed tax revenues in 2015 and trust funds will be depleted in 2037. Without any changes, benefit payments could then continue at only 70 percent of the benefits owed under the current system.

## WHAT TO EXPECT FROM SOCIAL SECURITY

Given the wide range of possibilities for reform, it is impossible to know what the system will look like when you retire. However, for planning purposes, you should know what you are entitled to under the current system. Then, when the changes come, it should not be difficult to adjust your expectations accordingly.

Finding out what you will receive is easier than ever, now that the Social Security Administration has begun annual mailings of Social Security statements to workers age 25 and older. The statements include an estimate of retirement, survivor, and disability benefits and a record of your earnings history. Note that if you have worked and paid Social Security taxes fewer than 10 years, the minimum required to receive benefits, the administration will not estimate your retirement benefits. Your statement should arrive each year about 3 months before your birthday. If it does not, or if it contains errors, call (800) 772-1213 or log on to *www.ssa.gov/mystatement/*.

## When Should You Retire?

Your Social Security retirement benefits are based on both your past earnings and the year in which you choose to retire. Full retirement age ranges from 65 to 67, depending on the year in which you were born. However, no matter what your full retirement age, you can begin drawing a reduced level of benefits as early as age 62. Table 6-1 outlines full retirement ages and the amount by which your benefits will be reduced for starting early.

The advantage of taking early retirement is that you will receive benefits for a longer period of time. The disadvantage is that your level of benefits is permanently reduced. While the monthly percentage reduction is designed to make the choices roughly equal over an average lifetime, each situation is different. If you live longer than average, you will collect the most by waiting until full retirement age to receive the maximum monthly benefit. If you do not live as long as expected, you may collect more in benefits by starting early.

**Retirement Dilemma**   Mike and Dave are twin brothers trying to decide when to begin taking their Social Security benefits. Born in 1943, both will turn 62 in 2005. According to their annual Social Security statements, they will each be eligible for $1500 per month at age 66, their full retirement age. Will they be better off beginning to collect their payments earlier or later?

**Solution**   It depends on how long they live after retirement. If Mike chooses to take benefits at age 62, at a 25 percent reduction, he will receive $1125 per month in benefits. If Dave decides to wait until he is 66, he will receive the full $1500 per month.

Mike has a 48-month head start and will collect $54,000 before Dave collects a penny. However, once Dave begins to collect, he will catch up at a rate of $375 per month, or $4500 per year. After 12 years, at age, 78, they will be even. From that point on, Dave will be ahead by $4500 per year. If they live until age 90, Dave will collect $54,000 more than Mike.

**TABLE 6-1**

Social Security Full Retirement and Reductions by Age

| Year of Birth | Full Retirement Age | Months from Age 62 to Full Retirement | Monthly % Reduction for Early Retirement* | Total % Reduction for Retiring at 62 |
|---|---|---|---|---|
| 1937 or earlier | 65 | 36 | 0.555 | 20.00 |
| 1938 | 65 and 2 months | 38 | 0.548 | 20.83 |
| 1939 | 65 and 4 months | 40 | 0.541 | 21.67 |
| 1940 | 65 and 6 months | 42 | 0.535 | 22.50 |
| 1941 | 65 and 8 months | 44 | 0.530 | 23.33 |
| 1942 | 65 and 10 months | 46 | 0.525 | 24.17 |
| 1943–1954 | 66 | 48 | 0.520 | 25.00 |
| 1955 | 66 and 2 months | 50 | 0.516 | 25.84 |
| 1956 | 66 and 4 months | 52 | 0.512 | 26.66 |
| 1957 | 66 and 6 months | 54 | 0.509 | 27.50 |
| 1958 | 66 and 8 months | 56 | 0.505 | 28.33 |
| 1959 | 66 and 10 months | 58 | 0.502 | 29.17 |
| 1960 and later | 67 | 60 | 0.500 | 30.00 |

*Percentage monthly and total reductions are approximate due to rounding. The actual reductions are 0.555 or five-ninths of 1 percent per month for the first 36 months and 0.416 or five-twelfths of 1 percent for subsequent months.
*Source:* Social Security Administration.

In addition to the flexibility of taking early retirement, you may also choose to delay receiving your retirement benefits. Social Security offers an incentive to do so by increasing your benefits for each month that you delay between your full retirement age and age 70. Table 6-2 outlines the annual percentage increase in benefits for each year that you delay.

**TABLE 6-2**

The Benefits of Delaying Retirement

| Year of Birth | Yearly Increase in Benefits |
|---|---|
| 1929–1930 | 4.5% |
| 1931–1932 | 5.0 |
| 1933–1934 | 5.5 |
| 1935–1936 | 6.0 |
| 1937–1938 | 6.5 |
| 1939–1940 | 7.0 |
| 1941–1942 | 7.5 |
| 1943 or later | 8.0 |

*Source:* Social Security Administration.

## What Happens to Social Security Benefits If You Work?

Supplementing Social Security income with a full- or part-time job can make sense for many retirees. If you plan to work, consider the age at which you plan to begin receiving Social Security benefits carefully because working retirees under age 65 may lose some benefits.

The loss of benefits, commonly called an *earnings penalty,* depends on a retiree's income. For Social Security's purposes, income includes wages from your job or net profit for the self-employed, including bonuses, commissions, and vacation pay. It does not include pensions, annuities, investment income, interest, or veterans' or other government or military retirement benefits.

The Senior Citizens Right to Work Act of 2000 eliminated the earnings penalty for retirees at full retirement age or older, but it is still in place for anyone collecting benefits between age 62 and full retirement. For those who collect before full retirement age, $1 in benefits is lost for every $2 in earnings above $11,520 per year (2003 rules). In the year you reach full retirement, $1 in benefits is lost for every $3 in earnings above $30,720 per year (2003 rules). Table 6-3 outlines the rules.

## TABLE 6-3

Social Security Retirement Earnings Test

| Age of Retiree | 2003 Annual Earnings Exemption | 2003 Monthly Earnings Exemption | Penalty: $1 in Benefits for Every: |
|---|---|---|---|
| Under full retirement age | $11,520 | $ 960 | $2 in earnings |
| Year you reach full retirement* | 30,720 | 2,560 | $3 in earnings |

\* The earnings test applies only to the months prior to reaching full retirement age. There is no earnings penalty beginning in the month an individual attains full retirement age.

*Source:* Social Security Administration.

**Retirement Dilemma**   Vickie is 62 and is entitled to $600 per month ($7200 per year) in Social Security benefits. She is working, earning $20,000 ($8480 over the $11,520 earnings limit) per year. How much will she receive in benefits if she elects to begin them this year?

**Solution**   If she takes Social Security benefits at age 62, not only will she collect at a lower payout rate because she has not reached full retirement age, she will have to give up $4240 of her $7200 in benefits. This is $1 for every $2 over the earnings limit ($8480 divided by 2). She will receive only $2960 in benefits.

What if Vickie were 64, reaching age 65 in August of this year, and had earned $70,000 during the year? If she earned half of it ($35,000) in the months January through July, she would have to give up $1 for every $3 of the $4280 she earned over the $30,720 limit, or $1427. Her benefits for the first 7 months of the year at $600 per month would be $4200 less $1427, or $2773. She would receive the full $600 per month for the remainder of the year.

What if Vickie made $90,000 in the year she turned 65? She wouldn't receive any benefits for the first 7 months. At $45,000 in earnings for the period, she would be over the $30,720 limit by $14,280. Losing benefits at a rate of $1 for every $3 creates a penalty of $4760. Since she would be due only $4200, she would not receive benefits until the month she turned 65, at which time she would begin to receive her $600 per month.

> **Retirement Tip** If you continue to work while you are receiving Social Security benefits, the SSA will check your record every year to see if the additional earnings will increase your monthly payment. If there is an increase, you will be notified.

## Will You Have to Pay Taxes on Your Benefits?

Once you reach full retirement age, you will not be subject to an earnings penalty, but you may have to pay income taxes on your Social Security benefits, depending on your income. For purposes of the taxation test, your retirement income equals one-half of your Social Security income plus all taxable pensions, wages, interest, dividends, and any other taxable income. Add to this amount any tax-exempt income, such as interest from municipal bonds. Compare this amount to your *base amount*, as defined below. If your income is less than or equal to your base amount, none of your benefits are taxable.

Your base amount (2002 rules) is:

- $25,000 if you are single, head of household, or qualifying widow(er)
- $25,000 if you are married, filing separately, and lived apart from your spouse for all of the previous year
- $32,000 if you are married, filing jointly
- $0 if you are married, filing separately, and lived with your spouse at any time during the previous year

If your income is greater than the base amount, some of your benefits may be taxable. If your income is greater than the base amount but less than $34,000 for those filing singly or $44,000 for those filing jointly, one-half of your Social Security benefits will be taxable. If your income is over the limits just described or you were married, filing separately, and lived with your spouse at any time in the previous year, 85 percent of your benefits may be taxable. You can find more information on the taxability of Social Security benefits in IRS Publication 915. A worksheet to compute your taxable benefits is included in the instructions for Form 1040 and 1040A tax returns.

## APPLYING FOR SOCIAL SECURITY

The Social Security Administration recommends that you apply for retirement benefits 3 months before you want them to begin. You can apply for benefits at your local Social Security office, by telephone, or online. To locate your local office, check your phone book, or use the online Social Security Office Locator at *s00dace.ssa.gov/pro/fol/fol-home.html*. The locator is available during the following hours (EST):

> Monday through Friday: All day (except between 2 a.m. and 3 a.m.)
>
> Saturday: 5 a.m. to 11 p.m.
>
> Sunday: 8 a.m. to 10 p.m.

You can speak to a service representative or make an appointment to apply by telephone if you call toll-free (800) 772-1213 from 7 a.m. to 7 p.m. (EST), Monday through Friday. Recorded information is available on this line 24 hours a day. For those who are deaf or hard of hearing, the TTY number is (800) 325-0778.

You can apply online by completing the Internet Retirement Insurance Benefits Application. Locate it through the home page of Social Security Online at *www.ssa.gov*.

When you apply for retirement benefits, you will need to provide the following:

- Your Social Security number
- Your birth certificate
- Your W-2 forms or self-employment tax return for the previous year
- Your military discharge papers if you served in the military
- Proof of U.S. citizenship or lawful alien status if you were not born in the United States
- The name of your bank and your account number so benefits can be deposited directly into your account

## SUMMARY

While the current Social Security system is not viable without reform, it is inconceivable that politicians would allow it to go bankrupt. You may not receive benefits at the level your parents did, and you may not even get back what you paid in, but you will get something. It is key to know what will be due to you and how reforms may affect you. This knowledge will allow you to plan accordingly and voice an informed opinion to your legislators.

# CHAPTER 7

# Your Retirement Funds as Part of an Investment Plan

**A**fter saving for years, your retirement funds could turn into your single biggest asset, potentially larger than the value of your home or any of your other investments. This is why it is critical to invest each and every dollar carefully. This chapter will help you put investment choices in their proper perspective. It isn't a complicated, technical process. In fact, with time and practice, it is a highly manageable procedure. We will use a step-by-step process to make choosing new options or analyzing old ones much easier.

> **Retirement Tip**  When it comes to financial decisions, many people can tell you what to do *once*, but it is critical for you to know what to do, when to do it, and why, all on a regular basis.

## THREE STEPS TO FINANCIAL SUCCESS

The hardest part is getting started. Begin by blocking off a few hours of quiet time to work with your financial resources. Take time to find out exactly where you are financially, think about where you want to go, and plan how you are going to get there. It takes time, but it's worth it. We call this process the *Three Steps to Financial Success*. It involves evaluating your personal financial situation and learning how to select good investments using a step-by-step sequence. The steps identify Where You Are, Where You Are Going, and How to Get There.

1. *Where You Are* requires you to compile a list of your investible funds and find out exactly what you own.
2. *Where You Are Going* is deciding what your financial goals and needs are.
3. *How to Get There* is choosing among your investment options in order to reach those goals.

## Step 1: Where You Are

In step 1, you will create your own *personal investment pyramid*. You will first need to have a clear understanding of the *investment pyramid*. This is a commonly used visual aid that helps investors categorize the relative risks and expected total return of different investments. In each successive level, as you move from the bottom of the pyramid to the top, investments are characterized by more risk and a higher expected total return.

Examples of investments that fit in each level of the investment pyramid are shown in Figure 7-1. We will discuss the various levels of the pyramid along with each level's investment objectives, risks, and expected returns. Keep in mind as you read that this is a general format that has been adapted for use by many professionals. If your retirement plan sponsor or financial advisor uses a slightly different pyramid, try to combine its content with the pyramid you see here, rather than throwing either one out.

---

**Retirement Tip**  When comparing returns of unlike investments, use *total return*, a combination of the income from an investment and any change in principal value. For example, if you purchase a stock for $10.00, it pays dividends of $0.20 during the year, and at the end of the year you sell it for $11.00, your total return will be $1.20:

$0.20 dividends + $1.00 increase in principal = $1.20

On a percentage basis, it would be 12 percent:

$1.20 ÷ $10.00 invested = 12 percent

---

**FIGURE 7-1**

The Investment Pyramid

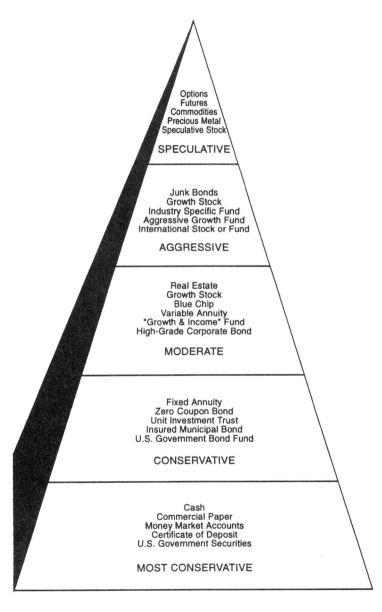

## The Investment Pyramid
### *Level 1: Most Conservative*

*Investment Objective.* Income and preservation of principal.

These investments are designed for income and preservation of principal. They are generally short term, and they have high liquidity and low total return. Examples are cash, money market accounts, certificates of deposit (CDs), and U.S. government securities. Your emergency reserves should be invested at this level and should equal 3 to 6 months of living expenses (not income). Your total return will be interest, not price appreciation. We recommend that you never have more than 15 percent of your investible funds in this level.

---

**Retirement Tip**   If emergency reserves (3 to 6 months of living expenses) exceed 15 percent of your investible funds, this is an acceptable deviation from the guideline.

---

### *Level 2: Conservative*

*Investment Objective.* Income.

These investments carry a little more risk and promise a little more total return. Like the investments in level 1, they are designed primarily for income and preservation of principal. Examples are U.S. government zero coupon bonds, insured municipal bonds, unit investment trusts (UITs), fixed annuities, U.S. government bond mutual funds, and some high-grade corporate bonds. The total return of the investments in this level will be mostly interest, but there may be some fluctuation in principal value.

---

**Retirement Tip**   The market value of a bond will change with fluctuations in interest rates. However, as long as you can hold a good-quality bond until it returns your principal at maturity, you will not lose money.

---

## Level 3: Moderate

*Investment Objective.* Growth and income.

These investments are designed for growth, and their total return is expected to come from moderate change in principal with modest income. Because these investments are growth oriented, their prices will fluctuate more, and they may be less liquid than investments in the bottom two levels. For this reason, your outlook should be long term (3 to 5 years) for any investment in the moderate level.

Examples of investments are some variable annuities, diversified U.S. equity (stock) mutual funds in categories such as "growth and income," "blue-chip growth," and "S&P 500 index," individual blue-chip stocks, and possibly investment real estate (other than your home).

## Level 4: Aggressive

*Investment Objective.* Aggressive growth.

These investments are designed for long-term growth in principal and a higher total return. A change in principal value is the primary component of total return in this level. Common stocks in this level may provide little or no dividend income and will carry significant risk along with their equally significant projected return. They may be very volatile and/or have very low liquidity. Examples of aggressive investments include international stocks and bonds and low-grade domestic corporate bonds (a.k.a. "junk bonds"). Stocks in this level are growth stocks, and they may be in high-tech or biotech industries, or they may be stocks of small companies whose track records are not established. Mutual funds include those which are industry specific (funds that invest in the stock of companies in a particular industry, such as telecommunications or health care) mutual funds labeled "aggressive growth," or those that invest in international stocks and/or bonds.

## Level 5: Speculative

*Investment Objective.* Speculation.

Invest in the speculative level only with money you can afford to lose. If you win, it's great; if you lose, it won't change your life. These investments are very risky; and though they make exciting stories, the losers far outnumber the winners. The total return in this level comes from stock price change (which can go to zero as quickly as it can double), rarely from income. Examples of speculative investments are futures, options, commodities, precious metals, speculative stocks, and penny stocks (stocks whose price per share is less than $5).

---

**Retirement Tip**  If you invest in the speculative level, try this strategy. Set a limit on the amount you are willing to lose, much as you might on a trip to a casino. Invest that amount. *If you win*, cash out, and take your profits and invest them at a less risky level of the pyramid. Reinvest your original principal in another speculative investment. *If you lose*, don't buy any more speculative investments this year. During the Internet stock bubble of 2000, speculating under this system could have yielded plenty of profits when those stocks exploded in price and would have limited losses when they crashed.

---

Never have more than 5 percent of your investible funds invested in the speculative level.

## Your Personal Investment Pyramid

No matter how much or how little money you have, everyone has a personal pyramid. To find out what yours looks like, you must compile all of your financial records and look at the whole picture. Only your *investible funds* belong in your personal investment pyramid. They are all of your assets *except* your primary residence and any art, jewelry, or collectibles, unless you have purchased them with the idea of selling them later for a profit. (If you wouldn't sell it for cash to invest, don't include it in your investible funds.) We include the money you put aside for emergencies, savings, checking, CDs, retirement plans such as 401(k)s or 403(b)s or IRAs, stocks, bonds, mutual funds, the cash value of life insurance policies—*everything* you own to generate income or growth. Each of your investments can be categorized in one of the five levels of the investment pyramid, and the end result will be your own personal portfolio in the shape of a pyramid.

How is this done?

- List everything you own on the appropriate level of the blank pyramid in Figure 7-2, approximating each item's current market value.
- Calculate the total of what you own in each individual level.
- Calculate the total of all levels combined.
- Calculate the percentage of your total investible funds that is in each level by dividing each level's total by the pyramid total.

**FIGURE 7-2**

Your Personal Pyramid Worksheet

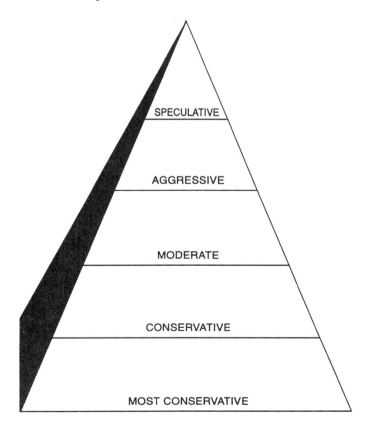

> **Retirement Tip**  Complete and analyze your personal pyramid on an annual basis so that when planning each year or making an important financial decision, you can begin with Where You Are. This snapshot of your financial condition is an annual report card, showing your progress.

Completing your pyramid may take several hours, and as is true of many endeavors, the first time is the hardest. While it is difficult to keep current with today's complex market, if you have this framework and know where you are, you can make better decisions. The most common problems with money are not knowing what you have and not making your money work for you. With the annual analysis of your personal pyramid, you will always know exactly what you have and how it is working. Note that while this book concentrates on the money you are investing in your retirement plans, your personal pyramid deals with *all* your investible funds because your retirement savings fit into a big picture.

## Step 2: Where You Are Going

The second step to financial success is to determine *Where You Are Going*. This involves determining which of the four financial stages (not ages) of life you are in and what percentage of your money should be invested at each level of your personal investment pyramid based on your stage. The recommended percentages are your investment goals, or where you are going. See Figure 7-3.

> **Retirement Dilemma**  Mark said to us, "I am 40 years old; this is how much money I have. How should it be invested?"
>
> **Solution**  Without knowing more about him, we couldn't offer any suggestions. Why? Because people have different financial situations and needs, even at the same age. At 40, he might have children who are 18 and 20 years old or children who are 2 and 4. Or he might not have any. His goal might be to retire in 5 years at 45 or in 25 years at age 65. Your personal circumstances and goals, not your age, determine your stage of life and, in turn, how you should invest your money.

**FIGURE 7-3**

Personal Pyramid Goals for the Four Financial Stages of Life

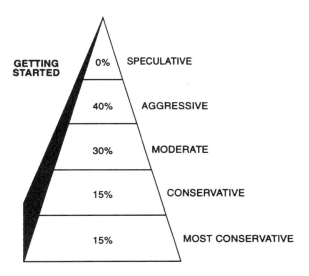

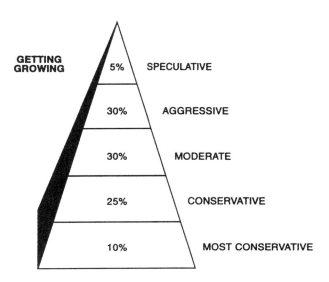

## **FIGURE 7-3 (Continued)**

Personal Pyramid Goals for the Four Financial Stages of Life

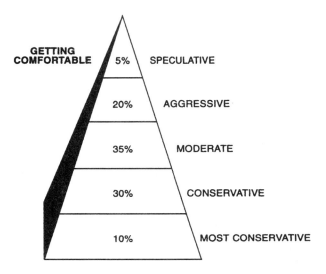

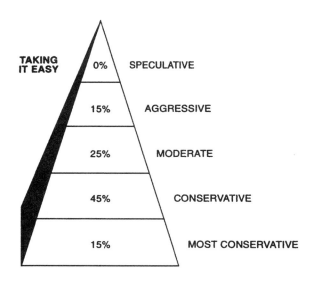

## The Four Financial Stages of Life

Take the next 5 minutes to decide which financial stage fits you best. Here are some guidelines to help:

**Getting Started.**   The first financial stage of life is Getting Started. During this stage you are establishing a career; determining your budget for living and saving expenses; buying furniture and cars; saving for a home; and, most important, establishing an emergency fund of 3 to 6 months of living expenses in a highly liquid investment, such as a money market account.

In this stage you are constructing a strong financial base. You may not have much extra cash after paying living expenses, but it is imperative to start your financial future by *earning some interest*, even if you must pay some interest to others. Save what you can, and watch it grow. Invest the maximum allowed in your employer's retirement plan and a Roth IRA. At 25, a single investment of $3000 has time to grow to nearly $20,000 over the next 40 years at 8 percent. Your investment outlook for this stage of life is long term. Seventy percent of your investments should be in the growth (top three) levels of the pyramid, and 30 percent should be in the income (bottom two) levels of the pyramid.

**Getting Growing.**   In the second stage, Getting Growing, you begin to make more money and to spend more on large items such as your first home. This stage may include getting married, having children, and saving for their education; dual incomes may be necessary to support growing families. Even with the high cost of living in this stage, you should be investing actively for retirement. Your investment outlook for this stage is long term. Sixty-five percent of your investments should be in the growth (top three) levels of the pyramid, and 35 percent should be in the income (bottom two) levels of the pyramid.

**Getting Comfortable.**   The third financial stage of life is Getting Comfortable. This stage begins after major responsibilities and high living expenses are over. If you have children, they have left the nest and no longer need your support. Now is the time to invest larger amounts of money for retirement, making sure your dollars are growing effectively to provide adequate support when you need it. Since you still may be years away from retirement, your investment outlook is long term, but you take less risk because you cannot afford to lose principal. However, you should continue to own some moderate- and aggressive-level growth investments to protect yourself against inflation. Sixty percent of your investments should be in the growth (top three) levels of the pyramid, and 40 percent should be in the income (bottom two) levels of the pyramid.

Some families will skip the Getting Comfortable stage. If you have children later in life, you may move from Getting Growing right into Taking It Easy when your children leave the nest at the onset of retirement. If you think this will happen to you, it is imperative to save more for retirement while you are in the earlier stages.

---

**Retirement Tip**   Having a family when you are older and more financially secure makes sense, but don't fall into the trap of spending money on college costs in the Getting Comfortable stage while neglecting to invest for your retirement. There are loans and scholarships available for college but not for retirement.

---

***Taking It Easy.***   In the fourth financial stage of life, Taking It Easy, retirement begins. You may be 50 or you may be 70. Whatever your age, this could be the longest stage of your life.

---

**Retirement Tip**   The biggest mistake people make in the Taking It Easy stage is saying, "I don't need to manage my money; I'm retired." WRONG! If you don't earn an income, that money you aren't managing is all you have.

---

Similar to the previous stage, Getting Comfortable, you will need a percentage of growth investments during retirement to protect you from inflation. A hamburger doesn't cost what it did

30 years ago; what do you think it will cost in 2020? The growth portion of your personal pyramid protects your buying power. The income portion protects your principal. Forty percent of your investments should be in the growth (top three) levels of the pyramid, and 60 percent should be in the income (bottom two) levels of the pyramid.

---

**Retirement Tip**  Saving for retirement isn't accumulating dollars; it's accumulating buying power to support a desired standard of living.

---

## Step 3: How to Get There—Comparing Pyramids

Once you have created your personal pyramid, compare it with the goal pyramid for your financial stage of life. See anything wrong? The two pyramids are probably not the same. Don't worry; that's why we have step 3, How to Get There; it allows you to make the changes necessary to bring your personal pyramid closer to your goal pyramid. By comparing percentages in each level of your personal pyramid to your goals, you can see which levels need more of your total funds and which levels need less. Anything within 5 percent of the recommended percentage is fine.

Let's take the Youngs' personal pyramid in Figure 7-4 as an example. They have listed all their investible funds and allocated each item to its proper level on the pyramid. They have subtotaled each level, and divided each of those numbers by the pyramid total to find a percentage for each level. The results are:

  0 percent speculative

30 percent aggressive

15 percent moderate

30 percent conservative

25 percent most conservative

This is their personal pyramid; in other words, this is where they are.

Next, they will take step 2. Their children are in high school, and they are beginning to think about retirement. The Youngs are

## FIGURE 7-4

Youngs' Personal Pyramid

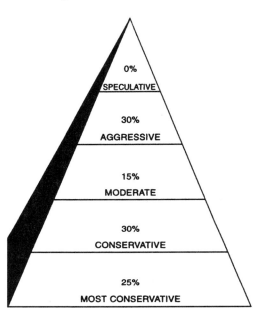

0%
SPECULATIVE

30%
AGGRESSIVE

15%
MODERATE

30%
CONSERVATIVE

25%
MOST CONSERVATIVE

in the Getting Growing stage of life, and their goal pyramid looks like this:

0 to 5 percent speculative

30 percent aggressive

30 percent moderate

25 percent conservative

10 percent most conservative

In step 3, they compare the pyramids (see Figure 7-5) to see what they should change.

The speculative level is fine at 0 percent compared with a goal of 0 to 5 percent.

The aggressive-level goal is 30 percent, and they have 30 percent; again, no change is necessary here.

**FIGURE 7-5**

Three Steps to Financial Success

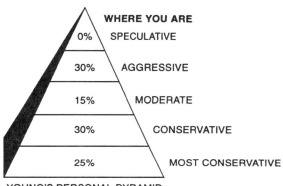

YOUNG'S PERSONAL PYRAMID

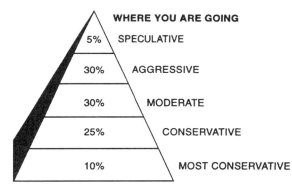

GETTING GROWING GOAL PYRAMID %

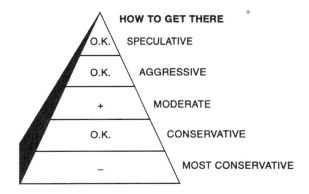

Their moderate level is 15 percent of their pyramid total, and the goal is 30 percent. We'll mark a plus (+) on that level because it is below the guideline.

The conservative level is 30 percent versus a goal of 25 percent. That one gets an OK because it is within 5 percent of the guideline.

The most conservative level is overconcentrated at 25 percent. Because the goal is only 10 percent, a minus (–) goes on that level.

Now the Youngs know just what to do the next time they are faced with an important financial decision. If they are adding to their investible funds due to a bonus, or maybe just more in monthly savings, where should they invest? That's right. They should invest in the moderate level.

---

**Retirement Dilemma**   If the Youngs have CDs or U.S. government bonds that are maturing in the most conservative level, should they reinvest in the same level?

**Solution**   No, since they need to decrease their concentration in the most conservative level. They should take these proceeds and reinvest them where they need more, in the moderate level.

---

To help you evaluate your own personal financial situation, see Figure 7-6, which is a worksheet of the three steps to complete for yourself.

## SUMMARY

At least once a year and again every time you make an investment decision, you should complete your personal pyramid and compare it to the goal pyramid for your stage of life. Individual investments can change, your financial stage of life may change, and investing habits and opportunities can change, not to mention interest rates, the stock market, and the economy.

**FIGURE 7-6**

Three Steps to Financial Success Worksheet

WHERE YOU ARE

____% SPECULATIVE

____% AGGRESSIVE

____% MODERATE

____% CONSERVATIVE

____% MOST CONSERVATIVE

Using a system like this takes some of the emotion out of investing. Investors who were caught up in the go-go Internet and high-tech markets of 1998 and 1999 put the bulk of their investible funds in the aggressive level of the pyramid. While they may have earned high returns for a short time, many saw their profits and even principal evaporate as the bubble burst in 2000 and 2001. Maintaining an evenly distributed pyramid may seem boring in a roaring market, but it can protect you in the inevitable downturns.

You may have noticed how the percentages change as you move through the four stages of life. In the first stage, you should

## FIGURE 7-6 (Continued)

Three Steps to Financial Success Worksheet

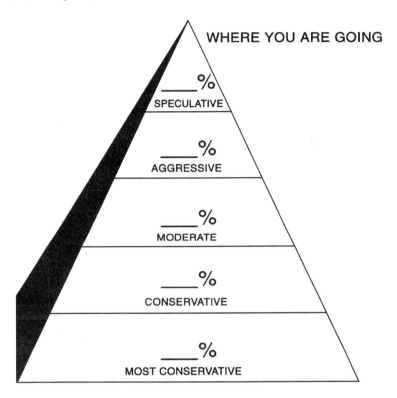

WHERE YOU ARE GOING

_____ %
SPECULATIVE

_____ %
AGGRESSIVE

_____ %
MODERATE

_____ %
CONSERVATIVE

_____ %
MOST CONSERVATIVE

have 70 percent in the top three (growth) levels of the pyramid and 30 percent in the bottom (income) two. As you reach the Taking It Easy stage, your percentages shift to 60 percent in the bottom two levels and 40 percent in the top three. The key is to give your personal pyramid proper attention throughout your life, set goals, and follow percentage guidelines. Then in retirement, you can worry less about how you spend your money and more about how you spend your time.

**FIGURE 7-6 (Continued)**

Three Steps to Financial Success Worksheet

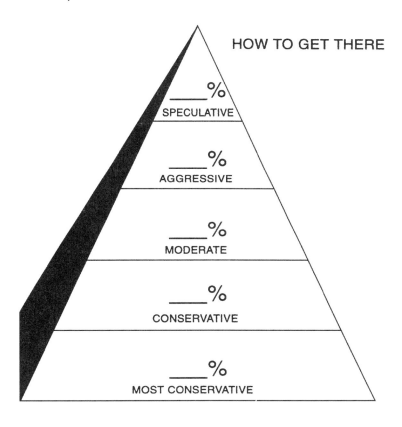

HOW TO GET THERE

_____%
SPECULATIVE

_____%
AGGRESSIVE

_____%
MODERATE

_____%
CONSERVATIVE

_____%
MOST CONSERVATIVE

# CHAPTER 8

# Your Investment Options: Where's the Risk?

**S**tock funds, bond funds, company stock, and money markets—which one or which combination is right for you? You'll probably never get it perfect, but after some analysis, you should be able to get close. John Templeton, the famous mutual fund manager, says that when it comes to choosing investments, his goal is to be right two out of every three times. We all make mistakes, but doing nothing is the biggest mistake you can make.

---

**Retirement Mistakes**

1. Investing too conservatively at an early age
2. Not becoming more conservative as retirement nears
3. Trying to be a market-timer (buying and selling frequently on short-term market news)
4. Not diversifying among investment options
5. Investing with a short-term rather than a long-term outlook
6. Investing without sufficient knowledge (investing in something you don't understand)

---

Deciding how to invest your retirement funds can be difficult, but don't agonize over it. What is important is to make educated, well-reasoned decisions. In an employer-sponsored plan, you will

typically be offered at least six investment options. Once you completely understand how they work, you'll be able to make the most
of your money. Sure, it is much easier to simply ask a coworker
what investment options to choose rather than digging in and
doing the research for yourself. Just remember everyone has different needs and objectives, so investments that are good for a
coworker may not be right for you. You wouldn't count on someone else to take care of you in retirement, so take the time to get
involved with your money.

---

**Retirement Tip**   No one will watch your money the way you will.

---

Begin by taking a few hours to use the Three Steps to Financial
Success we outlined in Chapter 7. This will give you a direction for
making individual investment choices. Only then will you be
ready to look at the options within your plan and start choosing
how to allocate the money.

Before you analyze each option, you will need to learn more
about the relationship between risk and reward. Whether you love
to bungee jump, drive race cars, play blackjack, and shoot white-
water river rapids, or look for nothing but peace and tranquility
out of your daily life, you should be aware of the risks that you
face when you invest. Determining your attitude about risk and
deciding which type of reward best matches your retirement goals
will help you follow through with a financial strategy. You don't
have to be a high-roller to take risks; all investments, even cash,
have some risk. No matter what the investment, it is imperative
that you learn what can go wrong and how to manage the possibilities.

---

**Retirement Tip**   There is always a risk/return trade-off. The
greater an investment's expected return, the greater the risk to your
principal. If you think of just one thing each time you consider an
investment, think of this.

---

# FIVE TYPES OF RISK

In this section we will define five types of investment risk. As you analyze your own investments, you will be able to identify and balance each type of risk in addition to balancing your goal pyramid levels.

## Inflation Risk

You experience inflation risk every day with anything you purchase. Will a dollar's worth of goods today be worth a dollar 5 years from now, or for an investment, will the dollars returned from an investment be worth less than the dollars invested? For example, if you earn 4 percent on your investments but lose 5 percent of their value to inflation, you have less purchasing power at the end of a year than when you started.

Using the Consumer Price Index as the rate of inflation, you would have to spend $2.18 in 2002 to buy the same things that $1 would buy in 1980.[*] That's twice as much in just over 20 years! In investment terms, your dollar lost more than half its value. What would you say if someone told you that you would probably lose half the value of an investment in 20 years without realizing it? You can. You face this risk with any investment that pays back a fixed dollar amount in the future, without chance of growth in principal. This includes CDs, bonds, money market accounts, and fixed annuities. In contrast, hard assets, such as real estate, collectibles, and precious metals, often rise in value with inflation. Investments such as stocks have the potential for growth in principal value, which can offset the loss in purchasing power of the dollar.

## Interest Rate Risk

The one thing you can bank on when it comes to interest rates is that they rarely stay the same from year to year. As they fluctuate, their movements will affect the value of your investments. Interest rate risk generally applies to fixed-income investments such as

---

[*] *Source:* Department of Labor Inflation Calculator at *www.dol.gov*

bonds or CDs and can be divided into two categories: *value* and *reinvestment rate risk.*

## Value Risk

When interest rates rise, bond prices usually fall, and vice versa. Thus, if you own a bond and market interest rates rise, the bond's market value (what you could sell it for) goes down. Why? Let's say you have a bond that pays 7 percent interest, and after 1 year, new bonds are paying 8 percent interest. Is your bond as valuable as one that pays a higher rate? Certainly not. A buyer would not be willing to pay as much for a bond with a lower-than-average rate. If market interest rates had gone down, your bond would have become more valuable because it would be paying more in interest than would other available bonds. If you own individual bonds and their market price goes down, it doesn't mean you need to sell. If you bought them for fixed income and you still expect to receive the full face value at maturity, you will not lose money by holding them. The risk lies in the event that you need to sell before maturity, and you receive a lower price than you paid.

Bond mutual funds are especially vulnerable to the value form of interest rate risk because they have no maturity date. If you own an ordinary bond that has lost value due to rising interest rates, you can hold on to it until maturity and receive the full face value. Handle the situation this way and you will not lose money. But because bond mutual funds do not have a maturity date, there is no promise of receiving the full value at maturity. They are priced at the current market value, which may mean the depressed market price of the individual bonds held in the fund. If discouraged investors cash out, the fund managers may be forced to sell bonds, locking in the loss in principal.

## Reinvestment Rate Risk

This is the risk that if interest rates fall after you make an investment, you will be reinvesting the interest payments that you receive at a lower rate. It also means that when the investment matures, or if it is called before maturity, your choices of reinvesting the principal could result in your earning a lower rate of interest.

> **Retirement Tip**  Callable bonds are especially vulnerable to rein-vestment rate risk because the issuer has the right to call the bonds (that is, pay them off) before maturity. The issuer will naturally do this when interest rates fall because it can issue new bonds and pay a lower rate, just as you do when refinancing your home. When bondholders get their investments back unexpectedly, they face a lower rate of return for reinvestment.

## Business Risk

Business risk is encountered in investments such as common stocks and corporate bonds. This is the risk that faces an individual cor-poration, from such diverse sources as management errors, faulty products, poor financial planning, and marketing mistakes. If the numbers on the balance sheet or income statement start to get in the "red," your investments may be in trouble; the most extreme result of business risk is bankruptcy. If you hold common stock, you are at the bottom of the list behind lawyers, the IRS, banks, bondholders, and preferred stockholders when it comes to getting any money back, which means that you probably won't.

The best way to avoid business risk is by practicing the prin-ciple of *diversification.* When you own stocks of individual compa-nies, buy 15 or more different stocks individually or through mutual funds. Experts say that the business risk of any one com-pany is effectively diversified away when you have the cushion of 14 others.

The principle of diversification is probably not news to you. However, many who understand it choose to ignore it. Before Enron collapsed, 58 percent of the employees' 401(k) assets were in Enron stock. Yes, some of it was matching funds that employees were required to keep in stock, but much of it was elective contributions that employees *chose* to invest in the stock. Enron employees were not alone. According to a 2001 study by the newsletter *DC Plan Investing,* seven U.S. 401(k) plans have concentrations of 80 percent or more in company stock. (See Table 8-1.) While the employees of Anheuser-Busch were feeling pretty smart with their 3-year stock

## TABLE 8-1

401(k) Plans with High Concentrations of Company Stock

| Percentage of 401(k) Assets in Company Stock | |
| Company | % of Assets |
| --- | --- |
| Procter & Gamble | 94.7 |
| Sherwin-Williams | 91.8 |
| Abbot Labs. | 90.2 |
| Pfizer | 85.5 |
| BB&T | 81.7 |
| Anheuser-Busch | 81.6 |
| Coca-Cola | 81.5 |

*Source:* DC Plan Investing.

return of 41.3 percent, the employees of Coca-Cola weren't crowing as loudly after losing 31.8 percent in the same period.* The moral of the story? Diversify your business risk. If company matching funds are paid in stock, invest your contributions elsewhere.

## Market Risk

The type of risk that remains in a diversified portfolio is *market risk* (a.k.a. *economic risk*)—that is, the risk that financial markets, or the economy as a whole, will perform poorly, thus causing investments to change in value, regardless of the fundamentals of individual investments. (See Figure 8-1.) The stock market crash of 1987 or the bear market of 2000 to 2002 are examples of market risk. This risk cannot be controlled by the investor or diversified away, and it will affect virtually all investments.

## Liquidity Risk

This is the risk that you cannot sell an investment quickly without losing principle. The appraised value of your home or your collection

* Returns as of November 30, 2001.

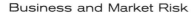

**FIGURE 8-1**

Business and Market Risk

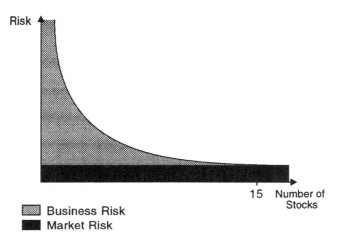

of Chinese porcelain won't put cash in your pocket if you cannot find a buyer. Liquidity risk affects investments that do not have active secondary markets and investments that are in very volatile or cyclical markets such as real estate.

**Retirement Dilemma**  Jon and Kathy have $100,000 of investible funds. They are in the Getting Growing stage of life and have the following investments:

- $25,000 in a money market account
- $10,000 in U.S. saving bonds
- $15,000 in growth stock mutual funds
- $50,000 in Jon's company stock

What risks do they face?

**Solution**  They have 35 percent of their portfolio in fixed-income investments (bonds and money market) that are subject to inflation risk and 65 percent (stock funds and company stock) in investments that are subject to market risk. But business risk from the 50 percent in

company stock is their most dangerous risk. Jon is counting on this
company for a paycheck as well as for one-half of the value of their
investments. If the company were to have problems and he were to be
fired without notice, they would lose an income while at the same time
their investments in the company stock could be losing value. Unless
the investment is in profit sharing or a company 401(k) matching program in which they have no choice, they should diversify this holding.

Don't be an armchair quarterback; get involved. The danger
in investment risk is the unknown. Being aware of the risks you
face can help you to diversify the risk you take.

## SAMPLE INVESTMENT OPTIONS

All retirement plans are different, so we'll offer a few sample
investment options, some of which you may find in your plan. We
will highlight where each fits in the investment pyramid along
with its advantages and risks.

### Fund A: Money Market Fund

This is a pool of investments that yields current short-term interest
rates by investing in short-term debt securities such as U.S. Treasury
bills. It seeks to maintain a consistent value of $1 per share. Money
market funds are often called *cash equivalents* because of their stability.

*Pyramid Level.*  Most conservative.

*Advantages.*  Safety; there is little or no chance of losing
principal.

*Disadvantages/Risk.*  While this is a safe investment in terms
of stability of principal, the rate of inflation can exceed your
earnings, making it possible to lose purchasing power.

*Your Objective.*  Use it as short-term shelter because it cannot
provide growth.

### Fund B: Fixed-Income Fund

This fund may include bonds, mortgages, preferred stocks,
investment contracts with insurance companies (GICs), and/or

other fixed-income securities such as U.S. Treasury bonds, U.S. Treasury bills, certificates of deposit (CDs), or money market accounts.

*Pyramid Level.*   Conservative.

*Advantages.*   Relative safety with low fluctuation of principal.

*Disadvantages/Risk.*   While fixed-income funds are generally considered to be very safe, they can lose principal quickly if market interest rates rise (interest rate risk). They also suffer from inflation risk.

*Your Objective.*   To obtain diversification when other funds are exposed to stock market fluctuations or to assume more principal stability as you reach retirement age.

## Fund C: Guaranteed Investment Contract (GIC)

A *guaranteed investment contract* (GIC) is a fixed-rate investment offered by an insurance company. Investors get a fixed yield for 1 to 5 years, and the promise is that they will not lose principal, similar to the terms of a CD. Sounds good, but the guarantee behind a GIC is only as good as the insurance company issuing the contract. See more about insurance companies in Chapter 5.

*Pyramid Level.*   Conservative.

*Advantages.*   Safety and preservation of principal.

*Disadvantages/Risk.*   The possibility that the issuing insurance company could become insolvent (business risk). If you are locked into long-term contracts, you could also miss out on higher returns in a period of rising interest rates (reinvestment rate risk).

*Your Objective.*   Fixed income and safety of principal.

## Fund D: Balanced Fund

A balanced fund provides a compromise between investing in stocks and in bonds, by investing in both. A balanced fund generally tries to maintain a mixture of large and small company stocks and long- and short-term bonds or preferred stocks. The rationale is that stock and bond markets often rise and fall at different times. The management style is designed to take advantage of the growth potential of stocks while limiting stock market risk with income and price stability from bonds or preferred stocks.

*Pyramid Level.*  Conservative to moderate, depending on the mix of stocks and bonds.

*Advantages.*  Diversification, with the average total return being leveraged to the upside by the growth potential of the stocks and tempered on the downside by the stability of principal and steady interest income from bonds and preferred stocks.

*Disadvantages/Risk.*  Your principal value may fluctuate due to changes in the stocks held in the portfolio, resulting from general malaise in the stock market (market risk) or poor stock choices by the fund manager (business risk). It may also fluctuate due to changes in the value of the bonds held in the portfolio, most often caused by movements in market interest rates (interest rate risk). The stock and bond markets often move independently, lowering your risk in a portfolio that holds both stocks and bonds. However, in some cases the markets may move together. For example, an increase in interest rates will cause bond prices to fall and may forecast falling stock prices because investors move out of stocks and into bonds when the returns are high.

*Your Objective.*  A long-term outlook with a balance of safety and growth.

## Fund E: Indexed Equity Fund

This fund is designed to mirror the performance of a common stock index, often the Standard & Poor's 500 Index (a.k.a. *S&P 500*), an index of 500 common stocks. When you hear that "the market" did well today, usually people are referring to either the S&P 500 Index or the Dow Jones Industrial Average Index (DJIA), an index of 30 blue-chip stocks. Though the stock market can be volatile, it has outperformed other investments over time. For example, from 1926 through 2001, the S&P 500 has had an average annualized return of approximately 12 percent every year. Even with the bear market of 2000 to 2002, a 10-year annualized return for the period ending June 30, 2002, was just over 11 percent. If you have been burned, you may pass up this investment option because the stock market seems too risky. Remember that your time horizon is very important. You need time to weather the storms.

*Pyramid Level.*   Moderate.

*Advantages.*   Growth of principal and a higher average historic total return.

*Disadvantages/Risk.*   The fluctuation in principal due to movements in stock market (market risk). There are no guarantees that the principal will increase in value.

*Your Objective.*   Long-term growth of principal through capital appreciation.

## Fund F: Company Stock Fund

Companies whose common stock is publicly traded may offer the employer's stock as one of their 401(k) plan investment options. Employers often encourage investment in this fund, feeling that employees who are owners of the company will work harder and take an interest in the bottom line. Many employees like it for similar reasons. More than a paycheck, daily work becomes a means to build your company and profit through an increased stock price.

*Pyramid Level.*   Moderate, aggressive, or speculative depending on the financial stability of the company. Read "Your Company Stock" later in Chapter 9 for more information about analyzing your stock's investment potential.

*Advantages.*   The potential to increase the value of your investment as your company grows. As an integral part of your firm, you should have a genuine feel for how the stock should perform. You hear about your company's strengths and at the same time understand its weaknesses. You know how the business works and what could make or break long-range plans. This is a true advantage because many people buy stock and never know more than the company's stock symbol. Being both an employee and a shareholder definitely gives you an edge, but be careful that loyalty doesn't blind you to financial concerns.

*Disadvantages/Risk.*   Counting on a paycheck as well as investing where you work means you are putting a lot of your eggs in one basket. If your company should have financial difficulties, you could find yourself without a job (or faced with salary freezes) at the same time your retirement savings in company stock are losing value due to falling prices. Also, because you own all of the same issue, you are facing a higher risk of price fluctuation and loss of principal than you would in a mutual fund in which there are many different types of stocks whose prices fluctuate independently of one another. A company stock fund is most obviously subject to business risk, but it is also affected by market and possibly liquidity risk if the stock is not actively traded.

*Your Objective.*   To take advantage of what you believe is excellent growth potential. Your hard work is reflected in the value of your investment.

## Fund G: Aggressive Fund

Different aggressive funds may be made up of small-company stocks, stocks of companies in a particular industry, or possibly international stocks. They are designed to provide high investor returns through rapid growth.

*Pyramid Level.*   Aggressive.

*Advantages.*   You expect a higher return on your invested dollars by assuming aggressive risk.

*Disadvantages/Risk.*   The price you pay for high potential return is high risk. These funds may fluctuate widely in value due to the business risk of small, new companies, the risk of stocks concentrated in one industry, or the different risks of international trade. International funds face the risk of currency fluctuation as well as business market and liquidity risks. Do not invest here if your time horizon is less than 5 years because these investments are highly volatile.

*Your Objective.*   A long-term outlook with maximum growth in principal.

## Your Plan Pyramid

How do all these funds fit in the investment pyramid? Now that we know more about each, match their investment objectives with the proper level of the pyramid to determine where they belong:

Level 5: Speculative               Fund F*
Level 4: Aggressive                Funds F* and G
Level 3: Moderate                  Funds E and F*
Level 2: Conservative              Funds B, C, and D
Level 1: Most conservative         Fund A

See Figure 8-2 for a sample plan pyramid.

## FIGURE 8-2

Sample Plan Pyramid

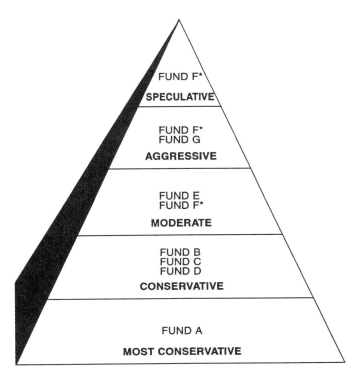

---

* The company stock fund could be in the moderate, aggressive, or speculative level of the pyramid depending on its financial stability and current condition.

## SUMMARY

In the 20-year history of 401(k) plans, 2001 was the second year in which the average 401(k) account dropped in value. The first year was 2000. Did you escape the carnage? Probably not if you were exposed to market risk. However, if your assets were spread over the investment pyramid and you tried to diversify among the different types of risk as well, you came out better than most. If you continue in the same vein, rather than running to money market for fear of losing principal (don't forget inflation risk) or dumping it into aggressive funds in hopes of a quick turnaround, you'll continue to do better than most.

## CHAPTER 9

# Analyzing Your Investment Options

**Y**our plan may have a wide array of investment choices, including some that sound very familiar and some you have never heard of. How can you choose between two mutual funds with comparable descriptions or among several in the same level of the investment pyramid? How do you know whether your company stock is a good buy or a dog? What do you need to know about annuity choices to make a good decision?

This chapter will help you with all of these dilemmas. We will explain the three most common types of retirement plan investment options: mutual funds, stocks, and annuities. You will find questions to ask when investigating each investment option and sources of objective rating information. While our discussion will focus on the options in your employer-sponsored plan, this information can just as easily be used to make decisions for your IRA or other investment accounts.

## MUTUAL FUNDS

What is a mutual fund? A mutual fund is an investment company that makes investments on behalf of individuals and institutions. Each fund can be a combination of stocks, bonds, or other securities that are managed by professionals and offer investors a simple, convenient, and relatively inexpensive method of investing.

The mutual fund pools money from many different investors who have similar objectives, and a professional money manager makes investment decisions designed to meet the stated objectives of the fund. Each share of the fund represents ownership in all of the fund's underlying securities, so shareholders who invest a few hundred dollars receive the same investment return per dollar as the shareholders who invest hundreds of thousands.

Advantages of investing in mutual funds include the following:

*Diversification.* Owning many different securities, which limits the risk of any single security, is one of the biggest advantages to investing in mutual funds.

*Professional Management.* Professional money management has long been available to institutions and wealthy investors. Investing in a mutual fund allows you to reap the benefits of the manager's investment knowledge without having to pay the manager by yourself. In a mutual fund, you share the money management expense with many others no matter what amount you have invested.

*Flexible Investing.* You are able to invest any amount above the minimum requirement (some funds have no minimum) and move with ease between other choices within the fund family.

*Automatic Reinvestment.* This feature allows you to automatically purchase more shares of the fund with dividends or capital gains that you earn.

## Comparing Mutual Funds

When you are comparing mutual fund choices, whether they are privately managed by your 401(k) administrator or by well-known, publicly offered fund families, such as Fidelity Investments or Vanguard, there are several questions you can ask to be sure that you make an informed decision.

### What Is the Fund's Investment Objective?

Your 401(k) plan's fund objectives may or may not correspond to the seven sample investment objectives explained in Chapter 8. However, if you look closely, you will probably find that these are the main categories of investments offered and that your plan includes some variations on the same themes.

When you are comparing various funds, it is important that you compare apples to apples in terms of risk level. Each fund's investment objective is the main determinant in deciding in which level of the investment pyramid it belongs. Remember the basis for the investment pyramid: As you move from the bottom to the top, both your expected return and your risk increase.

---

**Retirement Dilemma**   Fred's plan offers four funds, with average annual returns of 4.2, 6.7, 9.8, and 24.3 percent. Fred doesn't have any trouble deciding which fund to choose—he wants the one with the highest return.

**Solution**   What mistake is he making? Not looking at each investment objective as part of his decision-making process. The fund with the highest return happens to be a high-tech, aggressive stock mutual fund, which has had years with big losses as well as years with big gains. Just 3 years from retirement, Fred is taking a big chance by choosing the riskiest fund offered.

---

Before you begin comparing rates of return, make sure that the investment objectives of the funds in question put them in the same level (that is, risk level) of the investment pyramid. For example, a *small company stock fund* and an *international stock fund* both belong in the aggressive level of the investment pyramid. If you have determined that you need to invest in this level, move on to the next question, knowing that their risk is comparable.

## How Well Has the Fund Performed in the Past?

If you don't have a crystal ball handy, you'll have to use past performance to anticipate what a fund could do in the future. While this isn't a foolproof method, past performance is the best predictor we have, and it can be a good way to compare two funds.

The terminology you will see most often is *average annual return*. This generally means total return (dividends or interest plus capital gain or loss), and it is a calculated average of the time period in question. *Total return* is an important theory because it tells you not only what you have earned from an investment (*current return*) but how much your original principal is worth (*capital gain or loss*). The sum of these two items is the total return:

$$
\begin{array}{ccc}
\text{Interest or} & & \text{Gain or loss} & & \text{Total} \\
\text{dividends received} & + & \text{of principal in} & = & \text{return} \\
& & \text{original investment} & &
\end{array}
$$

Think of the total return of an investment as you would the life of a tulip bulb. It yields blooms every spring throughout its lifetime, and it may stay constant as one bulb or multiply, providing many more. The bulb is like the principal of an investment, remaining constant or increasing in size and number or occasionallyof of dying. The blooms are like income that occurs at regular intervals throughout its lifetime. The total return from the tulip bulb is the sum of its yield in blooms and its remaining bulb or bulbs.

The 5-year average annual total return is computed by taking the fund's beginning value and its value after 5 years, then calculating what annual rate of return, 5 years in a row, would have produced the ending value. While the individual year's rates of total return may fluctuate, making them difficult to compare, the average annual return can give you a good idea of long-term performance.

When comparing funds, concentrate on the following time frames:

- 1-year total return
- 3-year total return
- 5-year total return
- 10-year total return

**Retirement Tip**  Disregard returns for periods of less than 1 year, due to their temporary nature. Even the 1-year return figure is less valuable than the others. Why? Because it is easy to be lucky with a few good picks that really boost performance once. But to have consistently good returns over 3, 5, or 10 years is more difficult—and requires a lot more than luck.

Given recent history in the stock market, a 5-year total return may be the most valuable figure for analyzing and comparing stock mutual funds. Because 1998 and 1999 were positive years for the market averages but 2000, 2001, and 2002 were down years for the markets, a 5-year total return gives you a good indicator of fund performance in a time period that included both up and down years for stock market averages.

## *Three Ways to Use Total Return Figures*

1. *When You Need Help in Deciding on a Pyramid Level.* When you have a fund that doesn't fit into a category easily, check its average annual total returns. For example, in what level of the pyramid would you place a *high-yield bond fund*? You might be tempted to say "conservative," which is where most U.S. government bond funds belong. But if the *high-yield bond fund* has total returns that are 3 to 5 percent higher than ordinary bond funds, you can assume that the fund is taking additional risk in order to earn that "high yield." Depending on how *much* higher the returns are, it might belong in either the moderate or aggressive level.

    In another application, it is often difficult to decide whether a growth fund is moderate or aggressive. One hint is to check the volatility of its year-to-year annual returns. Given two funds with similar 5- or 10-year total returns, the fund whose individual annual total returns fluctuate more widely is the more risky fund. High year-to-year volatility, especially with periodic negative annual total returns, indicates an aggressive-level fund.

2. *When You Are Comparing Several Funds in the Same Risk Level.* If your plan offers a large assortment of different funds or offers funds from several different families, you may have more than one fund to choose from in each level of the pyramid. If you have decided to invest in the moderate level, what is the best way to choose among three different moderate-level funds? Compare their performance, using previous total returns. For example,

## TABLE 9-1

Choosing Relative Performance

| Fund | 1-Year Total Return | 3-Year Annualized Total Return | 5-Year Annualized Total Return |
|------|---------------------|--------------------------------|--------------------------------|
| A    | 22.6%               | 10.1%                          | 8.3%                           |
| B    | 13.9                | 15.8                           | 14.2                           |
| C    | 10.7                | 12.9                           | 14.1                           |

given the three funds in Table 9-1, Fund B has the superior performance.

3. *When You Want to See How Well a Fund Has Performed in Comparison to Market Averages and Other Similar Funds.* Two common comparison benchmarks used are the Standard & Poor's 500 Average and a peer group of funds with the same investment objective. The S&P 500 is a group of 500 U.S. stocks that represent approximately 70 percent of the total market value of U.S. stocks and that are tracked by the Standard & Poor's Corporation. The average tells you how the market performed in any given year or time period, and it can be found in most libraries or financial newspapers. Here are some results you might expect from comparing a fund to this average:

   ■ *Aggressive Growth Funds.* Aggressive growth funds will tend to be more volatile on a year-to-year basis than the S&P 500. In a year in which the S&P 500 has good performance, an aggressive fund should have better. In a year in which the S&P 500 does poorly (even negative returns for the year), an aggressive fund may do even worse. In other words, total returns tend to be more extreme than the average. See Figure 9-1 for an example. This short-term volatility is part of what makes them risky. A *good* aggressive growth fund will outperform the S&P 500 over the long term.

**FIGURE 9-1**

Expected Aggressive Fund Performance

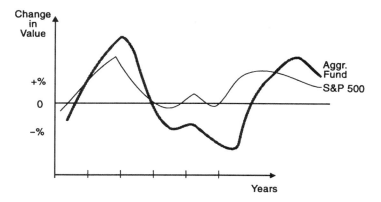

- *Growth Funds.*  Growth funds strive to outperform the S&P 500 on both an annual and a long-term basis. The good ones do. Their returns tend to follow the direction and volatility of the average.

- *Growth and Income Funds or Balanced Funds.*  The total returns of these funds should be less volatile than those of growth or aggressive growth funds. Due to the income portion of their holdings (bonds or dividend-paying stocks), they are cushioned in down-market years and often don't take full advantage of a raging stock market in up years. A performance graph might be just the opposite of that of an aggressive fund, showing under-performance of the S&P 500 in good years and out-performance in bad. See Figure 9-2 for an example. Due to their ability to control risk and volatility, many balanced or growth and income funds outperform the average over time.

- *Income Funds.*  Income funds, another name for bond funds, generally have no correlation to stock market averages such as the S&P 500. A better benchmark of performance for these funds is the Shearson/Lehman Bond Aggregate. Total return comparisons with either benchmark can be found in *Morningstar Mutual Funds.*

**FIGURE  9-2**

Expected Growth and Income Fund or Balanced Fund
Performance

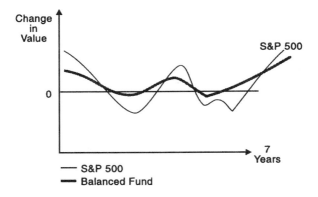

**Retirement  Dilemma**    Brigid's 401(k) plan offers one fund
choice in each level of the pyramid. She has completed her personal
pyramid and knows that she should add to either the moderate or
aggressive level. She wants to know how to decide between the
small company growth fund (aggressive) and the growth and
income fund (moderate).

**Solution**    Because these funds are in different risk levels of the
pyramid, she shouldn't compare them to each other but instead to a
group of their peers, to see how successful each is, given the risk that
it takes. She can choose to contribute to the best of the two, investing money outside her 401(k) plan in the level not chosen.

Comparing mutual funds to a group of their peers works for any
investment objective and is probably one of the best ways to determine the relative success of a fund manager.

**Retirement Tip**    When checking long-term results, keep an eye
out for changing a fund manager. Don't give a new manager credit
(or blame) for the previous manager's performance.

There are several sources of objective information that offer peer-group comparisons. One is the publication *Morningstar Mutual Funds,* which ranks funds within their investment objectives on a scale of 1 to 100. A score of 23 means the fund's total return ranked in the top 23 percent of all funds with the same investment objective for the time period in question. See Appendix C for Internet sites that analyze and rank mutual funds.

---

**Retirement Tip**   If your plan's funds are not publicly offered and are therefore not included in one of these publications, find a fund in the publication that has the same investment objective and a similar total return number. Use that fund to see where yours would have ranked had it been included in the survey.

---

## What Expenses and Commissions Must Be Paid?

In many cases, funds offered within a 401(k) plan are *no-load funds,* meaning that there are no commissions charged to investors to purchase or to sell shares. If your plan offers several public families of mutual funds, it is possible that there will be commissions involved and also possible that they will differ from family to family. (A family of funds is similar to a brand of cereal or salad dressing, with many different flavors produced by the same company.) There are even differences within a single family of funds. Fidelity Investments, for example, offers both load and no-load mutual funds.

Whether or not you pay a commission or load, each fund will have an *expense ratio*, which simply tells you how much of your total return goes to pay fund expenses. For a stock fund, a ratio of 0.75 percent or below is good; anything higher than 1.25 percent is a little excessive. For a bond or fixed-income fund, expense ratios should be well under 0.75 percent, with a target of 0.5 percent. International funds, due to the high cost of trading on foreign exchanges, may have expense ratios of 1.5 percent, which are considered acceptable.

## Help with Mutual Fund Analysis

Securities law requires that you receive a prospectus when you purchase a mutual fund. The prospectus is a lengthy document that
explains, in depth, what the fund invests in, what its fees are, who
makes decisions, who the managers are, and more. Unfortunately,
these are legal documents and, as such, are not generally written in
an easy-to-understand tone. They also do not include some important information for an investor, such as how the fund has performed against its peers. So, while you should *always* read the
prospectus, you should get additional information as well.

*Morningstar Mutual Funds* is an industry leader in providing
unbiased performance information about mutual funds. It is available at most libraries and on the Internet at *www.morningstar.com*.
Many other Web sites offer mutual fund data. See Appendix C for
suggestions.

# YOUR COMPANY'S STOCK

As an employee, you may be the best person or the worst person to
analyze the prospects of your company. Ideally, you are in the best
position to know whether your products are selling well, whether
you are reaching performance goals in terms of revenues and profits, and whether top management has a vision for the future. If you
can use this knowledge when evaluating your company's stock,
you will probably make good, fundamentally sound decisions. On
the other hand, it isn't unusual for employees to lose objectivity
about their company. Years of indoctrination about the quality of
your company's products or the level of its service versus those of
the competition can diminish your ability to make impartial judg-
ments. Selling or even just deciding not to buy your company's
stock can seem like a betrayal rather than a financial decision.

**Retirement Tip** Invest in the stock of your employer due to
sound fundamentals rather than loyalty. No matter how good the
stock looks, keep in mind that diversifying will protect you from
unforeseen disasters.

## Analyzing Your Company's Stock

In addition to your *feel* for the direction of your company's fortunes, analyze the facts and numbers that are available to all investors. Remember, perceptions of the investing public are a major force in determining stock prices. Ask yourself (or a trusted financial advisor) the following questions:

### What Are the Prospects for the Industry?

How will changes in the economy affect your industry? In times of economic expansion, *cyclical* industries such as automobile manufacturers, home and commercial builders, steel companies, and manufacturers of luxury items are expected to profit. In economic downturns, *defensive* industries—that is, those producing products that are consumed regardless of consumers' wealth—still pull in their revenues. Examples of such industries are beverage and food manufacturers and distributors, discount stores, and producers of home products, such as detergents and toiletries.

### What Is the Trend in Revenues at Your Company?

Check your company's annual report or Web site for last year's revenues. By looking at the quarterly numbers and computing percentage changes from year to year, you can get a good understanding of the direction of revenue growth. (Divide the difference in the two years' revenues by the earlier year's revenue to reach the percentage change.) Compare the latest year's change with 3- and 5-year growth rates.

- Is the rate of growth increasing or decreasing?
- How does it compare with other companies in the industry?

### What Is the Trend in Profits at Your Company?

Profits are what it's all about. How much money is your company making, and is it making more each year? It is important to look at profits on a per-share basis, which is called *earnings per share* (EPS). The EPS is simply the total net profit of the company divided by the outstanding number of shares of common stock. Because each share of stock represents ownership of the company, the EPS figure designates the earning power of each portion of ownership. For stockholders, the EPS is the most important profit figure because it

tells them how much their share of the company generated in profits. Check the growth in EPS just as you did the growth in revenues, looking at year-to-year trends and comparing the current
year's growth with long-term growth.

## What Is the Price-Earnings Ratio?

The first three questions can help you decide how well your company is performing. What they can't tell you is whether its stock is
a good buy at the current price. The price-earnings (P/E) ratio can
help you with this.

---

**Retirement Tip**   The price-earnings (P/E) ratio of a stock is its
price per share divided by its earnings per share (EPS).

Price ÷ EPS = P/E ratio

---

The ratio computes how many dollars per share you must pay
for each dollar of earnings per share. If all things are equal, a lower
P/E is better because you are paying less for each dollar of earnings. An analogy to comparing two stocks with the same earnings
per share but with different prices is that of shopping for two air-
conditioners that have the same cooling power. If one is on sale,
you get more cooling power for your purchase dollar. You might
consider the stock with a lower P/E ratio to be "on sale." If you
hear that a stock is selling "at a discount to the market," it has a
lower P/E ratio than the general market.

Why would anyone be willing to buy stocks with high P/E
ratios? Because they expect earnings growth. Let's look at an
example:

---

**Retirement Dilemma**   The Cushing Couch Company stock has
a price of $40 per share and an EPS of $2 per share. Its P/E ratio is
$40 divided by $2, or 20. A competitor, the Capshaw Couch
Company, also has an EPS of $2 per share, but its stock price is $60.
Its P/E ratio is $60 divided by $2, or 30.

---

Why would people be willing to buy the Capshaw Couch Company stock at $60 when they could get the same $2 in earnings per share with the Cushing Couch Company for just $40?

Probably because they believe that the EPS at Capshaw will soon grow. If the EPS grows to $3 per share, its P/E ratio will be 20 ($60 divided by $3, or 20), the same as the P/E ratio for Cushing.

What is the danger? That those $3 earnings won't materialize as expected. Then, to bring its P/E ratio into line with Cushing's and those of other companies in the industry, Capshaw's stock price would have to drop from $60 to $40.

To find out whether your company's P/E ratio is high, average, or low when compared to other stocks, check its *relative P/E ratio* on one of many investment Web sites. This figure compares a stock's P/E ratio to all others. A ratio of 1 is average, more than 1 shows a relatively high ratio, and less than 1, a low ratio. If you can't find a relative P/E ratio, check *Investor's Business Daily,* which publishes the average P/E ratio of the Dow Jones Industrial Average, and use this average P/E as a comparison figure.

Another rule of thumb compares the P/E ratio with the rate of growth in earnings per share in a ratio called the *price-earnings growth (PEG) ratio.* Following the concept that high P/E ratios are a result of expected growth in EPS, this rule contends that a company's P/E ratio should not be higher than its rate of growth in EPS. For example, a P/E ratio of 35 might not be considered too high for a company whose EPS is growing at the rate of 50 percent per year, but the same 35 P/E ratio is considered high for a company whose EPS growth is 15 percent. The PEG uses the P/E ratio as the numerator and the earnings growth rate as the denominator.

$$PEG = P/E \text{ ratio} \div EPS \text{ growth rate}$$

Using this rule of thumb, look for stocks with PEGs less than or equal to 1. While you can often find the P/E ratio in printed or Web site stock analysis material, you may have to compute the PEG ratio yourself. One Web site that provides the PEG is *SmartMoney* at *www.smartmoney.com.* Enter a symbol for a quote, and then click on the Earnings tab on the quote page to find the PEG.

## What Are the ROE and ROA?

The *return on equity* (ROE) and the *return on assets* (ROA) are measures of total return for the company, very similar to the measures of total return that you use to gauge the performance of your investments. Both of these ratios calculate the money returned (profits) on the money invested (equity or assets). Your annual report or any independent information source should have both of these ratios calculated for you. Analyze the numbers in two ways:

- Compare the numbers with other companies in the same industry.
- Compare year-to-year figures and trends.

Higher is better, and an increasing trend is generally a positive sign. In an exception to this rule, the ROE can increase due to rising debt levels. If you see your company's ROE move significantly higher, check to make sure that it isn't due to excessive borrowing. High levels of debt can cripple a company with interest payments.

### Help with Stock Analysis

The Internet has leveled the playing field when it comes to stock research. Just 10 years ago, up-to-date financial results and sophisticated comparisons were available only to those in the investment industry. Now, if you know the right Web sites, there is more information available than you could ever possibly use, and it is right at your fingertips. If you are just getting started, try the Research Wizard at MSN MoneyCentral for analysis and interpretation of many of the concepts discussed previously. You will find it at *www.money central.msn.com*. Appendix C provides an entire list of resources.

# ANNUITIES

An *annuity* is a contract with an insurance company that offers deferral of taxes on capital gains and income until you withdraw the funds. If your plan's investment options are annuities, your research and analysis task is very similar to what it would be for a plan that offers mutual funds. There is one striking difference, however, and that is the safety of the insurance company that provides the annuities. Because insurance companies are not just in the investment business but also in the property and casualty and life insurance business, they have many unknown risks and claims against their assets. This is a dimension of risk that you would not need to analyze before investing in mutual funds. Before investigating a particular annuity fund—its past performance and fees—you must check out the strength and stability of the insurance company that issues it.

Three companies—A.M. Best, Moody's Investor Services, and Standard & Poor's—rate insurance companies. Call the reference room of your local library or Standard & Poor's, (212) 553-0377, for the rating of any insurance company. A rating less than an A means that there are additional risks to investing your money with this company.

---

**Retirement Tip**   You should check this rating annually because circumstances and financial stability can change. Don't be the last to know that your insurance company is having difficulties.

---

## Analyzing Annuities

Once you are comfortable with the stability of the insurance company, begin to look at the different annuities offered within your plan. There are two basic types, fixed and variable.

### Fixed Annuities

*Fixed annuities* are similar in *structure* (not risk—CDs are FDIC insured, while annuities are not) to a certificate of deposit. You are guaranteed a particular rate of return for a certain time period. At the end of that time period, you can renew at the current rate available.

> *Advantages.*   You will always know the rate of return. Unless the insurance company becomes insolvent, your account will not lose money.
>
> *Disadvantages.*   As with any fixed-rate investment, you are not protected against inflation. If you invest in fixed annuities, beware of initial "teaser" rates, which entice new

investors but are not available to existing annuity holders. Upon renewal, you may find that your interest rate is much less attractive.

---

**Retirement Dilemma**   Genny had the option of choosing from two different annuity companies in her plan. Because she was nearing retirement, she decided on a fixed annuity. She chose Company A because its 1-year fixed rate was 7 percent, while Company B's rate was only 6.5 percent.

When it came time to renew at the end of 1 year, her renewal rate had dropped to only 6 percent, while the renewal rates at Company B were still 6.5 percent. What was her mistake?

**Solution**   Choosing a company with high teaser rates can sound good at the time but choosing on that basis alone can set you up for disappointment later. Existing policyholders can expect lower rates of return, which pay for the high returns being given to new customers.

---

Variable Annuities

*Variable annuities* are very much like mutual funds in their design. They include a pooled set of investments that are grouped according to investment objective and whose value is subject to the market value of the underlying securities. Unlike a fixed annuity, there is no guarantee of investment returns.

Just as with a mutual fund, begin your analysis with investment objectives. Complete your personal pyramid, compare it to the recommendations for your financial stage of life, and decide where (which level of the pyramid) you need to add. After you have chosen your pyramid level and narrowed your choices to a few investment objectives, begin analyzing past performance. Do this in the same way you studied performance for mutual funds. An independent source of information is *Morningstar Variable Annuity/Life Sourcebook*, which should be available in your library.

*Advantages.*   Variable annuities offer growth potential and many different investment choices.

*Disadvantages.*   Rates of return are not guaranteed, and values may fluctuate with market conditions.

You can read more about annuities in Chapter 5.

## SUMMARY

As you analyze your investment options, remember the following rules:

- Stay on track. A retirement plan is a long-term venture, and you won't get where you want to go using short-term vehicles. As the popular investment company advertisement says, "No one plans to fail; they just fail to plan." Check your progress quarterly and make changes as necessary.

- Unless you are on the verge of retirement, keep some growth investments in your portfolio. Over the past 60 years, stocks have averaged around 10 percent annualized return, while long-term bonds have lagged behind at 5 percent, and Treasury bills have turned in a 4 percent return. Growth protects against inflation and is critical to balancing your portfolio. Sure, the markets will move up and down over the years, but over the long term, growth investments win the race.

- Diversify among your investment options using your personal investment pyramid. Spreading out your retirement dollars and making periodic changes will help to secure the suitable asset mix you need.

- Collect all the available information about an investment *before* you spend your hard-earned money. Never invest in something you do not completely understand.

# CHAPTER 10

# Your Retirement Plan Hierarchy

**N**ancy and Jeff were in their mid-thirties, had just purchased a home, and were beginning to think seriously about putting some money away for retirement. They had been approached by several financial planners and were somewhat confused by the differing advice. Their employers were encouraging them to invest in Jeff's 403(b) plan and Nancy's 401(k) plan, and investment salespeople were pushing IRAs, annuities, and insurance policies. Their question was, "Should we start our retirement savings with an IRA or our 401(k) plans, or should we invest in mutual funds, insurance, or annuities?" We told them that retirement savings should be accumulated in this order, depending on their eligibility:

401(k)/403(b)/457 plan
↓
Roth IRA
↓
Tax-deductible traditional IRA (when they are near retirement)
↓
Nondeductible traditional IRA (maybe, for interest-bearing investments only)
↓
Tax-deferred investments, such as annuities (maybe, fixed annuities only)
↓
Growth and dividend-paying investments, such as stocks and stock mutual funds in taxable accounts

See Table 10-1 for income limits for eligibility on each plan type.

**TABLE 10-1**

Income Limits for Retirement Plan Contributions

| Retirement Account | Income Limits |
|---|---|
| Employer plan | No limit |
| Roth IRA | $95,000 single<br>$150,000 joint |
| Tax-deductible IRA | $34,000 single*<br>$54,000 joint* |
| Nondeductible IRA | No limit |
| Annuities or insurance | No limit |
| Other investments | No limit |

*These limits apply only if you contribute to an employer plan. If you do not contribute to an employer plan, there is no income limit for contributing to a tax-deductible IRA.

You should move down a level [that is, from 401(k)/403(b)/457 to Roth IRA] only when you have invested the maximum annual amount allowed by law in the previous level. You may choose to skip a level altogether.

## EMPLOYER PLANS

The generally accepted wisdom is to invest in your employer-sponsored plan before any other retirement plans, for the following advantages:

- Tax-deductible contributions
- High contribution limits
- Employer matching contributions
- Automatic payroll deductions

As we discussed in Chapter 4, contributions up to $12,000 (2003 rules) in your 401(k), 403(b), or 457 plan are tax deductible. This is much more than you can contribute to an IRA, and contributions are tax deductible regardless of income. Limits for years after 2003 can be found in Table 4-1. Keep in mind that the maximum combined employee and employer contribution is the lesser of $40,000 or 100 percent of your annual compensation. Therefore, you may reach your maximum well before the IRS limit due to your plan limits. For example, if your plan allows you to contribute a maximum of 10 percent of your $30,000 salary, the most you can contribute to your 401(k) account each year is $3000, not $12,000. If your employer matches 50 percent ($1500) of your contributions, the upper limit to your combined deposits is $4500, not $40,000.

The benefit of employer matching contributions can't be found in any other retirement plan. It amounts to an immediate return on your investment of your matching provision, often 25 or 50 percent. If other retirement plans, such as a Roth IRA, appeal to you, always contribute to your employer plan to the maximum that will be matched before investing in the Roth IRA. If you like the tax-exempt withdrawals of the Roth account, ask your employer whether Roth contribution accounts will become part of your plan when the law allows them.

Consider the convenience of payroll deductions when deciding how much to contribute to your employer plan. Paying yourself first is much easier when you don't ever have the money to spend. Besides the convenience, regular deductions take the emotion out of investing and provide dollar cost averaging (see Chapter 4). You buy more shares when prices are low and fewer shares when prices are high.

---

**Retirement Dilemma**   Amy is divorced and in her mid-forties. Her children have left the nest, and she has no retirement savings. She has just joined her 401(k) plan and is contributing the 10 percent maximum that her plan allows. Her salary is $30,000, and she contributes $3000 each year. Her biggest concern right now is saving enough to be able to retire comfortably. How should she do it?

**Solution**   She should plan to open either a Roth or a traditional tax-deductible IRA in addition to her 401(k). Under 2003 rules, as a single person with a salary of $30,000, she is eligible for either. This would allow her to contribute an additional $3000 per year. Even if the $3000 is more than she is able to put away each year, any amount up to the $3000 will bring her closer to her retirement goals.

## IRAs

If you do not have an employer plan or have contributed as much as you can, your next retirement savings consideration should be an IRA. The most that you can contribute for 2003 is $3000. See Chapter 3 for future increases in the limits. If you are eligible for both a Roth IRA and a tax-deductible traditional IRA, which is best? The decision involves trading the current tax break of the traditional IRA for the later tax break of the Roth IRA.

### Roth IRAs

If your income is under the IRS limits of $95,000 (for single filers) and $150,000 (filing jointly), you can contribute the maximum $3000 allowed annually to a Roth IRA. You can contribute lesser amounts if your single income is between $95,000 and $110,000 or if your joint income is between $150,000 and $160,000. See Chapter 3 for the computation of contribution limits between these income levels. While you won't get a current income tax deduction for your contributions to a Roth IRA, you won't have to pay taxes on withdrawals during retirement.

### Tax-Deductible IRAs

If neither you nor your spouse contributed to an employer plan, you can fully deduct your traditional IRA contribution. If you did contribute to an employer plan, you can fully deduct your contribution under the following conditions:

- If you are single and earned less than $40,000 in 2003
- If you are married and filing jointly, and you earned less than $60,000 in 2003

Contribution deductibility is subject to phase-outs for single filers who earned between $40,000 and $50,000 in 2003 and married joint filers with joint income between $60,000 and $70,000 for 2003. See Chapter 3 for more details.

## Roth IRAs versus Tax-Deductible IRAs

If you are in your twenties or thirties, the benefit of tax-free withdrawals during retirement will likely outweigh the benefit of a current income tax deduction. Try a calculator, such as the one at MSN (*www.moneycentral.msn.com/retire/home.asp*) to compare. The computation for the tax-deductible account includes the expectation that you will take the amount you saved each year in current income taxes and invest it in a taxable account.

**Retirement Dilemma**   Kip is 35, earns $50,000 per year, and isn't covered by a retirement plan at work. His wife doesn't work. Should he invest in a deductible IRA or a Roth IRA?

**Solution**   According to the calculator at MSN, he will be better off investing in the Roth IRA if he plans to retire when he's 60, live until he's 80, and his investments earn 9 percent pretax. Their estimate of his average yearly after-tax distribution during retirement is $16,710 for the Roth IRA versus $14,126 for the tax-deductible account.

The best way to decide which alternative will give you the most after-tax money to spend in your retirement is to run the numbers. Generally you will find that the younger you are and the higher your investment returns, the more favorable the Roth IRA will look.

**Retirement Tip**   Robert wanted to open an IRA last year, but couldn't because he didn't have $3000 on April 15. He decided that this year, he would contribute each month instead of trying to do it all at once. He started saving $166 per month, and he will easily reach his goal of $3000. Take the sting out of writing big checks by saving a little at a time.

## Nondeductible IRAs

If your income level makes you eligible for a Roth IRA, always choose that over a nondeductible traditional IRA. Neither provides a deduction for contributions, but qualified withdrawals from the Roth IRAs are not taxable. Withdrawals in excess of contributions from the traditional IRA are subject to current income tax.

If your income is too high for you to be eligible for a Roth IRA, always maximize contributions to your employer plan first, then consider a nondeductible traditional IRA. Be careful when doing so because investing in the nondeductible IRA has a distinct disadvantage when compared to investing in a taxable account. All investment income and capital gains are taxed at ordinary income tax rates when withdrawn from a traditional IRA. So, while deferring taxes on investment income is a bonus, you will pay ordinary income tax rates, up to 35 percent, on all dividends and capital gains rather than the 15 percent paid in taxable accounts. If your marginal rate is higher than 15 percent, you will pay more in taxes. The key in using the nondeductible IRA is to choose investments that will benefit from tax deferral while not suffering from the fact that returns will be taxed as current income. This means choosing investments that earn interest, which is taxed at ordinary income tax rates. Investments in the conservative and most conservative levels of the pyramid fall into this category. Investments in these levels are fixed-income securities, such as bonds, CDs, or bank money market accounts. They generally pay current interest and have little or no expected capital appreciation. Everyone needs investments in these levels due to their relative safety; choosing the right location for them will result in the lowest tax bill.

---

**Retirement Tip**  If you invest in a nondeductible IRA, you will be taxed only on the growth of the account at withdrawal, not the entire account value. Because the amount you initially invested has already been subject to taxes, only the amount in excess of your original investment will be taxed. To avoid any confusion upon withdrawal, do not mingle deductible and nondeductible IRAs.

---

## ANNUITIES AND INSURANCE

As we discussed at length in Chapter 5, there are numerous drawbacks to using annuities and insurance to invest for retirement, including high fees and the tax treatment of withdrawals. Just as with the nondeductible IRA, an annuity turns dividends and capital gains into ordinary income for tax purposes. However, like the nondeductible IRA, annuities and insurance provide tax deferral of investment earnings. Consider them if you have exhausted all employer plan and IRA limits and would still like tax deferral. They can make sense if you are willing to shop for low-load providers, expect to be in a lower tax bracket in retirement, are afraid you might outlive your income (you can annuitize your payments), and are willing to place interest-bearing (this means fixed annuities), rather than growth, investments in them so as to lessen the penalty of turning dividends and capital gains into ordinary income.

## TAXABLE GROWTH INVESTMENTS

Taxable investments that are simply earmarked for retirement don't have the sizzle of retirement plans, but they are still a necessary part of retirement planning. Most of us won't be able to retire on what we can contribute to retirement accounts, and Social Security isn't likely to pick up the slack. So unless you plan to inherit a big chunk of money (they *could* spend it all . . .) or win the lottery, other investing will have to do the trick.

The easiest way to invest for the long term is to pay yourself first, just as you make your contributions to your employer-sponsored retirement account. Have savings deducted before you get your paycheck or as soon as it hits your checking account, and most of the time, you won't even miss it. Most investment firms and many employers offer savings plans that will withdraw from your checking account or paycheck on a schedule that you dictate. Unless you want to live on leftovers in retirement, make it a habit to live on what is left over now.

Many of the investments you make early in life for other purposes can end up being retirement funds. The addition you never put on your house or the vacations you never had time to take can end up funding some of your retirement—you'll have plenty of time for vacations then! Keep this in mind when saving for your children's education. Yes, it is a wonderful gift to give your child an education, but don't shortchange your own retirement in the process. If you are committed to fully funding their college expenses, at least consider the fact that they might take another route or be talented or smart enough to earn scholarships. Investing in your own name rather than theirs frees up funds that aren't used. Then they can be spent on your retirement. When you invest in custodial accounts, those funds legally belong to the minor when he or she reaches the age of majority, usually 18 or 21, depending on your state law.

## INVESTING WITHIN THE RETIREMENT PLAN HIERARCHY

There are two main considerations when investing for retirement that may differentiate these investments from others that you might make. They are the long-term nature of retirement investments and the tax treatment of retirement accounts.

If you have more than 10 years until you expect to use the assets in your retirement account, you can afford to invest in securities that might be more volatile in the short term but are expected to offer greater long-term returns. Even with the bear market we have recently witnessed, investments in stocks have greatly outperformed investments in bonds over the last 70 years. Therefore, if you have plenty of time, a good portion of your retirement funds should be in diversified equity investments.

The tax treatment of retirement accounts affects how they should be invested if they are part of a retirement strategy that includes funds in taxable accounts as well. In Chapter 8, we discussed diversifying your investments across asset classes to reduce risk. So while you may want to concentrate retirement funds in equity investments, you will never want to put all your funds in the same asset class. As you diversify, you will include investments such as bonds or income-producing stocks, as well as stocks or funds whose returns are primarily capital gains.

Which assets should be in the traditional IRAs, 401(k)s, and annuities, and which outside or in Roth IRAs? When capital gains and dividends were taxed as ordinary income, conventional wisdom said the highest-returning assets, generally stocks, belonged in tax-deferred accounts in order to shelter the most income. This is no longer the case, now that capital gains and dividends are taxed at a maximum rate of 15 percent versus ordinary income tax rates that are as high as 35 percent. All investment gains in a traditional IRA or 401(k) are taxed as current income when withdrawn, raising the taxes due on capital gains and dividends by as much as 20 percent. Consider your personal pyramid when deciding how to invest, and place growth investments in taxable accounts so that you take maximum advantage of the tax break given to capital gains and dividends.

If you invest in mutual funds, look at the tax efficiency rating of a fund before you buy it. Tax-efficient funds don't trade often, allowing gains in taxable accounts to build, untaxed. Inefficient funds have high turnover, requiring you to fork out taxes every year on investment gains. If you are considering two funds with equal performance but different turnover, place high-turnover funds in tax-deferred retirement accounts and low-turnover funds in your taxable accounts.

Remember that withdrawals from employer plans and traditional, tax-deductible IRAs will be taxable as ordinary income. Roth IRAs are not taxed as they grow or upon withdrawal. Ordinary taxable accounts are taxed when income or capital gains are incurred, but withdrawals are not taxable unless you incur a capital gain in the process. Understanding these differences and the differences in tax rates and allocating the right investments to your various accounts will result in the best use of your money. See Table 10-2 for some suggestions.

## SUMMARY

With all the types of retirement plans available, it is often hard to know where to start. However, there are key advantages to each plan, so it is important that the money you save works hardest for you by being in the right investment vehicle. In general, always begin with your employer's retirement plan, especially if it offers matching. If you are not happy with the investment options offered, choose the best of the options available as you contribute up to the level that will be matched. Once you hit that level or if you have contributed the maximum allowed, consider IRAs next. You can review this chapter or Chapter 3 for the relative advantages of Roth IRAs and traditional deductible and nondeductible IRAs. If you are still interested in tax deferral,

TABLE 10-2

Investment Allocation of Tax-Deferred, Tax-Free, and Taxable
Retirement Funds

| Vehicle | Investments | Reason |
| --- | --- | --- |
| Roth IRA | ■ Those with the highest expected returns.<br>■ Growth portfolios with high turnover.<br>■ Interest-bearing securities and REITs | ■ Tax-free income on the largest gains.<br>■ No tax cost on gains from high turnover.<br>■ No taxes on income that would otherwise be taxed at ordinary income tax rates. |
| Retirement assets in taxable accounts | ■ Those whose total return will come primarily from capital gains and dividends.<br>■ Opt for a buy-and-hold strategy or low-turnover funds. | ■ Take advantage of the 15 percent dividends and capital gains tax rate.<br>■ Low turnover minimizes taxes. |
| Ordinary IRAs, employer plans, and annuities | ■ If your diversification plan includes interest-bearing investments or REITs, this is where they should be. | ■ Withdrawals will be taxed at ordinary income tax rates. |

consider insurance or annuities, but only after reading about the disadvantages and searching out low-cost providers. Last, don't forget that ordinary growth investments offer excellent opportunities for retirement planning. It is easy to max out plan contributions and consider yourself finished. For most of us, that won't be enough!

# CHAPTER 11

# Is Your Money Safe?

If you have read this far, you have determined where you are now, you know where you are going, and you know how you will get there. You have taken the time to wisely choose your investments, and you know how to analyze and compare total returns. But have you looked at your employer-sponsored plan to make sure your savings are safe? We aren't talking about the investment risks addressed in Chapter 8, like market risk or the effects of inflation. How do you know if your plan is at risk? What risks are inherent in your plan, your employer, or your trustee? In addition to those risks to principal, what fees pose risks to your investment return?

If you don't make an annual review of your retirement plan, how can you be sure? Chances are, your plan is in good shape, but if you file away those boring statements and prospectuses without even a glance, or worse yet, throw them away, you may be costing yourself money. This chapter is dedicated to helping you review and understand *everything* about your plan. You will learn the questions to ask to ensure that you get the answers you need. These questions won't change from year to year, but the answers certainly can. Use this chapter as your framework to make sure your financial foundation is solid.

The retirement planning and investment focus *is* shifting from employers' making choices (defined-benefit pension plans) to employees' making choices (defined-contribution plans). You are now the manager of your money, and it is your responsibility to periodically check out the plan's administrators, performance, and fees to make sure your money is safe. You may think, "Isn't that why we pay the manager? Why is it so important for *me* to check out my plan? I really don't have time for this." Well, you can't afford not to. Even though retirement plans follow many of the same laws, they can differ tremendously when it comes to proprietary contribution limits, matching funds, fees, and investment choices. Careful evaluation can assure you that your plan is being run properly and will give you the opportunity to voice an opinion about things that should be changed.

## THE PLAN DOCUMENT

Let's start at the beginning. You need to understand exactly how your plan works. The legal description of your plan is called the *plan document*. The user-friendly version is called the *summary plan description* (SPD). To get a copy, ask your benefits manager for one of the packets given to new employees. It has probably come in the mail or across your desk in the past, but you may not have given it a high reading priority. Now it is a high priority! Block off a few hours, and thoroughly read your plan documents. Yes, the reading is technical and a bit boring. We suggest you take notes and write down questions along the way to get the very most out of your time and effort. Going through this procedure is the only way you will know if your nest egg is safe.

---

**Retirement Tip**   A crisis is *not* the time to inquire into your plan's safety. It takes only a couple of hours to become familiar with your retirement plan, and it is well worth the time spent.

---

You may find the following definitions helpful as you read through your plan document or SPD:

*Plan Sponsor.*   This is your employer. As the plan sponsor, your employer is responsible for making sure your plan complies with the law. Your employer also handles making payroll deductions and any matching contributions that go into your retirement account. Payroll deductions belong to you throughout the process. Even if your employer files for bankruptcy after making a deduction but before transmitting the funds to your account, creditors of the company have no claim on your money.

*Plan Trustee.*   This is the trust company, bank, insurance company, or investment firm that handles the plan. The trustee is responsible for safeguarding the plan assets and keeping track of individual accounts. The trustee also directs investment of your retirement funds according to your instructions and the plan document.

*Plan Administrator.*   This is the individual, generally someone in the benefits department, who handles the daily administration of the plan.

## QUESTIONS FOR YOUR PLAN CHECKUP

1. **Who is the trustee? Is it a mutual fund company, bank, brokerage firm, or trust or insurance company?**

While it is true that you are in charge of your investment choices, you are not in control of the plan as a whole. Knowing more about the company that is the trustee and how it works is the first step to establishing a higher safety factor in your mind. Find out the company's history and how long it has been in business. This may entail just a few questions to your benefits department, or you may need to check resources available via the Internet or in your corporate or local library. You can use the Standard & Poor's Corporate Records to learn about the financial situation of your trustee. You are looking for a strong, healthy trustee with an S&P rating of A, A+, or A++. Remember, their financial stability can directly affect yours.

2. **If my 403(b) plan provides annuities as investments or my 401(k) or 457 plan includes guaranteed insurance contracts (GICs) or annuities, how stable is the insurance company backing the funds? What is its A.M. Best rating?**

It is important to obtain this information annually because a very high percentage of 401(k), 403(b), and 457 plan dollars is invested in guaranteed investment contracts (GICs) and annuities every year. Don't assume that because the rate is fixed like a CD rate, a GIC is as safe as a CD. They are similar in concept, as both CDs and GICs are designed to provide investors with a fixed yield for a fixed time period. However, a bank CD is backed by FDIC insurance in addition to the assets of the bank. A GIC is backed only by the assets of the insurance company. The security of your investment is only as secure as the insurance company itself.

To check an insurance company's financial condition, get its A.M. Best rating from your local library or over the Internet at *www.ambest.com*. Find out if the rating has changed over the past year. Just like a test score in school, A+ is the best, and the score can give you an indication of the financial stability of the insurance company. If the rating drops to a B– or C from an A+ over the period of a year, it is a red flag telling you to switch out of this fund. As you investigate your GICs and annuities, you will find out what the insurance company invests in and how it makes money with your money. The good news is that, to date, none of the insurers that offer contracts have defaulted on their GIC obligations. But there is always risk of the insurers loading their portfolios with bad investments, such as risky mortgages or junk bonds.

**Retirement Dilemma**  Mark checks his GIC account's latest rating and finds that one company has moved from an A+ to a B– rating. Upon further review through corporate records, he discovers that Star Insurance Company has invested heavily in junk bonds and real estate limited partnerships that have gone bad. What should Mark do? He has 25 percent of his 401(k) invested in the GIC option, and he is concerned that this insurance company will go into default.

**Solution**  He should find out whether his GIC is made up of many insurance company contracts or just one. If there are contracts from many companies, his risk is not as great, but he should continue to check its status on a regular basis and be able to move quickly to an account with a similar investment objective if necessary. If Star Insurance Company is the only company in the GIC or is a single investment outside his 401(k), he should definitely take action. Depending on individual state statutes, if the company were to become insolvent, the state's insurance guarantee fund might cover some of Mark's loss. However, it is possible that some states would not cover his GIC, and he could end up losing his entire investment. Checking the rating periodically could save him from an unfortunate situation.

### 3. Does the plan document allow me to diversify out of company stock? What are the parameters for selling?

When Enron collapsed into bankruptcy, its employees lost more than $1 billion in retirement plan assets due to the plunging price of Enron stock. While some blame falls on employees for not diversifying their elective contributions, many were simply stuck in the stock because they were not able to sell any stock acquired in company matches before the age of 50. Restrictions on selling stock are not limited to Enron, though many companies have changed their plans in the wake of the Enron disaster. According to CNN/Money, among those that have, Walt Disney now allows employees to sell stock without restriction. Previously, they had to wait until age 55. AOL Time Warner has also lifted its restrictions, from a previous requirement of age 50 and 5 years of service. Other companies that have made changes include Gannet, Gillette Co., Mellon Financial, and Viacom.[1] If your plan doesn't allow you to diversify out of your employer's stock, complain loudly, and enlist your coworkers to do the same. Keep an eye out for new laws that will require your plan to be more flexible. On April 11, 2002, a bill passed the House of Representatives that would require plans to allow employees to sell company stock after 3 years, defined by the plan as either 3 years of service or the sale of a share after owning it for 3 years.

### 4. What's the load or cost of my plan?

Keeping in mind that there is no free lunch, it is helpful to know the costs and understand where they are coming from. They usually break down into three different types. First, there are basic

---

[1] CNN/Money, "Your 401(k): Times are a-changin'," by Martine Costello, April 20, 2002.

bookkeeping costs (a.k.a. administrative fees), which depend mainly on the plan size. They could range from $25 per employee for a plan with 5000 participants to a much higher $100 per employee for smaller plans of 100 or fewer participants. Included in this figure are general overhead and management fees such as turning the lights on, answering phone calls, and sending out statements.

Second, there are asset management fees that change depending on the individual investment choices and their corresponding managers. For example, each mutual fund option within your plan may have a separate manager, and the stock growth fund may have a different management fee than the bond fund. What should you be paying? A normal range is 0.50 percent for a bond fund, 0.75 to 1.25 percent for a stock fund, and 1.50 to 1.75 percent for an international stock fund. A bond fund does not require as much management as a stock fund—hence the lower fee. Stock index funds will have lower expenses than other stock funds, because they are not actively managed. Since international funds may incur higher expenses due to trading on foreign stock exchanges, their fees are normally higher.

Last, you could incur a one-time sales charge or commission on your mutual fund options within your 401(k) plan. A *front-end load,* or sales charge, is a commission charged as a percentage of the total amount initially invested. By law, the rate cannot exceed 8.5 percent, and generally, there is a sliding scale so that larger investments are charged a lower percentage in commission. When you invest large amounts [generally outside your 401(k) plan], you may pay a lower commission. Investing enough to qualify for the lower rate is referred to as *hitting a breakpoint.* For example, a fund may charge 4 percent on the first $50,000 you invest, but reduce the charge to 3 percent once you invest $50,000 to $100,000 or more.

Another charge you may incur is a *back-end load,* also known as a *contingent deferred sales charge* (CDSC). This is simply a fancy way of saying the load or commission on the investment is paid when the shares are sold. It is computed as a percentage of the net asset value (NAV) at the time of redemption. For example, if you are selling shares of a fund worth $10,000 and there is a back-end load of 3 percent, you will pay $300, or $10,000 times 3 percent. Let's say when you opened the fund 3 years ago, you started with an investment of $8000. If you had paid a front-end load of 3 percent at the beginning, you would have paid only $240. Of course, you would pay less if the fund value dropped below the beginning balance of $8000.

---

**Retirement Tip**   Always know what it takes to get out of an investment before you get in.

---

Most funds with a CDSC have a declining fee scale that rewards you for owning the shares for a longer period of time. For example, the fee in the first year to sell your shares might be 6 percent, in the second year 5 percent, and so on. Many annuities are set up with back-end loads using the declining fee scale, which often start at 8 percent in the first year, and then decline by 1 percent each year to 0 percent. These fees can restrict your ability to make changes in your investment objectives or to move out of investments that are not performing well.

---

**Retirement Tip**   Be careful when you switch annuity assets into another investment choice (that is, a fixed annuity to a variable annuity) within the same insurance company. You may start the back-end load schedule all over again. For example, if you owned the original product for 5 or 6 years and were down to a redemption fee of only 2 to 3 percent, then switched, you might be locked into an 8 percent fee again.

---

If your plan uses *no-load* mutual funds, you don't have to worry about paying commissions because there is no fee to invest or to liquidate your investment.

### 5. What percentage of all fees is paid annually by my employer?

Often, employers pay for record keeping and basic administrative costs, while the employee pays for asset management. However, many plans assess an annual charge to each account to help defray administrative costs. These fees can change. It is up to the trustee of the plan to decide how and in what amount to raise fees. The larger your company, the more leverage it will have with the trustee to keep fees at reasonable amounts. We recommend looking at your plan's literature annually so that you know what fees are charged.

### 6. Are there any "hidden" fees?

A charge applied by many mutual funds within retirement plans is called a *12b-1 fee*. These fees, which are deducted annually from the total value of your account, are generally computed as a percent of net asset value, and they are paid to the broker of record. Annual fees of 0.25 to 0.35 percent are reasonable, but beware of the "no-load" funds that are advertised as applying no up-front charges but that actually charge an excessive 12b-1 of 1 percent or more annually. In *Morningstar Mutual Funds* reports, 12b-1 fees are included in the expense ratio, and because of this, the total returns also reflect their deduction. The Morningstar code for a 12b-1 fee is B.

**Retirement Dilemma**   June invests $1000 per year for 25 years in her 401(k) plan and earns an annual average of 9 percent. She should accumulate $78,668 assuming she pays only 0.5 percent in yearly fees. What if she has to pay three times that in fees, or 1.5 percent? Using the same assumptions as before, June would end up with $67,978, or $10,690 (14 percent) less for the extra 1 percent. Ouch!

The message is to be aware of the fees you are paying. Keep asking questions to find out exactly how your individual plan works and what fees you pay. You may not be able to single-handedly change the rules, but many voices will be heard. Making your employers know how you feel if your fees are high should put the pressure on providers. If you aren't aware, you can't make changes.

## DANGER SIGNS

You should read your plan document and any updates to the plan annually. Pick a logical time, such as on the anniversary of your enrollment or your first statement each year. However, don't sit back too comfortably in between. You should carefully read each statement as it comes in, either monthly or quarterly. If there is a problem with your plan, you will be ahead if you pay attention to the warning signs. Become concerned about any of the following:

- You repeatedly request a summary plan description or plan document and do not receive one.
- You make changes in your payroll deduction amount or your asset allocations, and they are not reflected on your statement. (Depending on your plan statement cycles, it may take two statements to see any changes.)
- You notice changes in payroll deductions or asset allocations that you did not authorize.
- The deductions from your paycheck do not match the deposits listed on your statement.
- There is a long lag time between payroll deduction and deposit into your account.
- A significant drop in the value of your account cannot be explained by normal market activity. (Compare the number of shares held to the number given on your last statement, and verify the stock or mutual fund share prices with an independent source, such as the newspaper or an investment broker.)
- Your statements cover a period of time more than 6 months past.
- The plan trustee and custodian are not financial institutions, separate from your employer.
- Former employees are having difficulty getting their distributions.
- You stop getting statements.

## YOUR RIGHTS UNDER ERISA

You have certain rights under the Employee Retirement Income Security Act of 1974 (ERISA), including the following:

- You can examine, without charge and at the plan administrator's office, all documents filed with the U.S. Department of Labor. This includes detailed annual reports and plan descriptions. Even though you can find detailed data about your plan administrator, the administrator is required to keep all information regarding your account confidential unless you give your permission to disclose information to someone you have designated or the records are subpoenaed by a court of law.

- You can obtain copies of all documents and other plan information upon written request to the plan administrator. The administrator may make a reasonable charge for the copies.
- You are entitled by law to receive a summary of the plan's annual financial report from the plan administrator.
- You can obtain a statement telling you what your benefit would be if you stopped working under the plan now. If you are not yet vested, the statement will tell you how many more years you have to work to be vested. This statement must be requested in writing, and it is not required to be given more than once per year. It must be provided free of charge.
- If you requested materials and did not receive them within 30 days, you may file suit in a federal court.
- Your employer cannot fire you to prevent you from receiving a benefit or exercising your rights under ERISA.

## Rule 404(c)

You may feel like the deck is stacked against you when it comes to your retirement plan, but there is hope. The Department of Labor has issued a voluntary guideline in Section 404(c) of the Employee Retirement Income Security Act (ERISA). The guideline recommends that employers do the following if they want to be relieved of fiduciary responsibility for the plan:

- Offer at least three diversified investment options with different levels of risk within a 401(k) plan (company stock purchase plans and GICs do not qualify as diversified).
- Allow employees to move money from one investment to another at least once every 3 months and at any time during the quarter, not just on a specified day.

- Provide prospectuses and education about each investment option.
- Provide education on investing principles as well as information on each of the choices offered by the plan.
- Reeducate employees if conditions within the plan change.

If you can't get a copy of your summary plan description, summary annual report, or the annual report of the plan from your plan administrator, contact the following office:

**U.S. Department of Labor**
Public Disclosure Room
Pension and Welfare Benefits Administration (PWBA)
200 Constitution Avenue, NY Suite N-5638
Washington, DC 20210
Phone: (202) 622-5164

If you have reason to believe assets are being mismanaged or misused, contact the nearest regional or district PWBA office. You can find addresses and phone numbers on the Web site *www.dol.gov*.

## SUMMARY

It isn't hard to decipher the basic information of your plan's reports if you are an interested individual who wants to make the most of each investment. You wouldn't expect a house to be maintenance free, so don't think your retirement account can go without maintenance checks and annual repairs either. Put in the proper due diligence, and make sure things are safe before you have a problem that can't be repaired. You should have questions for your benefits or human resource department and that's OK. Asking questions is the only way you can obtain data for financial decisions, and it is much better than contributing for 20 or 30 years without making sure your money is safe. It is the company's responsibility to provide you with information and answers, but it is up to you to ask the questions.

# CHAPTER 12

# Taking Your Money Out

**W**hen you deposit money into a retirement plan, your mindset should be one of locking up the deposit box and throwing away the key. Invest for the long term, and don't plan to use the money until your golden years. But even with the best intentions to let your money grow until retirement, circumstances—a new home, college education, or financial emergency—could arise for which you might need some of the funds before retirement. Then before you know it, it will be time to retire. In either case, you'll need to get your money out of those retirement plans.

In addition to withdrawing money, it's likely that you'll need to move a retirement plan at least once. At retirement, you'll have to decide what to do with the money in your employer plan. Before retirement, you could change jobs and be faced with a distribution from your employer plan, have an IRA that isn't performing up to your expectations, or be unhappy with the investments in your annuity.

This chapter outlines the different ways to get money out of your retirement plan, whether you plan to spend it or simply move it to another investment. Understanding these concepts now can prevent unnecessary taxes and penalties later.

# TRADITIONAL IRAS
## Premature Distributions

While we don't recommend it, you can take money out of your IRA before retirement simply by making a written request to your custodian. However, unless you meet certain exceptions, any money you withdraw from a traditional IRA before you reach the age of 59½ is subject to a 10 percent IRS penalty on the amount withdrawn. The exceptions to the penalty are the following:

- The withdrawal will be used to pay for qualified higher education expenses for the taxpayer, the taxpayer's spouse, or any child (including stepchild) or grandchild of the taxpayer or taxpayer's spouse. A child is not required to be a dependent. See Internal Revenue Code 151(c)(3) for a full definition. Eligible expenses include tuition, fees, books, supplies, and other necessary equipment required to attend an eligible postsecondary educational institution. The expenses must be net of any tax-free benefits such as scholarships and grants. IRC 529(e)(3) and IRC 529(e)(5) provide exact IRS definitions of eligible expenses and institutions.
- The withdrawal, up to a lifetime limit of $10,000, will be used for a first-time home purchase. A *first-time home buyer* is defined as anyone who has not had an ownership interest in a principal residence during the 2-year period ending on the date of acquisition. If married, the home buyer's spouse must also meet this condition.
- You become disabled as defined by the IRS.
- You die.
- You set up a schedule, based on your life expectancy, to take out substantially equal payments every year for the rest of your life. If you stop before taking payments for 5 years and before the age of 59½, you will owe back penalties plus interest.
- Your unreimbursed medical expenses exceed 7.5 percent of your adjusted gross income.
- You use the withdrawal to pay for medical insurance while you are unemployed.

- You reinvest (roll over) the money into an IRA or other qualified plan within 60 days.

In addition to any penalty, all withdrawals from a tax-deductible IRA are subject to ordinary income taxes. Withdrawals from non-deductible IRAs are taxable only to the extent that they exceed the amount contributed. In other words, only the investment earnings are taxed.

---

**Retirement Dilemma**   Chris, age 33, lost his job and had to withdraw $10,000 from his traditional, tax-deductible IRA to pay pressing bills. In addition to ordinary income taxes on $10,000 of income, he had to pay a $1000 IRS fine, which was 10 percent of the amount he withdrew.

---

## Moving Your IRA

### Transfers

Once you have chosen an IRA custodian, such as a bank, brokerage firm, or mutual fund, you are not locked into that decision for life. You may make a custodian-to-custodian transfer, sometimes called a *direct rollover*, in which the funds are sent from your existing custodian to a new custodian and you are never in possession of the funds. There is no limit to the number of transfers allowed and no IRS penalty or tax for a transfer. However, there may be fees and commissions charged by the sending or receiving custodian.

### Rollovers

In an IRA rollover, you withdraw funds from an IRA or other retirement plan, take possession of the money, and deposit it into the same or a different IRA. If you accomplish this within the 60-day time limit set by the IRS, you will not incur any taxes or penalties. The mandatory 20 percent IRS withholding that applies to employer plan distributions does not apply to IRA distributions. *The same money can only be rolled over once per year.*

**Retirement Tip**   You may have heard of someone who used an IRA rollover to cover a cash crunch by withdrawing money from an IRA, using it for 60 days, and then depositing it back into the same or a different IRA before the deadline. This is a perfectly legal rollover; just be careful that you will be able to deposit the money before the deadline. Failing to make the rollover in time will characterize your withdrawal as a distribution, and you will be subject to any applicable taxes and penalties.

In addition to transfers and rollovers to another IRA account, you can move money from an IRA into an employer plan as long as the plan document allows it. Be careful not to roll over or transfer after-tax (nondeductible) IRA contributions into a plan that contains only pretax funds. You could end up paying unnecessary taxes at withdrawal.

## Retirement

At any point after the age of 59½ you may withdraw your IRA funds without penalty. You must pay ordinary income tax on the amounts withdrawn, unless there are nondeductible contributions in your IRA. In that case, you will owe taxes only on the amounts in excess of the nondeductible contributions. Your basis (the amount of your contributions) comes out pro rata, or proportionately, in any distribution that is less than the entire account. See the following Retirement Dilemma for an example of how this works.

**Retirement Dilemma**   Over the years, Tina contributed $10,000 to a nondeductible IRA. Last year at age 60, she withdrew $5000. How much is taxable?

**Solution**   Her basis in the account is $10,000, the amount she contributed after tax. On December 31 of last year, after her withdrawal, the amount remaining in the account was $35,000. First, she should add her distribution to the fair market value of the account at the end of the year:

> $5000 + $35,000 = $40,000
>
> Then she divides her basis into that number to find the percentage of the account that is not taxable:
>
> $10,000 ÷ $40,000 = 25 percent
>
> Then she multiplies that percentage by the amount of the distribution:
>
> 25 percent × $5000 = $1250
>
> This is the amount of her distribution that is not taxable. The remaining $3750 is taxable.

The 10-year averaging option, available for employer plan distributions to those who qualify, is not available on IRA distributions.

## ROTH IRAS

You can withdraw *contributions* to a Roth IRA at any time without tax consequences or penalty, but the earnings withdrawn from the account are considered taxable income and may be subject to a 10 percent penalty if withdrawal requirements are not met. The requirements for tax-free, penalty-free withdrawals of earnings from a Roth IRA are the following:

1. The Roth IRA has existed for more than 5 years, *and* either:
   - You are over age 59½ *or*
   - It is for a qualified first-time home purchase (up to a lifetime limit of $10,000).

   OR

2. The withdrawal is made due to death or disability.

Withdrawals for qualified higher-education expenses (tuition, books, fees, and supplies, net of tax-free assistance such as grants and scholarships) can be made without penalty, but earnings withdrawn are taxable as income. For tax purposes, such withdrawals are treated as if all contributions are withdrawn first. If you have multiple Roth IRAs, but withdraw from just one, contributions to all accounts will be aggregated to determine whether any of the withdrawal is taxable.

**Retirement Dilemma**   Kathy has two Roth IRAs, the first of which has contributions of $4000 and a market value of $7500 and the second of which has contributions of $2000 and a market value of $2500. How much can she withdraw for college costs without paying taxes?

**Solution**   She can withdraw up to $6000 (the total of her contributions) before incurring any taxes. Even if she withdrew the entire $6000 from the first Roth IRA, $2000 more than she contributed to it, she would not owe any income taxes because the limit applies to the aggregate amount of contributions and is not calculated per account.

## EMPLOYER-SPONSORED RETIREMENT PLANS
### Premature Distributions

Of all the types of retirement plans, employer-sponsored plans make it the most difficult to spend your money before retirement. According to the law, you may not take a distribution from an employer retirement plan such as a 401(k), 403(b), or 457 plan unless you are terminated, become disabled, die, or are separated from service (that is, retire or quit). A *hardship distribution* may be the only way to take money out of your plan if you do not meet any of those criteria. For a distribution to qualify as a hardship distribution, it must satisfy two requirements:

- It must be due to the employee's immediate and heavy financial need, *and*
- It must be necessary to satisfy that need.

The following are examples of what is considered "immediate and heavy need":

- Medical expenses previously incurred by the employee or his or her spouse or dependents, in amounts necessary for any of these persons to obtain medical care
- Costs incurred in purchasing a principal residence (this does not include mortgage payments)
- Tuition and related educational expenses for the next year of postsecondary education for the employee or his or her spouse or dependents
- Payments to prevent eviction from or foreclosure on a principal residence

Hardship distributions are subject to ordinary income tax and the 10 percent IRS penalty for withdrawals before age 59½. Many plans that allow hardship distributions will not allow an employee to participate in the plan for 1 year following such a distribution.

---

**Retirement Dilemma**   Juliann had the bulk of her retirement savings locked up in her 401(k) plan, 80 percent of which she was required by her plan to invest in the company stock. Though she was happy with the stock's performance, the tales of Enron employees losing all their retirement savings concerned her. She called her benefits officer and found that there was nothing she could do to invest the funds differently.

**Solution**   While it seemed extreme, she quit her job. The only way she could diversify was to take a distribution from the plan and reinvest the funds elsewhere. Because she didn't qualify for a hardship distribution, she had to leave her job in order to take a distribution. Then she issued instructions for her employer to transfer her account to an IRA, where she could invest it as she chose.

---

## Retirement or Job Change

When you leave your employer, whether retiring or changing jobs, you have several choices for your retirement plan. While we can't tell you what to do, we can tell you what *not* to do. If at all possible, avoid taking either of the first two options. They will cost you money. Your options are the following:

1. **Take the distribution in cash; spend it or deposit it into an account that is not tax protected.**

If you take a distribution in cash from your retirement plan, you will be responsible for income taxes on everything except after-tax contributions, and you will be charged an additional 10 percent IRS early withdrawal penalty unless:

- You are under 55 and "separated from service."
- You are over age 59½.
- You are totally and permanently disabled as defined by your plan.
- You have a catastrophic medical need.
- You've selected to take the distribution in the form of annuitized payments.

If Uncle Sam's threats of taxes and penalties don't deter you from impulsively spending your retirement fund, maybe an example on the power of compounding can convince you.

> **Retirement Dilemma** Tonya is transferring to a new company, and she just received a lump-sum check for $15,000 from her retirement plan. Her son is dying for a new car. Should she incur the penalties and pay the taxes to spend the money now or deposit it into an IRA?
>
> **Solution** Any time you are dealing with money, simply run the numbers and let them speak for themselves. If she is 35 and plans to retire at age 65, $15,000 could grow to $261,741 by retirement, based on an average rate of return of 10 percent. Is her son's car worth $261,741? Probably not. Reinvest. Don't spend your distribution.

If you are over 59½ and are retiring, penalties won't apply on a cash distribution, but income taxes will. Because you probably won't need all your retirement plan money at once, consider immediately transferring the portion that you won't need (see transfers, following) into a tax-protected account, such as an IRA. Then you can withdraw as much as you need each year, thereby delaying income taxes on the amount held in the IRA for as long as possible. Not only will you delay paying taxes but you may also avoid paying at a higher rate, because taking the entire distribution at once could bump you into a higher marginal tax bracket.

### 2. Take your distribution as a rollover.

In a rollover, your distribution is issued in your name. To complete the rollover, you have 60 days from the date on which you receive your distribution to "roll it over" into a tax-deferred account such as an IRA or the retirement plan of a new employer. If you complete the rollover within the designated time frame, you will not be responsible for current income taxes (or any penalty if you are under 59½) on the distribution.

The tricky part of a rollover is that federal income tax law requires that employers who make retirement plan distributions withhold 20 percent of the value of the account and remit it to the IRS as a potential tax payment. You can get a refund of the withholding if you roll over, but not until you file your taxes.

If you elect to roll over your distribution, you have to come up with the missing 20 percent from other sources. If you do not, and you roll only the 80 percent that you received, the missing 20 percent will be taxed and penalized as an early distribution.

---

**Retirement Dilemma**   Genny is 42 and recently left her job. She had $40,000 in her company 401(k) plan. She hadn't decided how to invest the money, and thus she didn't give her former employer instructions for a transfer of the funds. One day she received a check in the mail. The check was for $32,000, which was the $40,000 value of the account less 20 percent withholding that had been sent directly to the IRS. To avoid taxes and penalties, she must roll over $40,000 (making up the $8000 difference herself) into an IRA within 60 days. Then she can file to get the $8000 back next April. If she deposits only the $32,000 into the IRA, she'll owe a 10 percent penalty plus current income taxes on the $8000.

---

In order to avoid this potential headache, have your distribution sent directly from the old custodian to the new custodian in what is called a *transfer*, not a rollover.

### 3. Transfer the funds to an IRA or a new employer's plan.

The easiest way to maintain the tax-protected status of your distribution is to transfer it into an IRA or the retirement plan of a new employer. In this transaction, your current custodian sends the funds from your account directly to your new custodian, based on your instructions.

---

**Retirement Tip**  While you may only roll over the same funds once per year, there are no limits on the number of transfers that you may have in any one year.

---

Once you have chosen a destination for your distribution, whether it is the retirement plan of a new employer or an IRA with a bank, brokerage firm, or mutual fund company, communicate this information in writing to the administrator of your current plan. If your employer doesn't have a distribution form, write a letter that includes the following information:

- Your plan account number
- Your Social Security number
- A copy of your last statement
- The date of your employment change
- The new custodian's address
- Your account number at the new custodian

It may be wise to include a reminder with the request stating that the transfer is a *direct transfer*, not a rollover. By completing your request in writing, you have a record of what was sent and when, not just a name on the other end of the phone line.

While most transfers are completed custodian to custodian without your ever having to handle a check, some custodians will mail a check to you, made out to your new custodian. Do not panic. Unless the check is made out to you, it is still a transfer, not a rollover.

It should read, "Money Center Bank, custodian for the IRA of James Hamby." You should then send it on to your new custodian.

---

**Retirement Dilemma**   When Cheryl left her employer, she promptly completed the paperwork for a transfer of her 401(k) distribution. One month later, she received a check (made out to her) in the mail from her employer. Realizing that they had made a mistake but not paying much attention, she simply endorsed the check and sent it to her new custodian.

**Solution**   What should she have done? She should have sent it back to her employer with a copy of her letter of instruction, directing them to issue another check, without withholding 20 percent, made out to her new custodian.

---

Remember, you do not have to choose how to invest your distribution when you make the transfer, only who will be the custodian. For example, if you like the Vanguard family of mutual funds but you are unsure of which specific funds you want to invest in, or you are concerned about the state of the stock market, you can transfer to an IRA at Vanguard and keep your money in a money market account until you make a decision. Don't let the prospect of designating a new custodian hurry you into making an investment decision. If you are not sure about a mutual fund company, open a self-directed IRA with a bank or brokerage firm and deposit the money into a money market fund or short-term certificate of deposit. Later, you can purchase stocks, bonds, or mutual funds as you choose.

---

**Retirement Tip**   If your retirement plan balance is between $1000 and $4999, your employer is required to transfer it to an IRA unless you specifically request a cash distribution.

---

### 4. Leave the funds in your plan.

Many plans will allow you to keep your account in the plan if its value is over $5000. Obviously, you will not continue to receive company matching, and you must consider whether this is the best place to leave your money. Are you happy with the performance of the investment options offered, or do you think you might be able to do better on your own? Consider any plan requirements to hold the stock of your former employer. Lack of ability to diversify may be reason enough to move. Investigate and decide which is better for you and your money. If you do leave the money there, periodically check your investments to make sure they are meeting your expectations.

### 5. Transfer the funds to your new employer's retirement plan.

If you already have a new job and there is not a waiting period to enroll in your new employer's 401(k), 403(b), or 457 plan, you may want to have your distribution transferred directly to it. Some employers will accept rollovers from another employer, but they will not accept direct transfers. Check to see what yours will allow. To avoid the 20 percent withholding due on a rollover distribution, transfer into an IRA temporarily, then perform a rollover into the new plan.

### 6. Take your distribution in the form of company stock.

You don't have to sell the company stock in your 401(k) plan just because you are retiring or leaving the company. If you have other investments in different levels of your personal pyramid and believe that your company stock is a good investment, consider taking your distribution in stock. Make sure that your investments are not so concentrated in the stock that any volatility in the price would threaten your retirement. Remember that you will no longer be a decision-making employee with a bird's-eye view of your company's prospects. If you are not retiring, transfer or roll over the stock to a self-directed IRA. In an exception to the 20 percent rollover withholding rule, distributions that are entirely employer contributions of the employer's company stock are excluded from withholding. In this case, it is as convenient to do a rollover as a direct transfer.

Another IRS exception, called the *trustee cost basis rule*, benefits those who take distributions of employer stock. If you are retir-

**TABLE 12-1**

The Trustee Cost Basis Rule

|  | Stock Distribution Use Trustee Cost Basis Rule | Sell Stock Take Distribution in Cash |
| --- | --- | --- |
| Market value of ABC stock in plan | $400,000 | $400,000 |
| Cost basis of ABC stock | 175,000 |  |
| Unrealized appreciation of ABC | 225,000 |  |
| Tax on distribution |  |  |
| Tax on cost basis of ABC at 35% | 61,250 |  |
| Tax on cash distribution at 35% |  | 140,000 |
| Capital gain on ABC stock | 225,000 |  |
| Capital gains tax at 15% | 33,750 |  |
| **Total tax** | **$95,000** | **$140,000** |

ing and will need the money from your plan in the next few years (that is, transferring your stock to an IRA is not an option), you can save a considerable amount in taxes on your distribution if you have a very low cost basis in your employer's stock. Under the rule, the income tax on your stock distribution is based on the cost basis, not the current market value of the stock. If you sell more than 1 year later, the difference between the cost basis and the market value is taxed at the capital gains rate of 15 percent. See Table 12-1 for an example.

### 7. Annuitize.

Many employer plans offer the option of annuitizing your account balance when you retire. When you do this, you elect to receive equal payments over a particular time period or the rest of your life (see the following list of different options). Should you choose this option, you lock in your investment rate of return, taking the risk of fluctuating market returns out of this portion of your retirement nest egg.

> *Life Annuity.* You will receive a monthly annuity for the rest of your life. After your death, no further payments will be made on your behalf. With a life annuity payment option, your trustee may purchase an annuity from an insurance

company with the balance of your retirement account or may simply annuitize the account if it is a TSA. The insurance company assumes all risk of investment performance and of your living a very long time.

*Life Annuity with Term Certain.* You will receive a monthly annuity for the rest of your life with this option, but in addition, if you die before the term (for example, 10 years) has passed, the remaining payments will be paid to a named beneficiary. If you die after the term is over, payments cease. Since there is a guarantee of at least a certain term of payments, each payment will generally be lower than those of a life annuity that does not have a term feature.

*Term Certain.* You will receive an annuity for a specified term under this option. With the term certain, it is possible to outlive the payments. If you die before the term has expired, the remaining payments will go directly to your named beneficiary. After you or your beneficiary has received payments for the entire term, the payments will stop. This option differs from the one preceding because you will not continue to receive the annuity for life.

*Life Annuity with a Cash Refund Feature.* This option pays a monthly annuity for life. You will be guaranteed to receive the amount your employer paid to the life insurance company to purchase the annuity. If you die before having received total annuity payments equal to the purchase price, any remaining value will be paid to your named beneficiary. If you die after receiving your guaranteed value, your annuity will work in the same way a life annuity would, by ceasing payments at your death.

*Joint and Survivor Annuity.* This annuity is paid until both you and your beneficiary die. No matter who dies first, the survivor continues to receive payments until his or her death, at which time payments cease.

## Plan—Don't Panic

Don't panic just yet. If you are leaving the company and have a 401(k) or 403(b) plan, do the following:

- Get a distribution form and any related information about your current plan.
- Find out the market value of your account and exactly how much you will be receiving and when.
- If you have a new employer, check to see if it has a retirement plan and if you can transfer funds into its plan.
- Investigate your current plan to see if you can leave your savings in that plan and whether there will be any additional fees.
- Learn about self-directed IRA accounts offered by your local banks and brokerage firms.
- Avoid rollovers with automatic 20 percent withholding by using a direct transfer.

## Loans

You may not borrow from an IRA or use it as collateral for a loan; however, many employers allow you to borrow a portion of your retirement plan account and pay yourself back, with interest. While it is not advisable to use your account for current expenses, in the case of financial emergency, it is better to borrow and repay than to withdraw and pay penalties and taxes.

---

**Retirement Dilemma**   Susan, age 35, has $30,000 in her 401(k) account and is thinking about taking a distribution of $20,000 when she changes jobs so that she can add a bedroom to her house. How will this affect her future?

**Solution**   First, the $20,000 she withdraws will be subject to 10 percent ($2000) in IRS penalties, and, assuming a 28 percent tax bracket, $5600 in current income taxes. She will net only $12,400 from the $20,000 withdrawal.

Second, the money that she takes out will not be growing to provide a secure retirement. At 8 percent, that $20,000 would grow to $201,253 in 30 years. Is an extra room worth *that*?

If she absolutely must have the addition and does not have enough home equity to finance it with a home equity loan, she should plan to *borrow* from her new employer's plan.

---

By law, a retirement plan loan cannot exceed the lesser of $50,000 or one-half of the present value of the employee's vested interest in the plan. An exception is provided for accounts whose value is less than $20,000. The loan maximum in those cases is $10,000. Loans must be repaid within 5 years, unless they are used to acquire a principal residence. In those cases, the loan may be amortized in equal payments, made not less than quarterly.

In Susan's case, she could borrow $15,000 from her plan, which would keep her at the 50 percent borrowing limit. She would have more to spend on the new room ($15,000 versus $12,400) *and* more left in her account ($15,000 versus $10,000).

---

**Retirement Tip**   Before you take a loan from your plan, consider the following hidden costs:

*Service Fees.*   There may be loan application and annual servicing fees, which could add up to as much as $200 over the life of a 5-year loan.

*Surrender Fees.*   If your plan invests in annuities, you may have to pay a surrender fee to terminate the contract early in order to withdraw cash. Fees can run as high as 7 percent, depending on how long your money has been invested.

*Losing Your Job.*   If your employment is terminated, your loan will come due immediately. If you can't pay it back, it will be considered a withdrawal and you will owe income taxes on the loan. If you are under 59½, you will owe a 10 percent penalty as well.

*Opportunity Cost.*   Paying yourself interest on a loan may sound appealing, but it isn't a good idea if you could have earned more on the money. Your account might be earning 8 percent on your interest payments, but what could it have earned in the stock market? If you could have made 12 percent in growth investments, you'll have $820 less after 5 years on a $10,000 loan.

*Cheaper Sources Elsewhere.*   If a home equity loan is a viable alternative for borrowing the money, it may be more cost effective. Remember that interest paid on a home loan is tax deductible. Compared to a 6 percent 401(k) loan that will cost the full 6 percent, a 6 percent home equity loan will cost only 4.32 percent after taxes if you are in a 28 percent tax bracket.

## Forward Averaging

If you were born before 1936 and are taking a lump-sum distribution from a 401(k) plan [distributions from 403(b) plans are not eligible], you may be able to use a special method of computing the income tax on your distribution called *10-year forward averaging.* You must have participated in your plan for at least 5 years, and you cannot have made an averaging election since 1986. Although it is called *averaging*, it is simply a special formula used by the IRS to figure the taxes due for the year of receipt. You pay the tax only once, not over the next 10 years as the name implies. The tax is in addition to the regular tax figured on your other income. The advantage is that you may pay less in taxes than you might otherwise. To elect forward averaging, complete IRS Form 4972 and attach it to your Form 1040 return.

> **Retirement Tip**  If you take more than one lump-sum distribution during the year, you must add them together using a special method. Refer to IRS Publication 575 for more specific tax information.

# REQUIRED DISTRIBUTIONS

Uncle Sam requires that you start distributions from non-Roth retirement plans by April 1 following the year you turn 70½. For example, if your seventieth birthday is between January and June, you will be considered 70½ that year, and you must take a distribution by April 1 of the following year. This is called your *required beginning date* (RBD). If you were born between July and December, you won't be considered 70½ until the next year, and you must take the first withdrawal in the following year. For subsequent years, you must take your distribution by December 31.

> **Retirement Dilemma**  Austin turned 70½ in October of this year. He did not want to take his first year's IRA distribution before December 31 because his income was already higher than usual this year.

**Solution**  He took advantage of the IRS grace period, which sets the deadline for the first year's withdrawal at April 1 of the following year. The rule requires that he then take the second year's withdrawal by December 31 of that year, resulting in two withdrawals within one calendar year. In Austin's case that was fine because he knew he would have considerably less income next year and it would not be a tax burden to take two withdrawals in the same year. However, a "double distribution" could move you into a higher tax bracket and subject your Social Security payments to higher taxes as well.

## Computing Your Required Minimum Distribution (RMD)

While you may always withdraw larger amounts, the IRS computes a required minimum withdrawal figure using either your life expectancy number or the joint life expectancy of you and your named beneficiary. The withdrawal factor is applied to your retirement plans as valued on December 31 of the year prior to the distribution. For example, distributions for the year 2004 are calculated on the account balance at the end of 2003. An exception may apply if one of your plans is an employer plan that uses another valuation date.

### Your Life Expectancy
If your beneficiary is anyone other than a spouse who is more than 10 years younger than you are, you will use the IRS Uniform Withdrawal Factor Table, which is found in Appendix A, to compute your required distribution. To do this, find the applicable divisor for your age in the year of the distribution. Divide your account balance by this number to compute your required distribution. For example, if you are 72 and have account balances totaling $200,000, use 25.6 as a divisor, for a required distribution of $7812.50.

### Yours and a Spouse
If your beneficiary is a spouse who is more than 10 years younger than you are and that spouse has been designated the beneficiary of your account for the entire year, you may use the IRS Joint Life

and Last Survivor Expectancy Table, which is found in Appendix B. Find your age and your spouse's age on your birthdays in the distribution year, and use the factor where the column and row intersect. (It will be the same regardless of whose age is on the row and whose is on the column.) Then divide your account balance by that factor. For example, if you are 73 and your spouse is 59, your factor is 27.5.

## More Than One Retirement Account
Don't worry if you have more than one retirement account. First, compute the required distribution for each (the factor may differ if you have different beneficiaries). For employer plans, you must take the required amount out of each plan. However for IRAs, you may add up the required distributions for several IRAs and take the total out of whichever accounts you choose, as long as you take at least the required total. You may also aggregate required distributions from *tax-deferred annuities* (TDAs) in the same way; however, you cannot mix IRAs and TDAs, nor may you aggregate inherited IRAs or TDAs with your own IRAs and TDAs.

---

**Retirement Tip**  If you have several retirement accounts, this is a perfect time to adjust your pyramid allocations. Once you decide which level of the pyramid to target, withdraw funds first from accounts that are earning the lowest returns while letting other accounts grow.

---

## Penalties for Noncompliance

Go to jail, directly to jail, and do not pass GO. Fortunately, that happens only when you are playing a game, but there are enormous penalties if you do not take your distribution on time or if you take less than the amount required. It is imperative to understand all of the retirement rules and tax ramifications *before* you reach 70½. Ready or not, Uncle Sam will penalize you 50 percent of the amount you should have removed plus any income taxes that would have been due on the required withdrawal amount. You will not receive any notification of your required beginning date or your required minimum distribution. It is up to you to know the rules and comply. Because the penalties for noncompliance are stiff, consider consulting a financial advisor when computing your required withdrawals. If you do make a mistake, you can request Form 5329 from the IRS, pay the penalties, and attach it to your next year's tax forms.

## WHAT HAPPENS WHEN YOU DIE?

### Your Beneficiary

If you die before retirement, your primary beneficiary is entitled to your retirement plan account balance. In the event that the primary beneficiary is no longer alive or chooses to disclaim the benefit, your contingent beneficiaries are entitled to the account. Why would anyone disclaim the benefit? See the following retirement dilemma.

> **Retirement Dilemma**   Bill recently died at the age of 55, and his wife Suzanne has considerable assets to live on. His hefty retirement plan named her as primary beneficiary. Because she doesn't need the assets, they will probably end up in her estate (subject to estate taxes) and be left to their children.
>
> **Solution**   Suzanne can disclaim her interest in the plan, allowing it to go directly to their children, who are contingent beneficiaries. Suzanne has until December 31 of the year of Bill's death to decide.

If your retirement plan is an IRA, you may name anyone as beneficiary. If your plan is an employer plan, such as a 401(k), and you are married, you may not name someone other than your spouse as beneficiary unless your spouse agrees in writing. The consent form must be notarized or witnessed by a plan representative. This form will specifically state what the agreement is. If it is a *general consent form*, you are permitted to change your beneficiary without again obtaining your spouse's permission. Your plan may or may not allow a spouse to take back consent once it has been given. Thus, signing such an agreement deserves special thought and should not be taken lightly.

> **Retirement Dilemma** Joe and his wife, Marla, have decided to change Joe's beneficiary to their daughter. Marla has given her general consent to allow this to happen. Later, if Joe decides to change it to their son, he can do this without Marla's consent. If you are Marla, be careful—he can also change it to anyone he pleases without your consent.

In many plans, you are allowed to name multiple primary beneficiaries, splitting the percentage of benefits among them as you choose. This can have drawbacks because all the beneficiaries will each be treated by the most restrictive rules that apply to any one beneficiary. For example, if you name your spouse and your children as multiple primary beneficiaries, all will be treated as nonspouse beneficiaries, depriving your spouse of the option of rolling over the account (see following sections).

## Taxes

Distributions from a retirement plan due to the death of the account holder are not subject to a 10 percent IRS penalty, regardless of the age of the account holder or the beneficiary. If the beneficiary does not roll over the plan assets into an IRA or other retirement plan (only a spouse has this option), ordinary income taxes will be due on the amount distributed.

## If You Die Before Age 70½

If you die before your RBD (generally April 1 of the year after you turn 70½), by law, your plan can be distributed using one of three methods: a spousal rollover, the life expectancy rule, or the 5-year rule. Remember that plan rules may be stricter than the law, and in those cases, plan rules govern. For example, your plan may not allow the life expectancy option even though the law allows it.

### Spousal Rollover
If your sole beneficiary is your spouse, he or she has an option that other beneficiaries do not. A spouse may roll over your retirement

plan distribution into an IRA or another retirement plan. This is the only way to postpone ordinary income taxes on the distribution.

## Life Expectancy Rule

The *life expectancy rule* permits your beneficiary to take distributions over his or her life expectancy as defined by IRS tables. Distributions generally must begin by the year after your death and continue until the account is depleted. A spouse beneficiary has the option of leaving the account in your name and delaying the onset of life expectancy distributions until the year in which you would have turned 70½. The distributions are then calculated based on the spouse's life expectancy.

> **Retirement Dilemma**   Tim is the beneficiary of his wife's, retirement plan, and she died at the age of 58. He is 10 years older than she and has plenty of assets to fund his retirement. If he rolls over her plan into his IRA, he will have to begin required distributions in just over 2 years, at the age of 70½.
>
> **Solution**   He can leave her retirement plan in her name and begin taking distributions in the year she would have turned 70½, a delay of 12 years.

## Five-Year Rule

The *five-year rule* stipulates that a nonspouse beneficiary must withdraw assets by December 31 of the fifth year following the account holder's death. The rule does not restrict how the distributions are to be taken. The beneficiary may decide, subject to plan rules, whether to take the entire distribution immediately, over the 5-year period, or by the December 31 deadline in the fifth year. This allows the beneficiary to make tax-planning decisions. Spreading distributions over the time period or taking large distributions in years when other income is low can result in a lower overall tax bill.

## If You Die After Age 70½

The rules on retirement plan distributions are different for beneficiaries if the account holder dies after the age of 70½. Once you have begun taking required minimum distributions from your account, your beneficiary must continue those distributions unless he or she is your spouse. In the year of your death, the required minimum distribution is computed as if you had lived until the end of the year. If you had not yet taken the distribution, your beneficiary must take it by December 31, regardless of spousal status.

## Spousal Rollover
Your spouse may choose to leave your plan in your name and apply his or her own life expectancy to required minimum distributions; however, most spouses choose to roll over the plan into a retirement plan in their own name. At that point the plan operates as if the spouse had owned it all along. Spouses under the age of 70½ may discontinue the required distributions until they reach their required beginning date.

---

**Retirement Tip**  Beneficiary spouses under the age of 59½ who might need income should consider leaving the account in the deceased's name. In that case, access to the funds from the deceased spouse's account is available to the beneficiary without a 10 percent penalty. However, if a spouse rolls the money over into an IRA or other plan in his or her name, this exception no longer exists. Check with an accountant to see whether current law dictates that taking a distribution means the account cannot be rolled over at a later date.

---

## Life Expectancy
Spouses may, and all other beneficiaries must, begin taking required distributions in the year after your death. The amount of the distributions is calculated using the beneficiary's life expectancy. If there are multiple beneficiaries on a single account, all beneficiaries must take distributions based on the shortest life expectancy (this results in the largest required distribution amount).

# DIVORCE
Retirement plans can play an important role in divorce proceedings because they are among many couples' most significant assets.

However, splitting a retirement plan is not as easy as dividing a bank account. There is a legal vehicle for making this adjustment, called a *Qualified Domestic Relations Order* (QDRO, pronounced "quadro").

### Qualified Domestic Relations Order (QDRO)

The QDRO was created by Congress to allow retirement plans to be used in property settlements, maintenance payments, and child support payments while minimizing tax penalties. To qualify for special penalty-free treatment, the QDRO must be issued or approved by the court, not simply agreed upon by the two parties.

For the recipient of a distribution under a QDRO, the following rules apply:

- You may roll over the distribution into an IRA or employer plan.
- The distribution will be subject to 20 percent mandatory withholding unless you make it a direct transfer, in which the funds move directly from the plan custodian to your new custodian.
- If you are under age 59½ and choose not to roll the distribution over, it is not subject to a 10 percent penalty. This exemption applies to employer plans and tax-deferred annuities, but not to IRAs.
- You must pay ordinary income tax on any portion of the distribution that you do not roll over.
- You may elect to use 10-year averaging when figuring the tax on your distribution if the plan participant (your former spouse) is eligible. (See the preceding section on forward averaging for eligibility requirements.)

## SUMMARY

Getting your money out of a retirement account is not as easy as putting it in. While this saves many a spendthrift from using retirement money before its time, it can be frustrating to navigate the rules and regulations of rollovers and transfers. During retirement, when it should be easy to spend your retirement savings, it can still be complicated, as you consider tax issues, required minimum withdrawals, and a beneficiary's ability to access your plan.

Know the rules before you invest, and you'll save yourself time and money when you need your funds. We have given you the current restrictions, but they can change. You must pay attention to changes in the law as they occur. "I didn't know" is no excuse for being stuck with an unexpected tax bill, or worse, a penalty that could have been avoided. Take time to read the mailings that arrive with your IRA or employer plan statements. In many cases, these will give you good explanations of any changes in retirement plan laws and how they will affect you.

# Internal Revenue Service Uniform Withdrawal Factor Table (2002)

To figure your required minimum distribution (RMD) for the current year, divide the total balance of your qualified retirement plans (exclude Roth IRAs) on December 31 of the previous year by the factor for your age as of your birthday in the current year.

| Your Age | RMD Factor |
|----------|------------|
| 70 | 27.4 |
| 71 | 26.5 |
| 72 | 25.6 |
| 73 | 24.7 |
| 74 | 23.8 |
| 75 | 22.9 |
| 76 | 22.0 |
| 77 | 21.2 |
| 78 | 20.3 |
| 79 | 19.5 |
| 80 | 18.7 |
| 81 | 17.9 |
| 82 | 17.1 |
| 83 | 16.3 |
| 84 | 15.5 |
| 85 | 14.8 |
| 86 | 14.1 |

| Your Age | RMD Factor |
|:---:|:---:|
| 87 | 13.4 |
| 88 | 12.7 |
| 89 | 12.0 |
| 90 | 11.4 |
| 91 | 10.8 |
| 92 | 10.2 |
| 93 | 9.6 |
| 94 | 9.1 |
| 95 | 8.6 |
| 96 | 8.1 |
| 97 | 7.6 |
| 98 | 7.1 |
| 99 | 6.7 |
| 100 | 6.3 |
| 101 | 5.9 |
| 102 | 5.5 |
| 103 | 5.2 |
| 104 | 4.9 |
| 105 | 4.5 |
| 106 | 4.2 |
| 107 | 3.9 |
| 108 | 3.7 |
| 109 | 3.4 |
| 110 | 3.1 |
| 111 | 2.9 |
| 112 | 2.6 |
| 113 | 2.4 |
| 114 | 2.1 |
| 115 and older | 1.9 |

*Source:* IRS Publication 590, Appendix E, "Table for Determining Applicable Divisor for MDIB."

# Internal Revenue Service Joint Life and Last Survivor Expectancy Table

## Table II

### (Joint Life and Last Survivor Expectancy)
#### (For Use by Owners Whose Spouses Are More Than 10 Years Younger)

| Ages | 20 | 21 | 22 | 23 | 24 | 25 | 26 | 27 | 28 | 29 |
|------|------|------|------|------|------|------|------|------|------|------|
| 20 | 70.1 | 69.6 | 69.1 | 68.7 | 68.3 | 67.9 | 67.5 | 67.2 | 66.9 | 66.6 |
| 21 | 69.6 | 69.1 | 68.6 | 68.2 | 67.7 | 67.3 | 66.9 | 66.6 | 66.2 | 65.9 |
| 22 | 69.1 | 68.6 | 68.1 | 67.6 | 67.2 | 66.7 | 66.3 | 65.9 | 65.6 | 65.2 |
| 23 | 68.7 | 68.2 | 67.6 | 67.1 | 66.6 | 66.2 | 65.7 | 65.3 | 64.9 | 64.6 |
| 24 | 68.3 | 67.7 | 67.2 | 66.6 | 66.1 | 65.6 | 65.2 | 64.7 | 64.3 | 63.9 |
| 25 | 67.9 | 67.3 | 66.7 | 66.2 | 65.6 | 65.1 | 64.6 | 64.2 | 63.7 | 63.3 |
| 26 | 67.5 | 66.9 | 66.3 | 65.7 | 65.2 | 64.6 | 64.1 | 63.6 | 63.2 | 62.8 |
| 27 | 67.2 | 66.6 | 65.9 | 65.3 | 64.7 | 64.2 | 63.6 | 63.1 | 62.7 | 62.2 |
| 28 | 66.9 | 66.2 | 65.6 | 64.9 | 64.3 | 63.7 | 63.2 | 62.7 | 62.1 | 61.7 |
| 29 | 66.6 | 65.9 | 65.2 | 64.6 | 63.9 | 63.3 | 62.8 | 62.2 | 61.7 | 61.2 |
| 30 | 66.3 | 65.6 | 64.9 | 64.2 | 63.6 | 62.9 | 62.3 | 61.8 | 61.2 | 60.7 |
| 31 | 66.1 | 65.3 | 64.6 | 63.9 | 63.2 | 62.6 | 62.0 | 61.4 | 60.8 | 60.2 |
| 32 | 65.8 | 65.1 | 64.3 | 63.6 | 62.9 | 62.2 | 61.6 | 61.0 | 60.4 | 59.8 |
| 33 | 65.6 | 64.8 | 64.1 | 63.3 | 62.6 | 61.9 | 61.3 | 60.6 | 60.0 | 59.4 |
| 34 | 65.4 | 64.6 | 63.8 | 63.1 | 62.3 | 61.6 | 60.9 | 60.3 | 59.6 | 59.0 |
| 35 | 65.2 | 64.4 | 63.6 | 62.8 | 62.1 | 61.4 | 60.6 | 59.9 | 59.3 | 58.6 |
| 36 | 65.0 | 64.2 | 63.4 | 62.6 | 61.9 | 61.1 | 60.4 | 59.6 | 59.0 | 58.3 |
| 37 | 64.9 | 64.0 | 63.2 | 62.4 | 61.6 | 60.9 | 60.1 | 59.4 | 58.7 | 58.0 |

| | | | | | | | | | |
|---|---|---|---|---|---|---|---|---|---|
| **38** | 64.7 | 63.9 | 63.0 | 62.2 | 61.4 | 60.6 | 59.9 | 59.1 | 58.4 | 57.7 |
| **39** | 64.6 | 63.7 | 62.9 | 62.1 | 61.2 | 60.4 | 59.6 | 58.9 | 58.1 | 57.4 |
| **40** | 64.4 | 63.6 | 62.7 | 61.9 | 61.1 | 60.2 | 59.4 | 58.7 | 57.9 | 57.1 |
| **41** | 64.3 | 63.5 | 62.6 | 61.7 | 60.9 | 60.1 | 59.3 | 58.5 | 57.7 | 56.9 |
| **42** | 64.2 | 63.3 | 62.5 | 61.6 | 60.8 | 59.9 | 59.1 | 58.3 | 57.5 | 56.7 |
| **43** | 64.1 | 63.2 | 62.4 | 61.5 | 60.6 | 59.8 | 58.9 | 58.1 | 57.3 | 56.5 |
| **44** | 64.0 | 63.1 | 62.2 | 61.4 | 60.5 | 59.6 | 58.8 | 57.9 | 57.1 | 56.3 |
| **45** | 64.0 | 63.0 | 62.2 | 61.3 | 60.4 | 59.5 | 58.6 | 57.8 | 56.9 | 56.1 |
| **46** | 63.9 | 63.0 | 62.1 | 61.2 | 60.3 | 59.4 | 58.5 | 57.7 | 56.8 | 56.0 |
| **47** | 63.8 | 62.9 | 62.0 | 61.1 | 60.2 | 59.3 | 58.4 | 57.5 | 56.7 | 55.8 |
| **48** | 63.7 | 62.8 | 61.9 | 61.0 | 60.1 | 59.2 | 58.3 | 57.4 | 56.5 | 55.7 |
| **49** | 63.7 | 62.8 | 61.8 | 60.9 | 60.0 | 59.1 | 58.2 | 57.3 | 56.4 | 55.6 |
| **50** | 63.6 | 62.7 | 61.8 | 60.8 | 59.9 | 59.0 | 58.1 | 57.2 | 56.3 | 55.4 |
| **51** | 63.6 | 62.6 | 61.7 | 60.8 | 59.9 | 58.9 | 58.0 | 57.1 | 56.2 | 55.3 |
| **52** | 63.5 | 62.6 | 61.7 | 60.7 | 59.8 | 58.9 | 58.0 | 57.1 | 56.1 | 55.2 |
| **53** | 63.5 | 62.5 | 61.6 | 60.7 | 59.7 | 58.8 | 57.9 | 57.0 | 56.1 | 55.2 |
| **54** | 63.5 | 62.5 | 61.6 | 60.6 | 59.7 | 58.8 | 57.8 | 56.9 | 56.0 | 55.1 |
| **55** | 63.4 | 62.5 | 61.5 | 60.6 | 59.6 | 58.7 | 57.8 | 56.8 | 55.9 | 55.0 |
| **56** | 63.4 | 62.4 | 61.5 | 60.5 | 59.6 | 58.7 | 57.7 | 56.8 | 55.9 | 54.9 |
| **57** | 63.4 | 62.4 | 61.5 | 60.5 | 59.6 | 58.6 | 57.7 | 56.7 | 55.8 | 54.9 |
| **58** | 63.3 | 62.4 | 61.4 | 60.5 | 59.5 | 58.6 | 57.6 | 56.7 | 55.8 | 54.8 |
| **59** | 63.3 | 62.3 | 61.4 | 60.4 | 59.5 | 58.5 | 57.6 | 56.7 | 55.7 | 54.8 |

## Table II (continued)

### (Joint Life and Last Survivor Expectancy)
(For Use by Owners Whose Spouses Are More Than 10 Years Younger)

| Ages | 20 | 21 | 22 | 23 | 24 | 25 | 26 | 27 | 28 | 29 |
|------|------|------|------|------|------|------|------|------|------|------|
| 60 | 63.3 | 62.3 | 61.4 | 60.4 | 59.5 | 58.5 | 57.6 | 56.6 | 55.7 | 54.7 |
| 61 | 63.3 | 62.3 | 61.3 | 60.4 | 59.4 | 58.5 | 57.5 | 56.6 | 55.6 | 54.7 |
| 62 | 63.2 | 62.3 | 61.3 | 60.4 | 59.4 | 58.4 | 57.5 | 56.5 | 55.6 | 54.7 |
| 63 | 63.2 | 62.3 | 61.3 | 60.3 | 59.4 | 58.4 | 57.5 | 56.5 | 55.6 | 54.6 |
| 64 | 63.2 | 62.2 | 61.3 | 60.3 | 59.4 | 58.4 | 57.4 | 56.5 | 55.5 | 54.6 |
| 65 | 63.2 | 62.2 | 61.3 | 60.3 | 59.3 | 58.4 | 57.4 | 56.5 | 55.5 | 54.6 |
| 66 | 63.2 | 62.2 | 61.2 | 60.3 | 59.3 | 58.4 | 57.4 | 56.4 | 55.5 | 54.5 |
| 67 | 63.2 | 62.2 | 61.2 | 60.3 | 59.3 | 58.3 | 57.4 | 56.4 | 55.5 | 54.5 |
| 68 | 63.1 | 62.2 | 61.2 | 60.2 | 59.3 | 58.3 | 57.4 | 56.4 | 55.4 | 54.5 |
| 69 | 63.1 | 62.2 | 61.2 | 60.2 | 59.3 | 58.3 | 57.3 | 56.4 | 55.4 | 54.5 |
| 70 | 63.1 | 62.2 | 61.2 | 60.2 | 59.3 | 58.3 | 57.3 | 56.4 | 55.4 | 54.4 |
| 71 | 63.1 | 62.1 | 61.2 | 60.2 | 59.2 | 58.3 | 57.3 | 56.4 | 55.4 | 54.4 |
| 72 | 63.1 | 62.1 | 61.2 | 60.2 | 59.2 | 58.3 | 57.3 | 56.3 | 55.4 | 54.4 |
| 73 | 63.1 | 62.1 | 61.2 | 60.2 | 59.2 | 58.3 | 57.3 | 56.3 | 55.4 | 54.4 |
| 74 | 63.1 | 62.1 | 61.2 | 60.2 | 59.2 | 58.2 | 57.3 | 56.3 | 55.4 | 54.4 |
| 75 | 63.1 | 62.1 | 61.1 | 60.2 | 59.2 | 58.2 | 57.3 | 56.3 | 55.3 | 54.4 |
| 76 | 63.1 | 62.1 | 61.1 | 60.2 | 59.2 | 58.2 | 57.3 | 56.3 | 55.3 | 54.4 |
| 77 | 63.1 | 62.1 | 61.1 | 60.2 | 59.2 | 58.2 | 57.3 | 56.3 | 55.3 | 54.4 |

| | | | | | | | | | | |
|---|---|---|---|---|---|---|---|---|---|---|
| 78 | 63.1 | 62.1 | 61.1 | 60.2 | 59.2 | 58.2 | 57.3 | 56.3 | 55.3 | 54.4 |
| 79 | 63.1 | 62.1 | 61.1 | 60.2 | 59.2 | 58.2 | 57.2 | 56.3 | 55.3 | 54.3 |
| 80 | 63.1 | 62.1 | 61.1 | 60.1 | 59.2 | 58.2 | 57.2 | 56.3 | 55.3 | 54.3 |
| 81 | 63.1 | 62.1 | 61.1 | 60.1 | 59.2 | 58.2 | 57.2 | 56.3 | 55.3 | 54.3 |
| 82 | 63.1 | 62.1 | 61.1 | 60.1 | 59.2 | 58.2 | 57.2 | 56.3 | 55.3 | 54.3 |
| 83 | 63.1 | 62.1 | 61.1 | 60.1 | 59.2 | 58.2 | 57.2 | 56.3 | 55.3 | 54.3 |
| 84 | 63.0 | 62.1 | 61.1 | 60.1 | 59.2 | 58.2 | 57.2 | 56.3 | 55.3 | 54.3 |
| 85 | 63.0 | 62.1 | 61.1 | 60.1 | 59.2 | 58.2 | 57.2 | 56.3 | 55.3 | 54.3 |
| 86 | 63.0 | 62.1 | 61.1 | 60.1 | 59.2 | 58.2 | 57.2 | 56.2 | 55.3 | 54.3 |
| 87 | 63.0 | 62.1 | 61.1 | 60.1 | 59.2 | 58.2 | 57.2 | 56.2 | 55.3 | 54.3 |
| 88 | 63.0 | 62.1 | 61.1 | 60.1 | 59.2 | 58.2 | 57.2 | 56.2 | 55.3 | 54.3 |
| 89 | 63.0 | 62.1 | 61.1 | 60.1 | 59.1 | 58.2 | 57.2 | 56.2 | 55.3 | 54.3 |
| 90 | 63.0 | 62.1 | 61.1 | 60.1 | 59.1 | 58.2 | 57.2 | 56.2 | 55.3 | 54.3 |
| 91 | 63.0 | 62.1 | 61.1 | 60.1 | 59.1 | 58.2 | 57.2 | 56.2 | 55.3 | 54.3 |
| 92 | 63.0 | 62.1 | 61.1 | 60.1 | 59.1 | 58.2 | 57.2 | 56.2 | 55.3 | 54.3 |
| 93 | 63.0 | 62.1 | 61.1 | 60.1 | 59.1 | 58.2 | 57.2 | 56.2 | 55.3 | 54.3 |
| 94 | 63.0 | 62.1 | 61.1 | 60.1 | 59.1 | 58.2 | 57.2 | 56.2 | 55.3 | 54.3 |
| 95 | 63.0 | 62.1 | 61.1 | 60.1 | 59.1 | 58.2 | 57.2 | 56.2 | 55.3 | 54.3 |
| 96 | 63.0 | 62.1 | 61.1 | 60.1 | 59.1 | 58.2 | 57.2 | 56.2 | 55.3 | 54.3 |
| 97 | 63.0 | 62.1 | 61.1 | 60.1 | 59.1 | 58.2 | 57.2 | 56.2 | 55.3 | 54.3 |
| 98 | 63.0 | 62.1 | 61.1 | 60.1 | 59.1 | 58.2 | 57.2 | 56.2 | 55.3 | 54.3 |
| 99 | 63.0 | 62.1 | 61.1 | 60.1 | 59.1 | 58.2 | 57.2 | 56.2 | 55.3 | 54.3 |

## Table II (continued)
### (Joint Life and Last Survivor Expectancy)
### (For Use by Owners Whose Spouses Are More Than 10 Years Younger)

| Ages | 20 | 21 | 22 | 23 | 24 | 25 | 26 | 27 | 28 | 29 |
|------|------|------|------|------|------|------|------|------|------|------|
| 100 | 63.0 | 62.1 | 61.1 | 60.1 | 59.1 | 58.2 | 57.2 | 56.2 | 55.3 | 54.3 |
| 101 | 63.0 | 62.1 | 61.1 | 60.1 | 59.1 | 58.2 | 57.2 | 56.2 | 55.3 | 54.3 |
| 102 | 63.0 | 62.1 | 61.1 | 60.1 | 59.1 | 58.2 | 57.2 | 56.2 | 55.3 | 54.3 |
| 103 | 63.0 | 62.1 | 61.1 | 60.1 | 59.1 | 58.2 | 57.2 | 56.2 | 55.3 | 54.3 |
| 104 | 63.0 | 62.1 | 61.1 | 60.1 | 59.1 | 58.2 | 57.2 | 56.2 | 55.3 | 54.3 |
| 105 | 63.0 | 62.1 | 61.1 | 60.1 | 59.1 | 58.2 | 57.2 | 56.2 | 55.3 | 54.3 |
| 106 | 63.0 | 62.1 | 61.1 | 60.1 | 59.1 | 58.2 | 57.2 | 56.2 | 55.3 | 54.3 |
| 107 | 63.0 | 62.1 | 61.1 | 60.1 | 59.1 | 58.2 | 57.2 | 56.2 | 55.3 | 54.3 |
| 108 | 63.0 | 62.1 | 61.1 | 60.1 | 59.1 | 58.2 | 57.2 | 56.2 | 55.3 | 54.3 |
| 109 | 63.0 | 62.1 | 61.1 | 60.1 | 59.1 | 58.2 | 57.2 | 56.2 | 55.3 | 54.3 |
| 110 | 63.0 | 62.1 | 61.1 | 60.1 | 59.1 | 58.2 | 57.2 | 56.2 | 55.3 | 54.3 |
| 111 | 63.0 | 62.1 | 61.1 | 60.1 | 59.1 | 58.2 | 57.2 | 56.2 | 55.3 | 54.3 |
| 112 | 63.0 | 62.1 | 61.1 | 60.1 | 59.1 | 58.2 | 57.2 | 56.2 | 55.3 | 54.3 |
| 113 | 63.0 | 62.1 | 61.1 | 60.1 | 59.1 | 58.2 | 57.2 | 56.2 | 55.3 | 54.3 |
| 114 | 63.0 | 62.1 | 61.1 | 60.1 | 59.1 | 58.2 | 57.2 | 56.2 | 55.3 | 54.3 |
| 115+ | 63.0 | 62.1 | 61.1 | 60.1 | 59.1 | 58.2 | 57.2 | 56.2 | 55.3 | 54.3 |

Table II (continued)
(Joint Life and Last Survivor Expectancy)
(For Use by Owners Whose Spouses Are More Than 10 Years Younger)

| Ages | 30 | 31 | 32 | 33 | 34 | 35 | 36 | 37 | 38 | 39 |
|------|------|------|------|------|------|------|------|------|------|------|
| 30 | 60.2 | 59.7 | 59.2 | 58.8 | 58.4 | 58.0 | 57.6 | 57.3 | 57.0 | 56.7 |
| 31 | 59.7 | 59.2 | 58.7 | 58.2 | 57.8 | 57.4 | 57.0 | 56.6 | 56.3 | 56.0 |
| 32 | 59.2 | 58.7 | 58.2 | 57.7 | 57.2 | 56.8 | 56.4 | 56.0 | 55.6 | 55.3 |
| 33 | 58.8 | 58.2 | 57.7 | 57.2 | 56.7 | 56.2 | 55.8 | 55.4 | 55.0 | 54.7 |
| 34 | 58.4 | 57.8 | 57.2 | 56.7 | 56.2 | 55.7 | 55.3 | 54.8 | 54.4 | 54.0 |
| 35 | 58.0 | 57.4 | 56.8 | 56.2 | 55.7 | 55.2 | 54.7 | 54.3 | 53.8 | 53.4 |
| 36 | 57.6 | 57.0 | 56.4 | 55.8 | 55.3 | 54.7 | 54.2 | 53.7 | 53.3 | 52.8 |
| 37 | 57.3 | 56.6 | 56.0 | 55.4 | 54.8 | 54.3 | 53.7 | 53.2 | 52.7 | 52.3 |
| 38 | 57.0 | 56.3 | 55.6 | 55.0 | 54.4 | 53.8 | 53.3 | 52.7 | 52.2 | 51.7 |
| 39 | 56.7 | 56.0 | 55.3 | 54.7 | 54.0 | 53.4 | 52.8 | 52.3 | 51.7 | 51.2 |
| 40 | 56.4 | 55.7 | 55.0 | 54.3 | 53.7 | 53.0 | 52.4 | 51.8 | 51.3 | 50.8 |
| 41 | 56.1 | 55.4 | 54.7 | 54.0 | 53.3 | 52.7 | 52.0 | 51.4 | 50.9 | 50.3 |
| 42 | 55.9 | 55.2 | 54.4 | 53.7 | 53.0 | 52.3 | 51.7 | 51.1 | 50.4 | 49.9 |
| 43 | 55.7 | 54.9 | 54.2 | 53.4 | 52.7 | 52.0 | 51.3 | 50.7 | 50.1 | 49.5 |
| 44 | 55.5 | 54.7 | 53.9 | 53.2 | 52.4 | 51.7 | 51.0 | 50.4 | 49.7 | 49.1 |
| 45 | 55.3 | 54.5 | 53.7 | 52.9 | 52.2 | 51.5 | 50.7 | 50.0 | 49.4 | 48.7 |
| 46 | 55.1 | 54.3 | 53.5 | 52.7 | 52.0 | 51.2 | 50.5 | 49.8 | 49.1 | 48.4 |
| 47 | 55.0 | 54.1 | 53.3 | 52.5 | 51.7 | 51.0 | 50.2 | 49.5 | 48.8 | 48.1 |
| 48 | 54.8 | 54.0 | 53.2 | 52.3 | 51.5 | 50.8 | 50.0 | 49.2 | 48.5 | 47.8 |

# Table II (continued)

(Joint Life and Last Survivor Expectancy)
(For Use by Owners Whose Spouses Are More Than 10 Years Younger)

| Ages | 30 | 31 | 32 | 33 | 34 | 35 | 36 | 37 | 38 | 39 |
|---|---|---|---|---|---|---|---|---|---|---|
| 49 | 54.7 | 53.8 | 53.0 | 52.2 | 51.4 | 50.6 | 49.8 | 49.0 | 48.2 | 47.5 |
| 50 | 54.6 | 53.7 | 52.9 | 52.0 | 51.2 | 50.4 | 49.6 | 48.8 | 48.0 | 47.3 |
| 51 | 54.5 | 53.6 | 52.7 | 51.9 | 51.0 | 50.2 | 49.4 | 48.6 | 47.8 | 47.0 |
| 52 | 54.4 | 53.5 | 52.6 | 51.7 | 50.9 | 50.0 | 49.2 | 48.4 | 47.6 | 46.8 |
| 53 | 54.3 | 53.4 | 52.5 | 51.6 | 50.8 | 49.9 | 49.1 | 48.2 | 47.4 | 46.6 |
| 54 | 54.2 | 53.3 | 52.4 | 51.5 | 50.6 | 49.8 | 48.9 | 48.1 | 47.2 | 46.4 |
| 55 | 54.1 | 53.2 | 52.3 | 51.4 | 50.5 | 49.7 | 48.8 | 47.9 | 47.1 | 46.3 |
| 56 | 54.0 | 53.1 | 52.2 | 51.3 | 50.4 | 49.5 | 48.7 | 47.8 | 47.0 | 46.1 |
| 57 | 54.0 | 53.0 | 52.1 | 51.2 | 50.3 | 49.4 | 48.6 | 47.7 | 46.8 | 46.0 |
| 58 | 53.9 | 53.0 | 52.1 | 51.2 | 50.3 | 49.4 | 48.5 | 47.6 | 46.7 | 45.8 |
| 59 | 53.8 | 52.9 | 52.0 | 51.1 | 50.2 | 49.3 | 48.4 | 47.5 | 46.6 | 45.7 |
| 60 | 53.8 | 52.9 | 51.9 | 51.0 | 50.1 | 49.2 | 48.3 | 47.4 | 46.5 | 45.6 |
| 61 | 53.8 | 52.8 | 51.9 | 51.0 | 50.0 | 49.1 | 48.2 | 47.3 | 46.4 | 45.5 |
| 62 | 53.7 | 52.8 | 51.8 | 50.9 | 50.0 | 49.1 | 48.1 | 47.2 | 46.3 | 45.4 |
| 63 | 53.7 | 52.7 | 51.8 | 50.9 | 49.9 | 49.0 | 48.1 | 47.2 | 46.3 | 45.3 |
| 64 | 53.6 | 52.7 | 51.8 | 50.8 | 49.9 | 48.9 | 48.0 | 47.1 | 46.2 | 45.3 |
| 65 | 53.6 | 52.7 | 51.7 | 50.8 | 49.8 | 48.9 | 48.0 | 47.0 | 46.1 | 45.2 |
| 66 | 53.6 | 52.6 | 51.7 | 50.7 | 49.8 | 48.9 | 47.9 | 47.0 | 46.1 | 45.1 |

| | 53.x | 52.x | 51.x | 50.x | 49.x | 48.x | 47.x | 46.x | 45/46 | 44/45 |
|---|---|---|---|---|---|---|---|---|---|---|
| 67 | 53.6 | 52.6 | 51.7 | 50.7 | 49.8 | 48.8 | 47.9 | 46.9 | 46.0 | 45.1 |
| 68 | 53.5 | 52.6 | 51.6 | 50.7 | 49.7 | 48.8 | 47.8 | 46.9 | 46.0 | 45.0 |
| 69 | 53.5 | 52.6 | 51.6 | 50.6 | 49.7 | 48.7 | 47.8 | 46.9 | 45.9 | 45.0 |
| 70 | 53.5 | 52.5 | 51.6 | 50.6 | 49.7 | 48.7 | 47.8 | 46.8 | 45.9 | 44.9 |
| 71 | 53.5 | 52.5 | 51.6 | 50.6 | 49.6 | 48.7 | 47.7 | 46.8 | 45.9 | 44.9 |
| 72 | 53.5 | 52.5 | 51.5 | 50.6 | 49.6 | 48.7 | 47.7 | 46.8 | 45.8 | 44.9 |
| 73 | 53.4 | 52.5 | 51.5 | 50.6 | 49.6 | 48.6 | 47.7 | 46.7 | 45.8 | 44.8 |
| 74 | 53.4 | 52.5 | 51.5 | 50.5 | 49.6 | 48.6 | 47.7 | 46.7 | 45.8 | 44.8 |
| 75 | 53.4 | 52.5 | 51.5 | 50.5 | 49.6 | 48.6 | 47.7 | 46.7 | 45.7 | 44.8 |
| 76 | 53.4 | 52.4 | 51.5 | 50.5 | 49.6 | 48.6 | 47.6 | 46.7 | 45.7 | 44.8 |
| 77 | 53.4 | 52.4 | 51.5 | 50.5 | 49.5 | 48.6 | 47.6 | 46.7 | 45.7 | 44.8 |
| 78 | 53.4 | 52.4 | 51.5 | 50.5 | 49.5 | 48.6 | 47.6 | 46.6 | 45.7 | 44.7 |
| 79 | 53.4 | 52.4 | 51.5 | 50.5 | 49.5 | 48.6 | 47.6 | 46.6 | 45.7 | 44.7 |
| 80 | 53.4 | 52.4 | 51.4 | 50.5 | 49.5 | 48.5 | 47.6 | 46.6 | 45.7 | 44.7 |
| 81 | 53.4 | 52.4 | 51.4 | 50.5 | 49.5 | 48.5 | 47.6 | 46.6 | 45.7 | 44.7 |
| 82 | 53.4 | 52.4 | 51.4 | 50.5 | 49.5 | 48.5 | 47.6 | 46.6 | 45.6 | 44.7 |
| 83 | 53.4 | 52.4 | 51.4 | 50.5 | 49.5 | 48.5 | 47.6 | 46.6 | 45.6 | 44.7 |
| 84 | 53.4 | 52.4 | 51.4 | 50.5 | 49.5 | 48.5 | 47.6 | 46.6 | 45.6 | 44.7 |
| 85 | 53.3 | 52.4 | 51.4 | 50.4 | 49.5 | 48.5 | 47.5 | 46.6 | 45.6 | 44.7 |
| 86 | 53.3 | 52.4 | 51.4 | 50.4 | 49.5 | 48.5 | 47.5 | 46.6 | 45.6 | 44.6 |
| 87 | 53.3 | 52.4 | 51.4 | 50.4 | 49.5 | 48.5 | 47.5 | 46.6 | 45.6 | 44.6 |
| 88 | 53.3 | 52.4 | 51.4 | 50.4 | 49.5 | 48.5 | 47.5 | 46.6 | 45.6 | 44.6 |

Table II (continued)

(Joint Life and Last Survivor Expectancy)
(For Use by Owners Whose Spouses Are More Than 10 Years Younger)

| Ages | 30 | 31 | 32 | 33 | 34 | 35 | 36 | 37 | 38 | 39 |
|------|------|------|------|------|------|------|------|------|------|------|
| 89 | 53.3 | 52.4 | 51.4 | 50.4 | 49.5 | 48.5 | 47.5 | 46.6 | 45.6 | 44.6 |
| 90 | 53.3 | 52.4 | 51.4 | 50.4 | 49.5 | 48.5 | 47.5 | 46.6 | 45.6 | 44.6 |
| 91 | 53.3 | 52.4 | 51.4 | 50.4 | 49.5 | 48.5 | 47.5 | 46.6 | 45.6 | 44.6 |
| 92 | 53.3 | 52.4 | 51.4 | 50.4 | 49.5 | 48.5 | 47.5 | 46.6 | 45.6 | 44.6 |
| 93 | 53.3 | 52.4 | 51.4 | 50.4 | 49.5 | 48.5 | 47.5 | 46.6 | 45.6 | 44.6 |
| 94 | 53.3 | 52.4 | 51.4 | 50.4 | 49.5 | 48.5 | 47.5 | 46.6 | 45.6 | 44.6 |
| 95 | 53.3 | 52.4 | 51.4 | 50.4 | 49.5 | 48.5 | 47.5 | 46.5 | 45.6 | 44.6 |
| 96 | 53.3 | 52.4 | 51.4 | 50.4 | 49.5 | 48.5 | 47.5 | 46.5 | 45.6 | 44.6 |
| 97 | 53.3 | 52.4 | 51.4 | 50.4 | 49.5 | 48.5 | 47.5 | 46.5 | 45.6 | 44.6 |
| 98 | 53.3 | 52.4 | 51.4 | 50.4 | 49.5 | 48.5 | 47.5 | 46.5 | 45.6 | 44.6 |
| 99 | 53.3 | 52.4 | 51.4 | 50.4 | 49.5 | 48.5 | 47.5 | 46.5 | 45.6 | 44.6 |
| 100 | 53.3 | 52.4 | 51.4 | 50.4 | 49.5 | 48.5 | 47.5 | 46.5 | 45.6 | 44.6 |
| 101 | 53.3 | 52.4 | 51.4 | 50.4 | 49.5 | 48.5 | 47.5 | 46.5 | 45.6 | 44.6 |
| 102 | 53.3 | 52.4 | 51.4 | 50.4 | 49.5 | 48.5 | 47.5 | 46.5 | 45.6 | 44.6 |
| 103 | 53.3 | 52.4 | 51.4 | 50.4 | 49.5 | 48.5 | 47.5 | 46.5 | 45.6 | 44.6 |
| 104 | 53.3 | 52.4 | 51.4 | 50.4 | 49.5 | 48.5 | 47.5 | 46.5 | 45.6 | 44.6 |
| 105 | 53.3 | 52.4 | 51.4 | 50.4 | 49.4 | 48.5 | 47.5 | 46.5 | 45.6 | 44.6 |
| 106 | 53.3 | 52.4 | 51.4 | 50.4 | 49.4 | 48.5 | 47.5 | 46.5 | 45.6 | 44.6 |

| | 40 | 41 | 42 | 43 | 44 | 45 | 46 | 47 | 48 | 49 |
|---|---|---|---|---|---|---|---|---|---|---|
| 107 | 53.3 | 52.4 | 51.4 | 50.4 | 49.4 | 48.5 | 47.5 | 46.5 | 45.6 | 44.6 |
| 108 | 53.3 | 52.4 | 51.4 | 50.4 | 49.4 | 48.5 | 47.5 | 46.5 | 45.6 | 44.6 |
| 109 | 53.3 | 52.4 | 51.4 | 50.4 | 49.4 | 48.5 | 47.5 | 46.5 | 45.6 | 44.6 |
| 110 | 53.3 | 52.4 | 51.4 | 50.4 | 49.4 | 48.5 | 47.5 | 46.5 | 45.6 | 44.6 |
| 111 | 53.3 | 52.4 | 51.4 | 50.4 | 49.4 | 48.5 | 47.5 | 46.5 | 45.6 | 44.6 |
| 112 | 53.3 | 52.4 | 51.4 | 50.4 | 49.4 | 48.5 | 47.5 | 46.5 | 45.6 | 44.6 |
| 113 | 53.3 | 52.4 | 51.4 | 50.4 | 49.4 | 48.5 | 47.5 | 46.5 | 45.6 | 44.6 |
| 114 | 53.3 | 52.4 | 51.4 | 50.4 | 49.4 | 48.5 | 47.5 | 46.5 | 45.6 | 44.6 |
| 115+ | 53.3 | 52.4 | 51.4 | 50.4 | 49.4 | 48.5 | 47.5 | 46.5 | 45.6 | 44.6 |

## Table II (continued)

### (Joint Life and Last Survivor Expectancy)
### (For Use by Owners Whose Spouses Are More Than 10 Years Younger)

| Ages | 40 | 41 | 42 | 43 | 44 | 45 | 46 | 47 | 48 | 49 |
|---|---|---|---|---|---|---|---|---|---|---|
| 40 | 50.2 | 49.8 | 49.3 | 48.9 | 48.5 | 48.1 | 47.7 | 47.4 | 47.1 | 46.8 |
| 41 | 49.8 | 49.3 | 48.8 | 48.3 | 47.9 | 47.5 | 47.1 | 46.7 | 46.4 | 46.1 |
| 42 | 49.3 | 48.8 | 48.3 | 47.8 | 47.3 | 46.9 | 46.5 | 46.1 | 45.8 | 45.4 |
| 43 | 48.9 | 48.3 | 47.8 | 47.3 | 46.8 | 46.3 | 45.9 | 45.5 | 45.1 | 44.8 |
| 44 | 48.5 | 47.9 | 47.3 | 46.8 | 46.3 | 45.8 | 45.4 | 44.9 | 44.5 | 44.2 |
| 45 | 48.1 | 47.5 | 46.9 | 46.3 | 45.8 | 45.3 | 44.8 | 44.4 | 44.0 | 43.6 |
| 46 | 47.7 | 47.1 | 46.5 | 45.9 | 45.4 | 44.8 | 44.3 | 43.9 | 43.4 | 43.0 |
| 47 | 47.4 | 46.7 | 46.1 | 45.5 | 44.9 | 44.4 | 43.9 | 43.4 | 42.9 | 42.4 |

Table II (continued)

(Joint Life and Last Survivor Expectancy)
(For Use by Owners Whose Spouses Are More Than 10 Years Younger)

| Ages | 40 | 41 | 42 | 43 | 44 | 45 | 46 | 47 | 48 | 49 |
|------|------|------|------|------|------|------|------|------|------|------|
| 48 | 47.1 | 46.4 | 45.8 | 45.1 | 44.5 | 44.0 | 43.4 | 42.9 | 42.4 | 41.9 |
| 49 | 46.8 | 46.1 | 45.4 | 44.8 | 44.2 | 43.6 | 43.0 | 42.4 | 41.9 | 41.4 |
| 50 | 46.5 | 45.8 | 45.1 | 44.4 | 43.8 | 43.2 | 42.6 | 42.0 | 41.5 | 40.9 |
| 51 | 46.3 | 45.5 | 44.8 | 44.1 | 43.5 | 42.8 | 42.2 | 41.6 | 41.0 | 40.5 |
| 52 | 46.0 | 45.3 | 44.6 | 43.8 | 43.2 | 42.5 | 41.8 | 41.2 | 40.6 | 40.1 |
| 53 | 45.8 | 45.1 | 44.3 | 43.6 | 42.9 | 42.2 | 41.5 | 40.9 | 40.3 | 39.7 |
| 54 | 45.6 | 44.8 | 44.1 | 43.3 | 42.6 | 41.9 | 41.2 | 40.5 | 39.9 | 39.3 |
| 55 | 45.5 | 44.7 | 43.9 | 43.1 | 42.4 | 41.6 | 40.9 | 40.2 | 39.6 | 38.9 |
| 56 | 45.3 | 44.5 | 43.7 | 42.9 | 42.1 | 41.4 | 40.7 | 40.0 | 39.3 | 38.6 |
| 57 | 45.1 | 44.3 | 43.5 | 42.7 | 41.9 | 41.2 | 40.4 | 39.7 | 39.0 | 38.3 |
| 58 | 45.0 | 44.2 | 43.3 | 42.5 | 41.7 | 40.9 | 40.2 | 39.4 | 38.7 | 38.0 |
| 59 | 44.9 | 44.0 | 43.2 | 42.4 | 41.5 | 40.7 | 40.0 | 39.2 | 38.5 | 37.8 |
| 60 | 44.7 | 43.9 | 43.0 | 42.2 | 41.4 | 40.6 | 39.8 | 39.0 | 38.2 | 37.5 |
| 61 | 44.6 | 43.8 | 42.9 | 42.1 | 41.2 | 40.4 | 39.6 | 38.8 | 38.0 | 37.3 |
| 62 | 44.5 | 43.7 | 42.8 | 41.9 | 41.1 | 40.3 | 39.4 | 38.6 | 37.8 | 37.1 |
| 63 | 44.5 | 43.6 | 42.7 | 41.8 | 41.0 | 40.1 | 39.3 | 38.5 | 37.7 | 36.9 |
| 64 | 44.4 | 43.5 | 42.6 | 41.7 | 40.8 | 40.0 | 39.2 | 38.3 | 37.5 | 36.7 |
| 65 | 44.3 | 43.4 | 42.5 | 41.6 | 40.7 | 39.9 | 39.0 | 38.2 | 37.4 | 36.6 |

| | | | | | | | | | | |
|---|---|---|---|---|---|---|---|---|---|---|
| 66 | 44.2 | 43.3 | 42.4 | 41.5 | 40.6 | 39.8 | 38.9 | 38.1 | 37.2 | 36.4 |
| 67 | 44.2 | 43.3 | 42.3 | 41.4 | 40.6 | 39.7 | 38.8 | 38.0 | 37.1 | 36.3 |
| 68 | 44.1 | 43.2 | 42.3 | 41.4 | 40.5 | 39.6 | 38.7 | 37.9 | 37.0 | 36.2 |
| 69 | 44.1 | 43.1 | 42.2 | 41.3 | 40.4 | 39.5 | 38.6 | 37.8 | 36.9 | 36.0 |
| 70 | 44.0 | 43.1 | 42.2 | 41.3 | 40.3 | 39.4 | 38.6 | 37.7 | 36.8 | 35.9 |
| 71 | 44.0 | 43.0 | 42.1 | 41.2 | 40.3 | 39.4 | 38.5 | 37.6 | 36.7 | 35.9 |
| 72 | 43.9 | 43.0 | 42.1 | 41.1 | 40.2 | 39.3 | 38.4 | 37.5 | 36.6 | 35.8 |
| 73 | 43.9 | 43.0 | 42.0 | 41.1 | 40.2 | 39.3 | 38.4 | 37.5 | 36.6 | 35.7 |
| 74 | 43.9 | 42.9 | 42.0 | 41.1 | 40.1 | 39.2 | 38.3 | 37.4 | 36.5 | 35.6 |
| 75 | 43.8 | 42.9 | 42.0 | 41.0 | 40.1 | 39.2 | 38.3 | 37.4 | 36.5 | 35.6 |
| 76 | 43.8 | 42.9 | 41.9 | 41.0 | 40.1 | 39.1 | 38.2 | 37.3 | 36.4 | 35.5 |
| 77 | 43.8 | 42.9 | 41.9 | 41.0 | 40.0 | 39.1 | 38.2 | 37.3 | 36.4 | 35.5 |
| 78 | 43.8 | 42.8 | 41.9 | 40.9 | 40.0 | 39.1 | 38.2 | 37.2 | 36.3 | 35.4 |
| 79 | 43.8 | 42.8 | 41.9 | 40.9 | 40.0 | 39.1 | 38.1 | 37.2 | 36.3 | 35.4 |
| 80 | 43.7 | 42.8 | 41.8 | 40.9 | 40.0 | 39.0 | 38.1 | 37.2 | 36.3 | 35.4 |
| 81 | 43.7 | 42.8 | 41.8 | 40.9 | 39.9 | 39.0 | 38.1 | 37.2 | 36.2 | 35.3 |
| 82 | 43.7 | 42.8 | 41.8 | 40.9 | 39.9 | 39.0 | 38.1 | 37.1 | 36.2 | 35.3 |
| 83 | 43.7 | 42.8 | 41.8 | 40.9 | 39.9 | 39.0 | 38.0 | 37.1 | 36.2 | 35.3 |
| 84 | 43.7 | 42.7 | 41.8 | 40.8 | 39.9 | 39.0 | 38.0 | 37.1 | 36.2 | 35.3 |
| 85 | 43.7 | 42.7 | 41.8 | 40.8 | 39.9 | 38.9 | 38.0 | 37.1 | 36.2 | 35.2 |
| 86 | 43.7 | 42.7 | 41.8 | 40.8 | 39.9 | 38.9 | 38.0 | 37.1 | 36.1 | 35.2 |
| 87 | 43.7 | 42.7 | 41.8 | 40.8 | 39.9 | 38.9 | 38.0 | 37.0 | 36.1 | 35.2 |

## Table II (continued)
### (Joint Life and Last Survivor Expectancy)
### (For Use by Owners Whose Spouses Are More Than 10 Years Younger)

| Ages | 40 | 41 | 42 | 43 | 44 | 45 | 46 | 47 | 48 | 49 |
|------|------|------|------|------|------|------|------|------|------|------|
| 88   | 43.7 | 42.7 | 41.8 | 40.8 | 39.9 | 38.9 | 38.0 | 37.0 | 36.1 | 35.2 |
| 89   | 43.7 | 42.7 | 41.7 | 40.8 | 39.8 | 38.9 | 38.0 | 37.0 | 36.1 | 35.2 |
| 90   | 43.7 | 42.7 | 41.7 | 40.8 | 39.8 | 38.9 | 38.0 | 37.0 | 36.1 | 35.2 |
| 91   | 43.7 | 42.7 | 41.7 | 40.8 | 39.8 | 38.9 | 37.9 | 37.0 | 36.1 | 35.2 |
| 92   | 43.7 | 42.7 | 41.7 | 40.8 | 39.8 | 38.9 | 37.9 | 37.0 | 36.1 | 35.1 |
| 93   | 43.7 | 42.7 | 41.7 | 40.8 | 39.8 | 38.9 | 37.9 | 37.0 | 36.1 | 35.1 |
| 94   | 43.7 | 42.7 | 41.7 | 40.8 | 39.8 | 38.9 | 37.9 | 37.0 | 36.1 | 35.1 |
| 95   | 43.6 | 42.7 | 41.7 | 40.8 | 39.8 | 38.9 | 37.9 | 37.0 | 36.1 | 35.1 |
| 96   | 43.6 | 42.7 | 41.7 | 40.8 | 39.8 | 38.9 | 37.9 | 37.0 | 36.1 | 35.1 |
| 97   | 43.6 | 42.7 | 41.7 | 40.8 | 39.8 | 38.9 | 37.9 | 37.0 | 36.1 | 35.1 |
| 98   | 43.6 | 42.7 | 41.7 | 40.8 | 39.8 | 38.9 | 37.9 | 37.0 | 36.0 | 35.1 |
| 99   | 43.6 | 42.7 | 41.7 | 40.8 | 39.8 | 38.9 | 37.9 | 37.0 | 36.0 | 35.1 |
| 100  | 43.6 | 42.7 | 41.7 | 40.8 | 39.8 | 38.9 | 37.9 | 37.0 | 36.0 | 35.1 |
| 101  | 43.6 | 42.7 | 41.7 | 40.8 | 39.8 | 38.9 | 37.9 | 37.0 | 36.0 | 35.1 |
| 102  | 43.6 | 42.7 | 41.7 | 40.8 | 39.8 | 38.9 | 37.9 | 37.0 | 36.0 | 35.1 |
| 103  | 43.6 | 42.7 | 41.7 | 40.8 | 39.8 | 38.9 | 37.9 | 37.0 | 36.0 | 35.1 |
| 104  | 43.6 | 42.7 | 41.7 | 40.8 | 39.8 | 38.8 | 37.9 | 37.0 | 36.0 | 35.1 |
| 105  | 43.6 | 42.7 | 41.7 | 40.8 | 39.8 | 38.8 | 37.9 | 37.0 | 36.0 | 35.1 |

| Age | | | | | | | | | | |
|---|---|---|---|---|---|---|---|---|---|---|
| 106 | 43.6 | 42.7 | 41.7 | 40.8 | 39.8 | 38.8 | 37.9 | 37.0 | 36.0 | 35.1 |
| 107 | 43.6 | 42.7 | 41.7 | 40.8 | 39.8 | 38.8 | 37.9 | 37.0 | 36.0 | 35.1 |
| 108 | 43.6 | 42.7 | 41.7 | 40.8 | 39.8 | 38.8 | 37.9 | 37.0 | 36.0 | 35.1 |
| 109 | 43.6 | 42.7 | 41.7 | 40.7 | 39.8 | 38.8 | 37.9 | 37.0 | 36.0 | 35.1 |
| 110 | 43.6 | 42.7 | 41.7 | 40.7 | 39.8 | 38.8 | 37.9 | 37.0 | 36.0 | 35.1 |
| 111 | 43.6 | 42.7 | 41.7 | 40.7 | 39.8 | 38.8 | 37.9 | 37.0 | 36.0 | 35.1 |
| 112 | 43.6 | 42.7 | 41.7 | 40.7 | 39.8 | 38.8 | 37.9 | 37.0 | 36.0 | 35.1 |
| 113 | 43.6 | 42.7 | 41.7 | 40.7 | 39.8 | 38.8 | 37.9 | 37.0 | 36.0 | 35.1 |
| 114 | 43.6 | 42.7 | 41.7 | 40.7 | 39.8 | 38.8 | 37.9 | 37.0 | 36.0 | 35.1 |
| 115+ | 43.6 | 42.7 | 41.7 | 40.7 | 39.8 | 38.8 | 37.9 | 37.0 | 36.0 | 35.1 |

## Table II (continued)

### (Joint Life and Last Survivor Expectancy)
### (For Use by Owners Whose Spouses Are More Than 10 Years Younger)

| Ages | 50 | 51 | 52 | 53 | 54 | 55 | 56 | 57 | 58 | 59 |
|---|---|---|---|---|---|---|---|---|---|---|
| 50 | 40.4 | 40.0 | 39.5 | 39.1 | 38.7 | 38.3 | 38.0 | 37.6 | 37.3 | 37.1 |
| 51 | 40.0 | 39.5 | 39.0 | 38.5 | 38.1 | 37.7 | 37.4 | 37.0 | 36.7 | 36.4 |
| 52 | 39.5 | 39.0 | 38.5 | 38.0 | 37.6 | 37.2 | 36.8 | 36.4 | 36.0 | 35.7 |
| 53 | 39.1 | 38.5 | 38.0 | 37.5 | 37.1 | 36.6 | 36.2 | 35.8 | 35.4 | 35.1 |
| 54 | 38.7 | 38.1 | 37.6 | 37.1 | 36.6 | 36.1 | 35.7 | 35.2 | 34.8 | 34.5 |
| 55 | 38.3 | 37.7 | 37.2 | 36.6 | 36.1 | 35.6 | 35.1 | 34.7 | 34.3 | 33.9 |
| 56 | 38.0 | 37.4 | 36.8 | 36.2 | 35.7 | 35.1 | 34.7 | 34.2 | 33.7 | 33.3 |

# Table II (continued)

## (Joint Life and Last Survivor Expectancy)
### (For Use by Owners Whose Spouses Are More Than 10 Years Younger)

| Ages | 50 | 51 | 52 | 53 | 54 | 55 | 56 | 57 | 58 | 59 |
|---|---|---|---|---|---|---|---|---|---|---|
| 57 | 37.6 | 37.0 | 36.4 | 35.8 | 35.2 | 34.7 | 34.2 | 33.7 | 33.2 | 32.8 |
| 58 | 37.3 | 36.7 | 36.0 | 35.4 | 34.8 | 34.3 | 33.7 | 33.2 | 32.8 | 32.3 |
| 59 | 37.1 | 36.4 | 35.7 | 35.1 | 34.5 | 33.9 | 33.3 | 32.8 | 32.3 | 31.8 |
| 60 | 36.8 | 36.1 | 35.4 | 34.8 | 34.1 | 33.5 | 32.9 | 32.4 | 31.9 | 31.3 |
| 61 | 36.6 | 35.8 | 35.1 | 34.5 | 33.8 | 33.2 | 32.6 | 32.0 | 31.4 | 30.9 |
| 62 | 36.3 | 35.6 | 34.9 | 34.2 | 33.5 | 32.9 | 32.2 | 31.6 | 31.1 | 30.5 |
| 63 | 36.1 | 35.4 | 34.6 | 33.9 | 33.2 | 32.6 | 31.9 | 31.3 | 30.7 | 30.1 |
| 64 | 35.9 | 35.2 | 34.4 | 33.7 | 33.0 | 32.3 | 31.6 | 31.0 | 30.4 | 29.8 |
| 65 | 35.8 | 35.0 | 34.2 | 33.5 | 32.7 | 32.0 | 31.4 | 30.7 | 30.0 | 29.4 |
| 66 | 35.6 | 34.8 | 34.0 | 33.3 | 32.5 | 31.8 | 31.1 | 30.4 | 29.8 | 29.1 |
| 67 | 35.5 | 34.7 | 33.9 | 33.1 | 32.3 | 31.6 | 30.9 | 30.2 | 29.5 | 28.8 |
| 68 | 35.3 | 34.5 | 33.7 | 32.9 | 32.1 | 31.4 | 30.7 | 29.9 | 29.2 | 28.6 |
| 69 | 35.2 | 34.4 | 33.6 | 32.8 | 32.0 | 31.2 | 30.5 | 29.7 | 29.0 | 28.3 |
| 70 | 35.1 | 34.3 | 33.4 | 32.6 | 31.8 | 31.1 | 30.3 | 29.5 | 28.8 | 28.1 |
| 71 | 35.0 | 34.2 | 33.3 | 32.5 | 31.7 | 30.9 | 30.1 | 29.4 | 28.6 | 27.9 |
| 72 | 34.9 | 34.1 | 33.2 | 32.4 | 31.6 | 30.8 | 30.0 | 29.2 | 28.4 | 27.7 |
| 73 | 34.8 | 34.0 | 33.1 | 32.3 | 31.5 | 30.6 | 29.8 | 29.1 | 28.3 | 27.5 |
| 74 | 34.8 | 33.9 | 33.0 | 32.2 | 31.4 | 30.5 | 29.7 | 28.9 | 28.1 | 27.4 |

| | | | | | | | | | | |
|---|---|---|---|---|---|---|---|---|---|---|
| 75 | 34.7 | 33.8 | 33.0 | 32.1 | 31.3 | 30.4 | 29.6 | 28.8 | 28.0 | 27.2 |
| 76 | 34.6 | 33.8 | 32.9 | 32.0 | 31.2 | 30.3 | 29.5 | 28.7 | 27.9 | 27.1 |
| 77 | 34.6 | 33.7 | 32.8 | 32.0 | 31.1 | 30.3 | 29.4 | 28.6 | 27.8 | 27.0 |
| 78 | 34.5 | 33.6 | 32.8 | 31.9 | 31.0 | 30.2 | 29.3 | 28.5 | 27.7 | 26.9 |
| 79 | 34.5 | 33.6 | 32.7 | 31.8 | 31.0 | 30.1 | 29.3 | 28.4 | 27.6 | 26.8 |
| 80 | 34.5 | 33.6 | 32.7 | 31.8 | 30.9 | 30.1 | 29.2 | 28.4 | 27.5 | 26.7 |
| 81 | 34.4 | 33.5 | 32.6 | 31.8 | 30.9 | 30.0 | 29.2 | 28.3 | 27.5 | 26.6 |
| 82 | 34.4 | 33.5 | 32.6 | 31.7 | 30.8 | 30.0 | 29.1 | 28.3 | 27.4 | 26.6 |
| 83 | 34.4 | 33.5 | 32.6 | 31.7 | 30.8 | 29.9 | 29.1 | 28.2 | 27.4 | 26.5 |
| 84 | 34.3 | 33.4 | 32.5 | 31.7 | 30.8 | 29.9 | 29.0 | 28.2 | 27.3 | 26.5 |
| 85 | 34.3 | 33.4 | 32.5 | 31.6 | 30.7 | 29.9 | 29.0 | 28.1 | 27.3 | 26.4 |
| 86 | 34.3 | 33.4 | 32.5 | 31.6 | 30.7 | 29.8 | 29.0 | 28.1 | 27.2 | 26.4 |
| 87 | 34.3 | 33.4 | 32.5 | 31.6 | 30.7 | 29.8 | 28.9 | 28.1 | 27.2 | 26.4 |
| 88 | 34.3 | 33.4 | 32.5 | 31.6 | 30.7 | 29.8 | 28.9 | 28.0 | 27.2 | 26.3 |
| 89 | 34.3 | 33.3 | 32.4 | 31.5 | 30.7 | 29.8 | 28.9 | 28.0 | 27.2 | 26.3 |
| 90 | 34.2 | 33.3 | 32.4 | 31.5 | 30.6 | 29.8 | 28.9 | 28.0 | 27.1 | 26.3 |
| 91 | 34.2 | 33.3 | 32.4 | 31.5 | 30.6 | 29.7 | 28.9 | 28.0 | 27.1 | 26.3 |
| 92 | 34.2 | 33.3 | 32.4 | 31.5 | 30.6 | 29.7 | 28.8 | 28.0 | 27.1 | 26.2 |
| 93 | 34.2 | 33.3 | 32.4 | 31.5 | 30.6 | 29.7 | 28.8 | 28.0 | 27.1 | 26.2 |
| 94 | 34.2 | 33.3 | 32.4 | 31.5 | 30.6 | 29.7 | 28.8 | 27.9 | 27.1 | 26.2 |
| 95 | 34.2 | 33.3 | 32.4 | 31.5 | 30.6 | 29.7 | 28.8 | 27.9 | 27.1 | 26.2 |
| 96 | 34.2 | 33.3 | 32.4 | 31.5 | 30.6 | 29.7 | 28.8 | 27.9 | 27.0 | 26.2 |

Table II (continued)
(Joint Life and Last Survivor Expectancy)
(For Use by Owners Whose Spouses Are More Than 10 Years Younger)

| Ages | 50 | 51 | 52 | 53 | 54 | 55 | 56 | 57 | 58 | 59 |
|------|------|------|------|------|------|------|------|------|------|------|
| 97 | 34.2 | 33.3 | 32.4 | 31.5 | 30.6 | 29.7 | 28.8 | 27.9 | 27.0 | 26.2 |
| 98 | 34.2 | 33.3 | 32.4 | 31.5 | 30.6 | 29.7 | 28.8 | 27.9 | 27.0 | 26.2 |
| 99 | 34.2 | 33.3 | 32.4 | 31.5 | 30.6 | 29.7 | 28.8 | 27.9 | 27.0 | 26.2 |
| 100 | 34.2 | 33.3 | 32.4 | 31.5 | 30.6 | 29.7 | 28.8 | 27.9 | 27.0 | 26.1 |
| 101 | 34.2 | 33.3 | 32.4 | 31.5 | 30.6 | 29.7 | 28.8 | 27.9 | 27.0 | 26.1 |
| 102 | 34.2 | 33.3 | 32.4 | 31.4 | 30.5 | 29.7 | 28.8 | 27.9 | 27.0 | 26.1 |
| 103 | 34.2 | 33.3 | 32.4 | 31.4 | 30.5 | 29.7 | 28.8 | 27.9 | 27.0 | 26.1 |
| 104 | 34.2 | 33.3 | 32.4 | 31.4 | 30.5 | 29.6 | 28.8 | 27.9 | 27.0 | 26.1 |
| 105 | 34.2 | 33.3 | 32.3 | 31.4 | 30.5 | 29.6 | 28.8 | 27.9 | 27.0 | 26.1 |
| 106 | 34.2 | 33.3 | 32.3 | 31.4 | 30.5 | 29.6 | 28.8 | 27.9 | 27.0 | 26.1 |
| 107 | 34.2 | 33.5 | 32.3 | 31.4 | 30.5 | 29.6 | 28.8 | 27.9 | 27.0 | 26.1 |
| 108 | 34.2 | 33.3 | 32.3 | 31.4 | 30.5 | 29.6 | 28.8 | 27.9 | 27.0 | 26.1 |
| 109 | 34.2 | 33.3 | 32.3 | 31.4 | 30.5 | 29.6 | 28.7 | 27.9 | 27.0 | 26.1 |
| 110 | 34.2 | 33.3 | 32.3 | 31.4 | 30.5 | 29.6 | 28.7 | 27.9 | 27.0 | 26.1 |
| 111 | 34.2 | 33.3 | 32.3 | 31.4 | 30.5 | 29.6 | 28.7 | 27.9 | 27.0 | 26.1 |
| 112 | 34.2 | 33.3 | 32.3 | 31.4 | 30.5 | 29.6 | 28.7 | 27.9 | 27.0 | 26.1 |
| 113 | 34.2 | 33.3 | 32.3 | 31.4 | 30.5 | 29.6 | 28.7 | 27.9 | 27.0 | 26.1 |
| 114 | 34.2 | 33.3 | 32.3 | 31.4 | 30.5 | 29.6 | 28.7 | 27.9 | 27.0 | 26.1 |
| 115+ | 34.2 | 33.3 | 32.3 | 31.4 | 30.5 | 29.6 | 28.7 | 27.9 | 27.0 | 26.1 |

Table II (continued)

(Joint Life and Last Survivor Expectancy)
(For Use by Owners Whose Spouses Are More Than 10 Years Younger)

| Ages | 60 | 61 | 62 | 63 | 64 | 65 | 66 | 67 | 68 | 69 |
|---|---|---|---|---|---|---|---|---|---|---|
| 60 | 30.9 | 30.4 | 30.0 | 29.6 | 29.2 | 28.8 | 28.5 | 28.2 | 27.9 | 27.6 |
| 61 | 30.4 | 29.9 | 29.5 | 29.0 | 28.6 | 28.3 | 27.9 | 27.6 | 27.3 | 27.0 |
| 62 | 30.0 | 29.5 | 29.0 | 28.5 | 28.1 | 27.7 | 27.3 | 27.0 | 26.7 | 26.4 |
| 63 | 29.6 | 29.0 | 28.5 | 28.1 | 27.6 | 27.2 | 26.8 | 26.4 | 26.1 | 25.7 |
| 64 | 29.2 | 28.6 | 28.1 | 27.6 | 27.1 | 26.7 | 26.3 | 25.9 | 25.5 | 25.2 |
| 65 | 28.8 | 28.3 | 27.7 | 27.2 | 26.7 | 26.2 | 25.8 | 25.4 | 25.0 | 24.6 |
| 66 | 28.5 | 27.9 | 27.3 | 26.8 | 26.3 | 25.8 | 25.3 | 24.9 | 24.5 | 24.1 |
| 67 | 28.2 | 27.6 | 27.0 | 26.4 | 25.9 | 25.4 | 24.9 | 24.4 | 24.0 | 23.6 |
| 68 | 27.9 | 27.3 | 26.7 | 26.1 | 25.5 | 25.0 | 24.5 | 24.0 | 23.5 | 23.1 |
| 69 | 27.6 | 27.0 | 26.4 | 25.7 | 25.2 | 24.6 | 24.1 | 23.6 | 23.1 | 22.6 |
| 70 | 27.4 | 26.7 | 26.1 | 25.4 | 24.8 | 24.3 | 23.7 | 23.2 | 22.7 | 22.2 |
| 71 | 27.2 | 26.5 | 25.8 | 25.2 | 24.5 | 23.9 | 23.4 | 22.8 | 22.3 | 21.8 |
| 72 | 27.0 | 26.3 | 25.6 | 24.9 | 24.3 | 23.7 | 23.1 | 22.5 | 22.0 | 21.4 |
| 73 | 26.8 | 26.1 | 25.4 | 24.7 | 24.0 | 23.4 | 22.8 | 22.2 | 21.6 | 21.1 |
| 74 | 26.6 | 25.9 | 25.2 | 24.5 | 23.8 | 23.1 | 22.5 | 21.9 | 21.3 | 20.8 |
| 75 | 26.5 | 25.7 | 25.0 | 24.3 | 23.6 | 22.9 | 22.3 | 21.6 | 21.0 | 20.5 |

## Table II (continued)

(Joint Life and Last Survivor Expectancy)
(For Use by Owners Whose Spouses Are More Than 10 Years Younger)

| Ages | 60 | 61 | 62 | 63 | 64 | 65 | 66 | 67 | 68 | 69 |
|---|---|---|---|---|---|---|---|---|---|---|
| 76 | 26.3 | 25.6 | 24.8 | 24.1 | 23.4 | 22.7 | 22.0 | 21.4 | 20.8 | 20.2 |
| 77 | 26.2 | 25.4 | 24.7 | 23.9 | 23.2 | 22.5 | 21.8 | 21.2 | 20.6 | 19.9 |
| 78 | 26.1 | 25.3 | 24.6 | 23.8 | 23.1 | 22.4 | 21.7 | 21.0 | 20.3 | 19.7 |
| 79 | 26.0 | 25.2 | 24.4 | 23.7 | 22.9 | 22.2 | 21.5 | 20.8 | 20.1 | 19.5 |
| 80 | 25.9 | 25.1 | 24.3 | 23.6 | 22.8 | 22.1 | 21.3 | 20.6 | 20.0 | 19.3 |
| 81 | 25.8 | 25.0 | 24.2 | 23.4 | 22.7 | 21.9 | 21.2 | 20.5 | 19.8 | 19.1 |
| 82 | 25.8 | 24.9 | 24.1 | 23.4 | 22.6 | 21.8 | 21.1 | 20.4 | 19.7 | 19.0 |
| 83 | 25.7 | 24.9 | 24.1 | 23.3 | 22.5 | 21.7 | 21.0 | 20.2 | 19.5 | 18.8 |
| 84 | 25.6 | 24.8 | 24.0 | 23.2 | 22.4 | 21.6 | 20.9 | 20.1 | 19.4 | 18.7 |
| 85 | 25.6 | 24.8 | 23.9 | 23.1 | 22.3 | 21.6 | 20.8 | 20.1 | 19.3 | 18.6 |
| 86 | 25.5 | 24.7 | 23.9 | 23.1 | 22.3 | 21.5 | 20.7 | 20.0 | 19.2 | 18.5 |
| 87 | 25.5 | 24.7 | 23.8 | 23.0 | 22.2 | 21.4 | 20.7 | 19.9 | 19.2 | 18.4 |
| 88 | 25.5 | 24.6 | 23.8 | 23.0 | 22.2 | 21.4 | 20.6 | 19.8 | 19.1 | 18.3 |
| 89 | 25.4 | 24.6 | 23.8 | 22.9 | 22.1 | 21.3 | 20.5 | 19.8 | 19.0 | 18.3 |
| 90 | 25.4 | 24.6 | 23.7 | 22.9 | 22.1 | 21.3 | 20.5 | 19.7 | 19.0 | 18.2 |
| 91 | 25.4 | 24.5 | 23.7 | 22.9 | 22.1 | 21.3 | 20.5 | 19.7 | 18.9 | 18.2 |
| 92 | 25.4 | 24.5 | 23.7 | 22.9 | 22.0 | 21.2 | 20.4 | 19.6 | 18.9 | 18.1 |
| 93 | 25.4 | 24.5 | 23.7 | 22.8 | 22.0 | 21.2 | 20.4 | 19.6 | 18.8 | 18.1 |

| | 18.0 | 18.8 | 19.6 | 20.4 | 21.2 | 22.0 | 22.8 | 23.6 | 24.5 | 25.3 |
|---|---|---|---|---|---|---|---|---|---|---|
| 94 | 18.0 | 18.8 | 19.6 | 20.4 | 21.2 | 22.0 | 22.8 | 23.6 | 24.5 | 25.3 |
| 95 | 18.0 | 18.8 | 19.6 | 20.3 | 21.1 | 22.0 | 22.8 | 23.6 | 24.5 | 25.3 |
| 96 | 18.0 | 18.8 | 19.5 | 20.3 | 21.1 | 21.9 | 22.8 | 23.6 | 24.5 | 25.3 |
| 97 | 18.0 | 18.7 | 19.5 | 20.3 | 21.1 | 21.9 | 22.8 | 23.6 | 24.5 | 25.3 |
| 98 | 17.9 | 18.7 | 19.5 | 20.3 | 21.1 | 21.9 | 22.8 | 23.6 | 24.4 | 25.3 |
| 99 | 17.9 | 18.7 | 19.5 | 20.3 | 21.1 | 21.9 | 22.7 | 23.6 | 24.4 | 25.3 |
| 100 | 17.9 | 18.7 | 19.5 | 20.3 | 21.1 | 21.9 | 22.7 | 23.6 | 24.4 | 25.3 |
| 101 | 17.9 | 18.7 | 19.4 | 20.2 | 21.1 | 21.9 | 22.7 | 23.6 | 24.4 | 25.3 |
| 102 | 17.9 | 18.6 | 19.4 | 20.2 | 21.1 | 21.9 | 22.7 | 23.6 | 24.4 | 25.3 |
| 103 | 17.9 | 18.6 | 19.4 | 20.2 | 21.0 | 21.9 | 22.7 | 23.6 | 24.4 | 25.3 |
| 104 | 17.8 | 18.6 | 19.4 | 20.2 | 21.0 | 21.9 | 22.7 | 23.5 | 24.4 | 25.3 |
| 105 | 17.8 | 18.6 | 19.4 | 20.2 | 21.0 | 21.9 | 22.7 | 23.5 | 24.4 | 25.3 |
| 106 | 17.8 | 18.6 | 19.4 | 20.2 | 21.0 | 21.9 | 22.7 | 23.5 | 24.4 | 25.3 |
| 107 | 17.8 | 18.6 | 19.4 | 20.2 | 21.0 | 21.8 | 22.7 | 23.5 | 24.4 | 25.2 |
| 108 | 17.8 | 18.6 | 19.4 | 20.2 | 21.0 | 21.8 | 22.7 | 23.5 | 24.4 | 25.2 |
| 109 | 17.8 | 18.6 | 19.4 | 20.2 | 21.0 | 21.8 | 22.7 | 23.5 | 24.4 | 25.2 |
| 110 | 17.8 | 18.6 | 19.4 | 20.2 | 21.0 | 21.8 | 22.7 | 23.5 | 24.4 | 25.2 |
| 111 | 17.8 | 18.6 | 19.4 | 20.2 | 21.0 | 21.8 | 22.7 | 23.5 | 24.4 | 25.2 |
| 112 | 17.8 | 18.6 | 19.4 | 20.2 | 21.0 | 21.8 | 22.7 | 23.5 | 24.4 | 25.2 |
| 113 | 17.8 | 18.6 | 19.4 | 20.2 | 21.0 | 21.8 | 22.7 | 23.5 | 24.4 | 25.2 |
| 114 | 17.8 | 18.6 | 19.4 | 20.2 | 21.0 | 21.8 | 22.7 | 23.5 | 24.4 | 25.2 |
| 115+ | 17.8 | 18.6 | 19.4 | 20.2 | 21.0 | 21.8 | 22.7 | 23.5 | 24.4 | 25.2 |

## Table II (continued)

### (Joint Life and Last Survivor Expectancy)
### (For Use by Owners Whose Spouses Are More Than 10 Years Younger)

| Ages | 70 | 71 | 72 | 73 | 74 | 75 | 76 | 77 | 78 | 79 |
|------|------|------|------|------|------|------|------|------|------|------|
| 70 | 21.8 | 21.3 | 20.9 | 20.6 | 20.2 | 19.9 | 19.6 | 19.4 | 19.1 | 18.9 |
| 71 | 21.3 | 20.9 | 20.5 | 20.1 | 19.7 | 19.4 | 19.1 | 18.8 | 18.5 | 18.3 |
| 72 | 20.9 | 20.5 | 20.0 | 19.6 | 19.3 | 18.9 | 18.6 | 18.3 | 18.0 | 17.7 |
| 73 | 20.6 | 20.1 | 19.6 | 19.2 | 18.8 | 18.4 | 18.1 | 17.8 | 17.5 | 17.2 |
| 74 | 20.2 | 19.7 | 19.3 | 18.8 | 18.4 | 18.0 | 17.6 | 17.3 | 17.0 | 16.7 |
| 75 | 19.9 | 19.4 | 18.9 | 18.4 | 18.0 | 17.6 | 17.2 | 16.8 | 16.5 | 16.2 |
| 76 | 19.6 | 19.1 | 18.6 | 18.1 | 17.6 | 17.2 | 16.8 | 16.4 | 16.0 | 15.7 |
| 77 | 19.4 | 18.8 | 18.3 | 17.8 | 17.3 | 16.8 | 16.4 | 16.0 | 15.6 | 15.3 |
| 78 | 19.1 | 18.5 | 18.0 | 17.5 | 17.0 | 16.5 | 16.0 | 15.6 | 15.2 | 14.9 |
| 79 | 18.9 | 18.3 | 17.7 | 17.2 | 16.7 | 16.2 | 15.7 | 15.3 | 14.9 | 14.5 |
| 80 | 18.7 | 18.1 | 17.5 | 16.9 | 16.4 | 15.9 | 15.4 | 15.0 | 14.5 | 14.1 |
| 81 | 18.5 | 17.9 | 17.3 | 16.7 | 16.2 | 15.6 | 15.1 | 14.7 | 14.2 | 13.8 |
| 82 | 18.3 | 17.7 | 17.1 | 16.5 | 15.9 | 15.4 | 14.9 | 14.4 | 13.9 | 13.5 |
| 83 | 18.2 | 17.5 | 16.9 | 16.3 | 15.7 | 15.2 | 14.7 | 14.2 | 13.7 | 13.2 |
| 84 | 18.0 | 17.4 | 16.7 | 16.1 | 15.5 | 15.0 | 14.4 | 13.9 | 13.4 | 13.0 |
| 85 | 17.9 | 17.3 | 16.6 | 16.0 | 15.4 | 14.8 | 14.3 | 13.7 | 13.2 | 12.8 |
| 86 | 17.8 | 17.1 | 16.5 | 15.8 | 15.2 | 14.6 | 14.1 | 13.5 | 13.0 | 12.5 |
| 87 | 17.7 | 17.0 | 16.4 | 15.7 | 15.1 | 14.5 | 13.9 | 13.4 | 12.9 | 12.4 |

| | | | | | | | | | | |
|---|---|---|---|---|---|---|---|---|---|---|
| 88 | 17.6 | 16.9 | 16.3 | 15.6 | 15.0 | 14.4 | 13.8 | 13.2 | 12.7 | 12.2 |
| 89 | 17.6 | 16.9 | 16.2 | 15.5 | 14.9 | 14.3 | 13.7 | 13.1 | 12.6 | 12.0 |
| 90 | 17.5 | 16.8 | 16.1 | 15.4 | 14.8 | 14.2 | 13.6 | 13.0 | 12.4 | 11.9 |
| 91 | 17.4 | 16.7 | 16.0 | 15.4 | 14.7 | 14.1 | 13.5 | 12.9 | 12.3 | 11.8 |
| 92 | 17.4 | 16.7 | 16.0 | 15.3 | 14.6 | 14.0 | 13.4 | 12.8 | 12.2 | 11.7 |
| 93 | 17.3 | 16.6 | 15.9 | 15.2 | 14.6 | 13.9 | 13.3 | 12.7 | 12.1 | 11.6 |
| 94 | 17.3 | 16.6 | 15.9 | 15.2 | 14.5 | 13.9 | 13.2 | 12.6 | 12.0 | 11.5 |
| 95 | 17.3 | 16.5 | 15.8 | 15.1 | 14.5 | 13.8 | 13.2 | 12.6 | 12.0 | 11.4 |
| 96 | 17.2 | 16.5 | 15.8 | 15.1 | 14.4 | 13.8 | 13.1 | 12.5 | 11.9 | 11.3 |
| 97 | 17.2 | 16.5 | 15.8 | 15.1 | 14.4 | 13.7 | 13.1 | 12.5 | 11.9 | 11.3 |
| 98 | 17.2 | 16.4 | 15.7 | 15.0 | 14.3 | 13.7 | 13.0 | 12.4 | 11.8 | 11.2 |
| 99 | 17.2 | 16.4 | 15.7 | 15.0 | 14.3 | 13.6 | 13.0 | 12.4 | 11.8 | 11.2 |
| 100 | 17.1 | 16.4 | 15.7 | 15.0 | 14.3 | 13.6 | 12.9 | 12.3 | 11.7 | 11.1 |
| 101 | 17.1 | 16.4 | 15.6 | 14.9 | 14.2 | 13.6 | 12.9 | 12.3 | 11.7 | 11.1 |
| 102 | 17.1 | 16.4 | 15.6 | 14.9 | 14.2 | 13.5 | 12.9 | 12.2 | 11.6 | 11.0 |
| 103 | 17.1 | 16.3 | 15.6 | 14.9 | 14.2 | 13.5 | 12.9 | 12.2 | 11.6 | 11.0 |
| 104 | 17.1 | 16.3 | 15.6 | 14.9 | 14.2 | 13.5 | 12.8 | 12.2 | 11.6 | 11.0 |
| 105 | 17.1 | 16.3 | 15.6 | 14.9 | 14.2 | 13.5 | 12.8 | 12.2 | 11.5 | 10.9 |
| 106 | 17.1 | 16.3 | 15.6 | 14.8 | 14.1 | 13.5 | 12.8 | 12.2 | 11.5 | 10.9 |
| 107 | 17.0 | 16.3 | 15.6 | 14.8 | 14.1 | 13.4 | 12.8 | 12.1 | 11.5 | 10.9 |
| 108 | 17.0 | 16.3 | 15.5 | 14.8 | 14.1 | 13.4 | 12.8 | 12.1 | 11.5 | 10.9 |
| 109 | 17.0 | 16.3 | 15.5 | 14.8 | 14.1 | 13.4 | 12.8 | 12.1 | 11.5 | 10.9 |

## Table II (continued)

(Joint Life and Last Survivor Expectancy)
(For Use by Owners Whose Spouses Are More Than 10 Years Younger)

| Ages | 70 | 71 | 72 | 73 | 74 | 75 | 76 | 77 | 78 | 79 |
|---|---|---|---|---|---|---|---|---|---|---|
| 110 | 17.0 | 16.3 | 15.5 | 14.8 | 14.1 | 13.4 | 12.7 | 12.1 | 11.5 | 10.9 |
| 111 | 17.0 | 16.3 | 15.5 | 14.8 | 14.1 | 13.4 | 12.7 | 12.1 | 11.5 | 10.8 |
| 112 | 17.0 | 16.3 | 15.5 | 14.8 | 14.1 | 13.4 | 12.7 | 12.1 | 11.5 | 10.8 |
| 113 | 17.0 | 16.3 | 15.5 | 14.8 | 14.1 | 13.4 | 12.7 | 12.1 | 11.4 | 10.8 |
| 114 | 17.0 | 16.3 | 15.5 | 14.8 | 14.1 | 13.4 | 12.7 | 12.1 | 11.4 | 10.8 |
| 115+ | 17.0 | 16.3 | 15.5 | 14.8 | 14.1 | 13.4 | 12.7 | 12.1 | 11.4 | 10.8 |

## Table II (continued)

(Joint Life and Last Survivor Expectancy)
(For Use by Owners Whose Spouses Are More Than 10 Years Younger)

| AGES | 80 | 81 | 82 | 83 | 84 | 85 | 86 | 87 | 88 | 89 |
|---|---|---|---|---|---|---|---|---|---|---|
| 80 | 13.8 | 13.4 | 13.1 | 12.8 | 12.6 | 12.3 | 12.1 | 11.9 | 11.7 | 11.5 |
| 81 | 13.4 | 13.1 | 12.7 | 12.4 | 12.2 | 11.9 | 11.7 | 11.4 | 11.3 | 11.1 |
| 82 | 13.1 | 12.7 | 12.4 | 12.1 | 11.8 | 11.5 | 11.3 | 11.0 | 10.8 | 10.6 |
| 83 | 12.8 | 12.4 | 12.1 | 11.7 | 11.4 | 11.1 | 10.9 | 10.6 | 10.4 | 10.2 |
| 84 | 12.6 | 12.2 | 11.8 | 11.4 | 11.1 | 10.8 | 10.5 | 10.3 | 10.1 | 9.9 |
| 85 | 12.3 | 11.9 | 11.5 | 11.1 | 10.8 | 10.5 | 10.2 | 9.9 | 9.7 | 9.5 |
| 86 | 12.1 | 11.7 | 11.3 | 10.9 | 10.5 | 10.2 | 9.9 | 9.6 | 9.4 | 9.2 |
| 87 | 11.9 | 11.4 | 11.0 | 10.6 | 10.3 | 9.9 | 9.6 | 9.4 | 9.1 | 8.9 |
| 88 | 11.7 | 11.3 | 10.8 | 10.4 | 10.1 | 9.7 | 9.4 | 9.1 | 8.8 | 8.6 |

| | 11.5 | 11.1 | 10.6 | 10.2 | 9.9 | 9.5 | 9.2 | 8.9 | 8.6 | 8.3 |
|---|---|---|---|---|---|---|---|---|---|---|
| 89 | 11.5 | 11.1 | 10.6 | 10.2 | 9.9 | 9.5 | 9.2 | 8.9 | 8.6 | 8.3 |
| 90 | 11.4 | 10.9 | 10.5 | 10.1 | 9.7 | 9.3 | 9.0 | 8.6 | 8.3 | 8.1 |
| 91 | 11.3 | 10.8 | 10.3 | 9.9 | 9.5 | 9.1 | 8.8 | 8.4 | 8.1 | 7.9 |
| 92 | 11.2 | 10.7 | 10.2 | 9.8 | 9.3 | 9.0 | 8.6 | 8.3 | 8.0 | 7.7 |
| 93 | 11.1 | 10.6 | 10.1 | 9.6 | 9.2 | 8.8 | 8.5 | 8.1 | 7.8 | 7.5 |
| 94 | 11.0 | 10.5 | 10.0 | 9.5 | 9.1 | 8.7 | 8.3 | 8.0 | 7.6 | 7.3 |
| 95 | 10.9 | 10.4 | 9.9 | 9.4 | 9.0 | 8.6 | 8.2 | 7.8 | 7.5 | 7.2 |
| 96 | 10.8 | 10.3 | 9.8 | 9.3 | 8.9 | 8.5 | 8.1 | 7.7 | 7.4 | 7.1 |
| 97 | 10.7 | 10.2 | 9.7 | 9.2 | 8.8 | 8.4 | 8.0 | 7.6 | 7.3 | 6.9 |
| 98 | 10.7 | 10.1 | 9.6 | 9.2 | 8.7 | 8.3 | 7.9 | 7.5 | 7.1 | 6.8 |
| 99 | 10.6 | 10.1 | 9.6 | 9.1 | 8.6 | 8.2 | 7.8 | 7.4 | 7.0 | 6.7 |
| 100 | 10.6 | 10.0 | 9.5 | 9.0 | 8.5 | 8.1 | 7.7 | 7.3 | 6.9 | 6.6 |
| 101 | 10.5 | 10.0 | 9.4 | 9.0 | 8.5 | 8.0 | 7.6 | 7.2 | 6.9 | 6.5 |
| 102 | 10.5 | 9.9 | 9.4 | 8.9 | 8.4 | 8.0 | 7.5 | 7.1 | 6.8 | 6.4 |
| 103 | 10.4 | 9.9 | 9.4 | 8.8 | 8.4 | 7.9 | 7.5 | 7.1 | 6.7 | 6.3 |
| 104 | 10.4 | 9.8 | 9.3 | 8.8 | 8.3 | 7.9 | 7.4 | 7.0 | 6.6 | 6.3 |
| 105 | 10.4 | 9.8 | 9.3 | 8.8 | 8.3 | 7.8 | 7.4 | 7.0 | 6.6 | 6.2 |
| 106 | 10.3 | 9.8 | 9.2 | 8.7 | 8.2 | 7.8 | 7.3 | 6.9 | 6.5 | 6.2 |
| 107 | 10.3 | 9.8 | 9.2 | 8.7 | 8.2 | 7.7 | 7.3 | 6.9 | 6.5 | 6.1 |
| 108 | 10.3 | 9.7 | 9.2 | 8.7 | 8.2 | 7.7 | 7.3 | 6.8 | 6.4 | 6.1 |
| 109 | 10.3 | 9.7 | 9.2 | 8.7 | 8.2 | 7.7 | 7.2 | 6.8 | 6.4 | 6.0 |
| 110 | 10.3 | 9.7 | 9.2 | 8.6 | 8.1 | 7.7 | 7.2 | 6.8 | 6.4 | 6.0 |

## Table II (continued)
### (Joint Life and Last Survivor Expectancy)
### (For Use by Owners Whose Spouses Are More Than 10 Years Younger)

| AGES | 80 | 81 | 82 | 83 | 84 | 85 | 86 | 87 | 88 | 89 |
|------|------|-----|-----|-----|-----|-----|-----|-----|-----|-----|
| 111 | 10.3 | 9.7 | 9.1 | 8.6 | 8.1 | 7.6 | 7.2 | 6.8 | 6.3 | 6.0 |
| 112 | 10.2 | 9.7 | 9.1 | 8.6 | 8.1 | 7.6 | 7.2 | 6.7 | 6.3 | 5.9 |
| 113 | 10.2 | 9.7 | 9.1 | 8.6 | 8.1 | 7.6 | 7.2 | 6.7 | 6.3 | 5.9 |
| 114 | 10.2 | 9.7 | 9.1 | 8.6 | 8.1 | 7.6 | 7.1 | 6.7 | 6.3 | 5.9 |
| 115+ | 10.2 | 9.7 | 9.1 | 8.6 | 8.1 | 7.6 | 7.1 | 6.7 | 6.3 | 5.9 |

## Table II (continued)
### (Joint Life and Last Survivor Expectancy)
### (For Use by Owners Whose Spouses Are More Than 10 Years Younger)

| AGES | 90 | 91 | 92 | 93 | 94 | 95 | 96 | 97 | 98 | 99 |
|------|-----|-----|-----|-----|-----|-----|-----|-----|-----|-----|
| 90 | 7.8 | 7.6 | 7.4 | 7.2 | 7.1 | 6.9 | 6.8 | 6.6 | 6.5 | 6.4 |
| 91 | 7.6 | 7.4 | 7.2 | 7.0 | 6.8 | 6.7 | 6.5 | 6.4 | 6.3 | 6.1 |
| 92 | 7.4 | 7.2 | 7.0 | 6.8 | 6.6 | 6.4 | 6.3 | 6.1 | 6.0 | 5.9 |
| 93 | 7.2 | 7.0 | 6.8 | 6.6 | 6.4 | 6.2 | 6.1 | 5.9 | 5.8 | 5.6 |
| 94 | 7.1 | 6.8 | 6.6 | 6.4 | 6.2 | 6.0 | 5.9 | 5.7 | 5.6 | 5.4 |
| 95 | 6.9 | 6.7 | 6.4 | 6.2 | 6.0 | 5.8 | 5.7 | 5.5 | 5.4 | 5.2 |
| 96 | 6.8 | 6.5 | 6.3 | 6.1 | 5.9 | 5.7 | 5.5 | 5.3 | 5.2 | 5.0 |
| 97 | 6.6 | 6.4 | 6.1 | 5.9 | 5.7 | 5.5 | 5.3 | 5.2 | 5.0 | 4.9 |

| | | | | | | | | | | |
|---|---|---|---|---|---|---|---|---|---|---|
| 98 | 6.5 | 6.3 | 6.0 | 5.8 | 5.6 | 5.4 | 5.2 | 5.0 | 4.8 | 4.7 |
| 99 | 6.4 | 6.1 | 5.9 | 5.6 | 5.4 | 5.2 | 5.0 | 4.9 | 4.7 | 4.5 |
| 100 | 6.3 | 6.0 | 5.8 | 5.5 | 5.3 | 5.1 | 4.9 | 4.7 | 4.5 | 4.4 |
| 101 | 6.2 | 5.9 | 5.6 | 5.4 | 5.2 | 5.0 | 4.8 | 4.6 | 4.4 | 4.2 |
| 102 | 6.1 | 5.8 | 5.5 | 5.3 | 5.1 | 4.8 | 4.6 | 4.4 | 4.3 | 4.1 |
| 103 | 6.0 | 5.7 | 5.4 | 5.2 | 5.0 | 4.7 | 4.5 | 4.3 | 4.1 | 4.0 |
| 104 | 5.9 | 5.6 | 5.4 | 5.1 | 4.9 | 4.6 | 4.4 | 4.2 | 4.0 | 3.8 |
| 105 | 5.9 | 5.6 | 5.3 | 5.0 | 4.8 | 4.5 | 4.3 | 4.1 | 3.9 | 3.7 |
| 106 | 5.8 | 5.5 | 5.2 | 4.9 | 4.7 | 4.5 | 4.2 | 4.0 | 3.8 | 3.6 |
| 107 | 5.8 | 5.4 | 5.1 | 4.9 | 4.6 | 4.4 | 4.2 | 3.9 | 3.7 | 3.5 |
| 108 | 5.7 | 5.4 | 5.1 | 4.8 | 4.6 | 4.3 | 4.1 | 3.9 | 3.7 | 3.5 |
| 109 | 5.7 | 5.3 | 5.0 | 4.8 | 4.5 | 4.3 | 4.0 | 3.8 | 3.6 | 3.4 |
| 110 | 5.6 | 5.3 | 5.0 | 4.7 | 4.5 | 4.2 | 4.0 | 3.8 | 3.5 | 3.3 |
| 111 | 5.6 | 5.3 | 5.0 | 4.7 | 4.4 | 4.2 | 3.9 | 3.7 | 3.5 | 3.3 |
| 112 | 5.6 | 5.3 | 4.9 | 4.7 | 4.4 | 4.1 | 3.9 | 3.7 | 3.5 | 3.2 |
| 113 | 5.6 | 5.2 | 4.9 | 4.6 | 4.4 | 4.1 | 3.9 | 3.6 | 3.4 | 3.2 |
| 114 | 5.6 | 5.2 | 4.9 | 4.6 | 4.3 | 4.1 | 3.9 | 3.6 | 3.4 | 3.2 |
| 115+ | 5.5 | 5.2 | 4.9 | 4.6 | 4.3 | 4.1 | 3.8 | 3.6 | 3.4 | 3.1 |

Table II (continued)

(Joint Life and Last Survivor Expectancy)
(For Use by Owners Whose Spouses Are More Than 10 Years Younger)

| AGES | 100 | 101 | 102 | 103 | 104 | 105 | 106 | 107 | 108 | 109 |
|---|---|---|---|---|---|---|---|---|---|---|
| 100 | 4.2 | 4.1 | 3.9 | 3.8 | 3.7 | 3.5 | 3.4 | 3.3 | 3.3 | 3.2 |
| 101 | 4.1 | 3.9 | 3.7 | 3.6 | 3.5 | 3.4 | 3.2 | 3.1 | 3.1 | 3.0 |
| 102 | 3.9 | 3.7 | 3.6 | 3.4 | 3.3 | 3.2 | 3.1 | 3.0 | 2.9 | 2.8 |
| 103 | 3.8 | 3.6 | 3.4 | 3.3 | 3.2 | 3.0 | 2.9 | 2.8 | 2.7 | 2.6 |
| 104 | 3.7 | 3.5 | 3.3 | 3.2 | 3.0 | 2.9 | 2.7 | 2.6 | 2.5 | 2.4 |
| 105 | 3.5 | 3.4 | 3.2 | 3.0 | 2.9 | 2.7 | 2.6 | 2.5 | 2.4 | 2.3 |
| 106 | 3.4 | 3.2 | 3.1 | 2.9 | 2.7 | 2.6 | 2.4 | 2.3 | 2.2 | 2.1 |
| 107 | 3.3 | 3.1 | 3.0 | 2.8 | 2.6 | 2.5 | 2.3 | 2.2 | 2.1 | 2.0 |
| 108 | 3.3 | 3.1 | 2.9 | 2.7 | 2.5 | 2.4 | 2.2 | 2.1 | 1.9 | 1.8 |
| 109 | 3.2 | 3.0 | 2.8 | 2.6 | 2.4 | 2.3 | 2.1 | 2.0 | 1.8 | 1.7 |
| 110 | 3.1 | 2.9 | 2.7 | 2.5 | 2.3 | 2.2 | 2.0 | 1.9 | 1.7 | 1.6 |
| 111 | 3.1 | 2.9 | 2.7 | 2.5 | 2.3 | 2.1 | 1.9 | 1.8 | 1.6 | 1.5 |
| 112 | 3.0 | 2.8 | 2.6 | 2.4 | 2.2 | 2.0 | 1.9 | 1.7 | 1.5 | 1.4 |
| 113 | 3.0 | 2.8 | 2.6 | 2.4 | 2.2 | 2.0 | 1.8 | 1.6 | 1.5 | 1.3 |
| 114 | 3.0 | 2.7 | 2.5 | 2.3 | 2.1 | 1.9 | 1.8 | 1.6 | 1.4 | 1.3 |
| 115+ | 2.9 | 2.7 | 2.5 | 2.3 | 2.1 | 1.9 | 1.7 | 1.5 | 1.4 | 1.2 |

## Table II (continued)
### (Joint Life and Last Survivor Expectancy)
### (For Use by Owners Whose Spouses Are More Than 10 Years Younger)

| AGES | 110 | 111 | 112 | 113 | 114 | 115+ |
|------|-----|-----|-----|-----|-----|------|
| 110  | 1.5 | 1.4 | 1.3 | 1.2 | 1.1 | 1.1  |
| 111  | 1.4 | 1.2 | 1.1 | 1.1 | 1.0 | 1.0  |
| 112  | 1.3 | 1.1 | 1.0 | 1.0 | 1.0 | 1.0  |
| 113  | 1.2 | 1.1 | 1.0 | 1.0 | 1.0 | 1.0  |
| 114  | 1.1 | 1.0 | 1.0 | 1.0 | 1.0 | 1.0  |
| 115+ | 1.1 | 1.0 | 1.0 | 1.0 | 1.0 | 1.0  |

233

## APPENDIX C

# Resources

## THE INTERNET

The Internet has leveled the playing field for individual investors. The advantage that institutional investors used to have was information, delivered immediately. Now, rather than read about it in the *Wall Street Journal* tomorrow, you have access to breaking news, such as earnings announcements and interest rate changes, as it is reported. You can learn about investment techniques, find financial data on public companies, and price your portfolio in real time. However, there are literally thousands of Web sites to choose from, and they change quickly. Finding the right resources for the information that you need can make the process much easier and less time consuming. The following lists, presented in alphabetical order, contain some of the best Web sites for investment information.

### Financial Megasites

These are the comprehensive sites, often a good place to start. Consider making one of them your home page, the first thing you see when you log onto the Net. They offer investment research, quotes, educational articles, and much more.

## CBS MarketWatch (cbsmarketwatch.com)

This site is one of the best for current financial news. Regular columns plus breaking features make it easy to stay abreast of the financial world. Set up portfolios and search through a library of articles using either symbols or keywords.

## MoneyCentral Investor (www.investor.msn.com)

A comprehensive financial site run by Microsoft, MoneyCentral is easy to navigate and provides good research. For those seeking news, a bonus is the link with MSNBC News and a synopsis of important *Wall Street Journal* articles for the day. The Research Wizard area provides a full fundamental analysis of any stock, complete with comparisons to others in the same industry.

## The Motley Fool (www.fool.com)

A good place for beginning to intermediate investors, this Web site is easy to navigate and packed full of educational articles. Try Fool's School and Personal Finance. The Fool's signature editorial style is a commonsense, sometimes irreverent, look at investing. Bulletin boards at this site are very popular.

## Quicken.com (www.quicken.com)

Sponsored by the software company of the same name, Quicken.com provides a wide variety of financial information, from household issues like mortgages, taxes, and insurance to investing in stocks and mutual funds. This is a good place to go if you want to learn about a particular topic.

## Smart Money (www.smartmoney.com)

This site, part of *Smart Money* magazine, offers a good mix of current news, columns, financial data, and education. Proprietary features, such as the Map of the Market, a green and red heat map of the daily performance in industries and individual stocks, make it worth the trip to this site.

## Stockpoint (www.investor.stockpoint.com)

Sponsored by Pinnacor, Stockpoint's best feature is its Investor Tools section. You can find the best and worst stocks and mutual funds or screen the database, using your own investment criteria.

It offers several retirement calculators to help you calculate when you can retire and how much to save, plus asset allocation for your retirement plan.

## Wall Street City (www.wallstreetcity.com)

One of the best on the Internet for stock research, this site is packed full of information to screen stocks and find out about those you have. The stock screener allows you to input 70 different criteria. A great section (13 different categories) of financial calculators includes the usual home mortgage and retirement calculators, plus less common finds, such as bond yield to maturity. Much of the site is accessible for no cost. ProStation, its subscription service, which offers real-time quotes and advanced charting, is $59.95 per month.

## Yahoo! Finance (finance.yahoo.com)

Yahoo! Finance is one of the most popular financial portals. Quote pages are not easy on the eye, but they are functional and full of information. From a quote you can go to many different research pages, including a company profile with a link to the company's own home page.

## Zacks.Com (www.zacks.com)

Though the home page is cluttered at first glance, it provides a useful composite of information, including a market synopsis, daily EPS and sales surprises, and personal portfolios with price targets and a progress chart. Try one of ten predefined screens, or input up to 96 different variables in the custom screen. The Dawn Patrol column gives daily insight into where the market might be headed, based on early futures trading and news or government reports already issued. It also notes the time of day that reports are expected.

## Retirement

Many financial sites, especially those of large mutual fund companies like Fidelity and Vanguard, offer excellent retirement information. This section includes only retirement-specific sites.

## 401(k) Help Center (www.401khelpcenter.com)

Geared more toward the retirement plan professional but still helpful for the participant, this site provides mountains of articles on current retirement plan topics. Especially well covered are current legislation and legal issues.

## 403(b)wise (www.403bwise.com)

This site was created by Southern California educators John Moore and Dan Otter after their search for unbiased, accurate information on 403(b) plans turned up few resources. Areas of interest include frequently asked questions (FAQs), calculators, and new tax laws. Don't miss Top Ten 403(b) Must Reads, which includes articles from "Ten Facts on 403(b)s" to "What's That Fishy Smell in the Teachers' Lounge," about financial planners.

## About.com Retirement Planning (www.retireplan.about.com)

This is a good educational site. Learn more about retirement planning and investing in general here. Be sure to try the different calculators, including one that will help you decide whether to borrow from your 401(k) plan.

## Employee Benefits Legal Resource Site (www.benefitsattorney.com)

Run by employee benefits attorney Carol Calhoun, this site is a good resource for new developments in 403(b) and 457 plans, and the Research Tools section includes IRS documents pertaining to employer plans.

## mPowercafe.com (www.mpowercafe.com)

This is an excellent site for information about 401(k), 403(b), and 457 plan rules and regulations. Begin with Features or Expert Q&A, and if you can't find what you need there, search the archives of articles or ask Ted Benna directly through the Web site's e-mail form. Benna, creator of the 401(k) plan, writes a plain-English column every week in which he answers questions submitted to the site.

## Plan Sponsor (www.plansponsor.com)

Here is a good resource for information about employer retirement plans. Look for articles about changes to rules and regulations or to find out what other companies are doing with their plans. The site also includes a comprehensive glossary of terms.

## Portfolio Survival Simulator (www.portfoliosurvival.com)
This is Bill Swerbenski's Web site, where you can learn about his *Portfolio Survival Simulator* and download it if you choose. Explanations for each of the three types of simulations are provided, as is an example of the results you might obtain.

## Quicken (www.quicken.com/retirement)
The retirement center at Quicken offers a wealth of information about retirement plans. Look here for calculators of nearly every type, from how much you should save for retirement to whether your spouse can afford to stop working.

## Retire on Your Terms (www.RetireOnYourTerms.com)
This site, sponsored by the National Association of Variable Annuities, is a good place to learn more about annuities. Be aware that the information provided casts a favorable light on annuities as retirement investments.

## Roth IRA Web site (www.rothira.com)
This site compiles articles about the Roth IRA. Much of it is designated for financial planning professionals, meaning it can get pretty technical. However, if you need specific information about rules and uses of the Roth IRA, this is a good place to start.

## Smart Money (www.smartmoney.com/retirement)
This site features articles about retirement planning as well as general information about retirement accounts. If you aren't contributing the maximum to your plan, be sure to try the 401(k) Contribution Calculator, which figures how your take-home pay will change if you increase or decrease your contributions.

## Tim Younkin (www.timyounkin.com)
This site, run by pharmacist and individual investor Tim Younkin, offers comprehensive coverage of news, rules, and legal aspects of 401(k) plans, 403(b) plans, and IRAs. It includes recommended reading and a host of links to other sites.

# News

Nearly all financial Web sites have some sort of market commentary and recent news articles; however, the sites whose primary focus is news are much more comprehensive and are generally updated more frequently.

## Bloomberg (www.bloomberg.com)
This is a cluttered but valuable source of breaking news and financial articles. Follow your favorite columnist or choose by topic. Includes key currency, bond, and commodity rates and prices.

## CNBC.com (www.cnbc.com)
CNBC is an easy-to-navigate financial news site with proprietary news stories plus stories from MSNBC and the *Wall Street Journal.* Find schedules for CNBC television plus lists of television show guest appearances. CNBC 101 gives a good explanation on reading a ticker tape for those who watch the television programs. The *Deluxe Portfolio Tracker*, available for download, is one of the best around.

## CNN/Money (www.cnnfn.com)
This site is packed with information in a layout that can make the numerous headlines and categories overwhelming. But once you take time to hit your areas of interest, the site becomes easy to navigate. Coverage of international markets is extensive. You can find a detailed schedule of television programs on CNNfn's cable station.

## The Financial Center (www.tfc.com)
Though its home page is something from the dark ages, The Financial Center has excellent columns. If you find a particular contributor that you like, you can click on that person's name for a daily column. A highlight is its *Market Mavens* radio show, which interviews experts on a variety of topics. Interviews are posted daily, and users have access to archives.

## The Street.com (www.thestreet.com)
A news site for the active trader, market commentary at The Street.com is updated frequently throughout the day. James Cramer, an opinionated hedge fund manager on Wall Street, is the

most popular and prolific columnist. Articles are easy to find, but many are reserved for paying subscribers only.

## Wall Street Journal (www.wsj.com)

All the information in the print version plus updates throughout the day. The full database of Dow Jones publications, including *Barron's*, is available for searching. A year's subscription is $79, or $39 for those already receiving the print version.

## Stock Research

### American Association of Individual Investors (AAII) (www.aaii.com)

A $49 annual membership in AAII includes 10 newsletters plus access to members-only areas of the Web site. The site offers advanced, in-depth articles on investing techniques as well as a good amount of basic information. The stock-screening tool can use preset parameters based on the investment criteria of respected investment gurus to offer up lists of stocks that fit those criteria.

### Big Charts (www.bigcharts.com)

Self-proclaimed as "The world's coolest investment charting and research site," Big Charts has both quick (preset) and interactive charting. The interactive charting allows you to change variables and compare results to other stocks, indices, and indicators. Once you have decided on your settings, you can save them for future visits. Other good research includes loads of industry data and Big Reports, which sorts a chosen market for price or volume movements.

### Briefing.com (www.briefing.com)

Popular for its market commentaries, which are part of the free package along with standard fare such as quotes and portfolios, Briefing.com offers two levels of service in addition to the free package. The Stock Analysis package, at $9.95 per month, provides information on upgrades and downgrades, company reports, and splits and earnings calendars. The Professional package, at $25 per month, is for bond traders, with yield curves, bond quotes, and fixed-income market analysis.

### ClearStation (www.clearstation.com)

Investors and traders using technical analysis will like this site. Charts are extensive, and each day's A-list has stocks with notations like "MACD bullish" or "Stochastic bullish." Below each chart is a message board of comments from other ClearStation devotees. You can compare up to 100 stocks on one chart. For newcomers to charting, the education center provides a tutorial.

### Investor's Business Daily (www.investors.com)

This site was developed by William O'Neil, founder of *Investor's Business Daily* and author of *How to Make Money in Stocks: A Winning System in Good Times or Bad*. His CANSLIM method of investing uses a combination of fundamental analysis to choose companies and technical analysis to time purchases and sales. The subscription portion of the site, Daily Graphs Online, provides fundamental and technical data on over 11,000 stocks. Subscriptions run from $199 to $1000 annually. CANSLIM enthusiasts who are active traders might want to try the 7-day trial for $19.95 (applicable to the first month's subscription).

### Earnings Whispers.com (www.earningswhispers.com)

A resource for the "whisper number" that you often hear about in statements such as, "XYZ company reported fourth-quarter earnings of $1.20 a share. That was a penny above the whisper number and 8 cents above consensus estimates." About 3 to 4 weeks before earnings announcements, this site publishes estimates that are alleged to be from inside sources. Enter the symbol for over 4000 stocks to see the whisper estimate, consensus estimates from investment analysts, earnings dates, and a bulletin board for each stock.

### FreeEDGAR (www.freeedgar.com)

Find SEC filings for publicly held corporations here. You can search by ticker symbol, company name, and by specified text. Register for the FreeEDGAR Watchlist to be notified by e-mail when companies on your watch list file new documents.

### Hoover's Online (www.hoovers.com)

Hoover is a well-known industry provider of detailed company financial profiles; in fact, much of the corporate financial information at other sites is provided by Hoover. The site provides a free synopsis of each company, and for a paid subscription, you can get the full report. Hoover's IPO Central has a calendar of upcoming IPOs and a scorecard of statistics and returns for IPOs by individual stock and by industry. This, as well as quotes and basic investor education, is free.

### Multex Investor Network (www.multexinvestor.com)
This site offers one-stop shopping for professional research reports from over 500 providers, including the likes of Morgan Stanley Dean Witter, Goldman Sachs, and Merrill Lynch. Reports are available for download ranging in price from $5 to $150. Most are $5 to $10. NetScreen, formerly found at MarketGuide.com, is available here, providing screens of over 9000 stocks using preset or user-chosen variables. Other tools, such as the What's Hot/What's Not page, provide lists of stocks whose prices have increased or decreased the most in 1- and 5-day periods.

### Stock Consultant (www.stockconsultant.com)
Enter the symbol and click on the Consult button to receive a several-page technical analysis of any stock. Bullish and bearish indicators are given as well as breakout points, resistance and support levels, and more. The candlestick charts used are explained in a linked article.

### Wright Investors (www.wisi.com)
This site has an incredible database of international stocks in its Research Center area. Reports on over 18,000 companies in 50 countries provide a Wright Quality Rating, company profile, research report, analysis summary, sales analysis, and earnings analysis. To make comparisons easier, there is a feature that will change all figures into the currency of your choice.

## Mutual Funds

Sifting through the attributes of the thousands of mutual funds available is exponentially easier when using an Internet search than when flipping through pages of research reports. The sites noted here are not related to mutual fund providers, though most have links to them.

## Brill's Mutual Funds Interactive (www.brill.com)

This site is full of links to providers of useful mutual fund information, as well as to the funds themselves. Fund News and Views contains articles about mutual funds from a variety of different sources and the Experts area keeps archives of articles categorized by author. Money Manager Profiles gives insight into the thought processes of your favorite fund managers.

## Fund Alarm (www.fundalarm.com)

This is a site not of the best mutual funds, but of the worst. The 3-Alarm Funds, which have underperformed their appropriate benchmarks for the past 12 months, 3 years, and 5 years, make up a good sell list. The Fund Alarm Honor Roll is a list of funds with no alarms. Data are updated monthly.

## IndexFunds.com (www.indexfunds.com)

This is the place to look for a comprehensive listing of index funds, both open ended (called "retail" here) and exchange traded. Data Central provides screens of indices, index mutual funds, and exchange-traded funds. You may input variables to get just the funds that pass your criteria or enter "all" for a complete listing.

## Morningstar (www.morningstar.com)

This is a good, all-around financial Web site from one of the leaders in mutual fund analysis. It includes stock and current market information as well as mutual fund articles and performance data. Basic interactive screens and preset screens are free. Advanced screens and other more in-depth information are available for a fee.

## Insurance

## A.M. Best (www.ambest.com)

A.M. Best is the leader in insurance company financial strength ratings. Though the site isn't particularly user-friendly, you can find company ratings here.

## Insurance.com (www.insurance.com)

This is a Fidelity Investments site where you can search for insurance and annuity quotes and even submit some applications online. The Insurance 101 articles and FAQ sections provide good basic information about the different types of insurance.

### Insure.com (www.insure.com)
This educational site has articles about insurance as well as calculators to help you decide how much you need. A search engine provided by Quotesmith.com compares quotes on life insurance and annuities after you enter your parameters.

## Bonds

Stocks get all the space in the financial news, and they seem to get all the space on the Internet too. There are, however, a few sites dedicated to bonds, though not nearly the variety and quality that can be found for stocks.

### Bonds Online (www.bondsonline.com)
This site has basic information on bond investing and links to other sites, such as rating agencies. Links under General Information and Q&A in The Bond Professor are helpful for the novice bond investor. The most valuable part of the site is its pricing area, which covers over 15,000 bonds. Prices and yields for Treasuries are real time, and offerings for other bonds are updated throughout the day.

### Bureau of the Public Debt (www.publicdebt.treas.gov)
Look no further for basic education about U.S. Treasury securities. Find the latest auction results and current savings bond yields. You can even buy Treasuries online through the TreasuryDirect service.

### ConvertBond.com (www.convertbond.com)
Operated by Morgan Stanley Dean Witter, this specialized site focuses only on convertible bonds and notes. For $120 per year (there is a 2-week free trial), you may perform 75 securities searches and view 150 detailed analysis reports.

### Investing in Bonds (www.investinginbonds.com)
Produced by the Bond Market Association, an industry trade group, this site is the best place for the beginner to learn about bonds and the bond markets. The municipal bond pricing area provides the

previous day's transactions for the state chosen, sorted by any one of seven variables (rating, volume, and so on). Individual transaction details are then available from the results page. Corporate bond transactions are available in a similar fashion.

## Government Resources

### Bureau of the Public Debt (www.publicdebt.treas.gov)

This is the home of TreasuryDirect, a service of the government that allows you to purchase U.S. Treasury securities online. The Savings Bond Connection, also located here, allows online purchases of U.S. Savings Bonds. In addition to transaction capabilities, this site is full of educational material concerning savings bonds and Treasury securities.

### Internal Revenue Service (www.irs.gov)

While no one would ever describe it as user-friendly, the IRS Web site can come in handy for forms and publications if you already know what you're looking for. You can place an order for most publications, and many are available for viewing in PDF format.

### Social Security Administration (www.ssa.gov)

Check this site for general information about Social Security. The Frequently Asked Questions (FAQ) area is good, and you can conduct some SSA business online. Try getting an estimate of your Social Security benefits with an online request for a Social Security Statement. You may be familiar with this form by its former name: Request for Personal Earnings and Benefits Estimate Statement. The results will be mailed to you in 2 to 3 weeks.

## Miscellaneous

### Investopedia (www.investopedia.com)

For definitions on investing terms, both quick and in-depth, look here. You can search by word or by topic.

### National Association of Investors Corporation (NAIC) (www.better-investing.org)

Don't forget this one ends in .org, not .com. This is the Web site for the NAIC, an organization devoted to investment clubs. You will find information about how to start a club, sample partnership agreements, and recommended IRS filings. The site also includes education based on NAIC investment principles and access to *Better Investing*, the NAIC newsletter, for members of the organization.

## TaxPlanet (www.taxplanet.com)

A good site for tax information, Tax Planet is strongest on current news and legislation, weakest on actual tax rules, making it a good complementary site to the IRS's site. An interesting feature is the proposed tax plans from political candidates.

## Risk Grades (www.riskgrades.com)

Enter your portfolio on this site and receive an evaluation of the risk characteristics of your investments. See how your risk changes over time with the RiskChart, or measure the risk of a single investment.

# TAX INFORMATION BY TELEPHONE

If you do not have access to the Internet or find that navigating the IRS Web site for help on tax questions is unproductive, you might try one of the prerecorded help topics available from the IRS. The service is available 24 hours a day, 7 days a week. The toll-free telephone number is (800) 829-4477. Some topics of interest include the following:

| Topic Number | Subject |
| --- | --- |
| 309 | Roth IRA contributions |
| 403 | Interest received |
| 404 | Dividends |
| 409 | Capital gains and losses |
| 410 | Pensions and annuities |
| 411 | Pensions: the general rule and the simplified method |
| 412 | Lump-sum distributions |
| 413 | Rollovers from retirement plans |
| 423 | Social Security and equivalent railroad retirement benefits |
| 424 | 401(k) plans |
| 428 | Roth IRA distributions |
| 451 | IRAs |
| 555 | Ten-year tax option for lump-sum distributions |
| 557 | Tax on early distributions from traditional and Roth IRAs |
| 558 | Tax on early distributions from retirement plans |
| 610 | Retirement savings contributions credit |

Understanding investment terminology is key to assessing the risks and potential rewards of securities. As Mark Twain aptly put it, "The difference between the right word and the almost right word is the difference between lightning and the lightning bug."

**10-K**  The financial report that companies are required to file with the SEC each year. The 10-K is much more detailed than the shareholders' annual report.

**1099-INT; 1099-DIV**  Payers of dividends and interest issue 1099s to the IRS and investors. These forms detail the amount of dividends or interest that the investors received during the year.

**1099-OID**  The 1099 form issued to owners of taxable original-issue discount securities for the amount of implied interest received during the year. Dictated by formula, the amount is roughly comparable to the amount by which a discounted security increases in value each year as it nears maturity.

**accrued interest**  Interest owed but not yet paid. If a bond is sold between semi-annual interest payments, the buyer must pay the seller for the interest accrued from the last interest payment through the purchase date. The buyer will be reimbursed at the next interest date when he or she receives interest for the entire 6 months, as if he or she had owned the bond the whole time.

**advance/decline index**  The cumulative total of the daily number of stocks advancing in price less the daily number of stocks declining. It is used by technical analysts as a measure of breadth. When graphically presented, it is called the *advance/decline line*.

**after-tax return**  The return on an investment calculated after payment of the required income and capital gains taxes.

**all-or-none order**  An order to purchase or sell a stock only if the entire order can be filled.

**alpha**  The mathematical estimate of the return on a security when the return on the market is zero.

**alternative minimum tax (AMT)**  An alternative method of computing taxable income that includes items normally excluded from the computation—specifically losses from passive investments and interest paid on municipal bonds. Retirees who don't have earned income can easily be subject to AMT.

**American depositary receipt (ADR)**  A certificate that represents ownership in a foreign stock. ADRs are traded on U.S. stock exchanges.

**annual report**  The annual financial statement issued by a corporation. Annual reports generally contain a balance sheet, income statement, cash flow statement, and statement of changes in shareholder equity, as well as supporting documentation.

**annuity**  (1) A stream of equal payments made at regular intervals. (2) A life insurance product that provides tax-deferred investment growth before retirement and a series of payments after retirement. Annuities may be *fixed*, with a set rate of return, or *variable*, with returns based on underlying investments.

**arbitrage**  The simultaneous purchase and sale of the same asset in two different markets or two substantially similar assets in the same or different markets in order to profit from their price differences.

**arbitration**  Settling a dispute by agreeing to the decision of an impartial third party. Most securities firms require clients to agree to arbitration rather than settle disputes through the court system.

**asked price**  The lowest price at which a dealer will sell a security.

**asset**  Anything of monetary value owned by an individual, business, or organization. A corporation's balance sheet lists the firm's assets and liabilities (debts).

**asset allocation**  The investment strategy of diversifying among asset types, such as cash, stocks, bonds, and real estate, in order to reduce risk.

**at-the-money option**  A put or call option whose strike price is equal to the price of the underlying stock.

**back-end load**  The common name for a contingent deferred sales charge. This is a commission charged when mutual fund or annuity shares are sold.

**basic shares outstanding**  The actual number of a corporation's shares that are held by the public.

**basis point**  One-hundredth of 1 percent, or 0.01 percent, the unit of measure used to differentiate bond yields. A bond yield that changes from 7.25 to 7.5 percent has risen 25 basis points.

**bear market**  A period of time in which securities prices decline.

**beta**  A statistical measure of the price volatility of a stock relative to market averages. A beta of 1.00 connotes volatility equal to that of the market. A beta of 1.5 predicts a 1.5 percent change in the stock's price for every 1 percent change in the market.

**blue chip**  A stock with a long history of stability in earnings and dividends.

**bond**  A debt security that allows the issuer to borrow the face value of the bond while promising to repay it upon maturity, plus periodic interest until that time. Bonds may be issued by corporations, the U.S. government, or state and local municipalities. A bond owner is a creditor of the issuer and does not have any ownership rights.

**bond rating**  A rating for creditworthiness as determined by a rating service, such as Standard & Poor's, Moody's, or Fitch. Ratings assess the issuer's ability to pay interest and repay principal and range from AAA or Aaa to D.

**book-entry security**  A security that is not issued in paper form, but is held in an account for the owner, who receives a receipt or confirmation. U.S. Treasury bills are book-entry securities.

**book value; book value per share**  The book value of a corporation is the liqui-dation value of the business according to the financial statements. Subtracting all liabilities from assets results in book value. Dividing book value by the outstand-ing shares gives the book value per share.

**breakpoints**  The dollar amounts that must be invested in order for a mutual fund commission rate to be reduced.

**breakup value**  The sum of the market values of the individual parts of a corpora-tion when valued as independent businesses. Firms may spin off divisions to share-holders when the breakup value exceeds current market value. Takeovers commonly occur when breakup values are high relative to current market values because the buying corporation can profit by operating or selling divisions independently.

**bull market**  A period of time in which securities prices are rising.

**buyback**  A company's repurchase of its own shares of stock.

**buying power**  The dollar value of securities that may be purchased in an investor's account without requiring additional cash to be deposited. This is the sum of cash in the account and the amount that can be borrowed on securities held.

**call**  (1) A contract that gives its owner the right but not the obligation to purchase 100 shares of the underlying security for a specified price until its expiration date. The seller of the call has the obligation to sell 100 shares of the security if the call owner chooses to exercise the contract. (2) The right of a bond issuer to repay prin-cipal before a bond's maturity date. The *call price* is the price that must be paid. The *call premium* is the excess of the call price over the bond's face value. *Call pro-tection* describes the period before the issuer can call the bond.

**capital gain**  The profit derived from selling an asset for more than its cost basis (usually the purchase price). Capital gains on assets held for over 1 year are con-sidered long term and are taxable at a 15 percent rate. Short-term capital gains on assets held for less than 1 year are taxable as ordinary income.

**capitalization**  (1) The market value of a corporation. It is computed by multi-plying the current share price by the number of outstanding shares. (2) The term *capitalization* also refers to the breakdown of financing used by a corporation.

**cash flow**  The amount of cash generated by a business, generally calculated as net income plus depreciation.

**certificate of deposit (CD)**  A deposit held by a financial institution with the promise to pay interest to the investor and repay the principal upon maturity. Withdrawing the principal before maturity results in a penalty.

**churning**  Excessive trading by a broker in order to generate commissions.

**closed-end mutual fund**  A mutual fund with a limited number of outstanding shares. Shares of closed-end funds trade on exchanges or in the over-the-counter market, as opposed to shares of open-end funds, which are purchased from and redeemed by the fund.

**collateral**  Assets pledged as security for a loan. Collateral may be sold to repay the loan if the borrower defaults.

**commission**   The fee charged by a brokerage firm for executing a transaction on behalf of a customer.

**commodity**   Industrial and agricultural goods that are traded in bulk, such as grains, metals, lumber, coffee, and beef.

**common stock**   The class of corporate ownership that is entitled to voting rights and the residual value of the corporation after all obligations have been paid.

**compound interest**   A method of computing interest in which interest earned in previous periods is added to the principal before computing the current period's interest.

**Consumer Price Index (CPI)**   A measure of inflation based on price increases for a basket of commonly purchased goods.

**contingent deferred sales charge (CDSC)**   A commission charged on some mutual funds and annuities at redemption. Schedules generally decline over time, beginning at 5 or 6 percent and falling by 1 percent each year that the asset is owned.

**contrarian investing**   A strategy of investing in securities that are out of favor with most investors under the theory that most investors overreact to bad news.

**convertible bond**   A bond that is convertible into the common stock of the issuing corporation at the choice of the bondholder. The *conversion ratio* is the number of shares that may be exchanged for each bond. The *conversion price* is the common stock price at which conversion is a breakeven proposition.

**correction**   A sharp, relatively short price decline in a security or an index that occurs in the middle of a general upward trend in prices.

**correlation**   A statistical measure of the tendency of two variables to move together. *High correlation* of securities classes means their prices tend to move together. *Low correlation* means they do not. *Negative correlation* means they move in opposite directions. The principal of diversification relies on investments with low or negative correlation.

**cost basis**   Also called *basis,* the amount that an investor paid for a security. The cost basis is subtracted from sales proceeds to determine a capital gain or loss.

**coupon**   The stated interest rate on a bond.

**current ratio**   A measure of the liquidity of a corporation and its ability to meet short-term obligations. The current ratio equals the current assets divided by the current liabilities. *Current assets* are those expected to be used within 1 year, and *current liabilities* are debts due within 1 year.

**current yield**   The annual interest or dividend paid on an investment divided by its current price.

**day order**   A securities order that expires at the end of the trading day if it is not executed.

**day trader**   A speculator who buys and sells securities for short-term profits. The term is derived from the fact that many day traders do not hold their positions overnight.

**debenture**  An unsecured bond, backed only by the financial strength of the issuing corporation.

**debt-to-equity ratio**  The amount of long-term debt owed by a corporation as a percentage of shareholder's equity. This measure is used to gauge risk due to high debt.

**default**  Failure to perform under the terms of a contract. Default may refer to the failure to pay interest or principal on a bond. Bonds termed *in default* are those on which interest is not being paid.

**deferred annuity**  An annuity purchased with the expectation that annuity payments will not begin until some time in the future.

**depreciation**  An accounting method that allows the expense of acquiring an asset to be considered over its depreciable life. Depreciation expense is a noncash charge.

**devaluation**  A reduction in the value of a currency relative to other currencies.

**diluted shares outstanding**  The total number of a corporation's shares of stock that would be outstanding if all convertible securities were converted into stock and all stock options were exercised.

**direct transfer**  The custodian-to-custodian transfer of the funds in an account in a qualified retirement plan. During the transfer, the account owner never has possession of the funds, and the event is not taxable.

**discount rate**  The interest rate that the Federal Reserve charges on loans to member banks. This is one of the Fed's policy-making tools.

**diversification**  The practice of investing in many different securities in order to limit the risk of any one security. To maximize risk reduction, diversification should occur across industries and asset classes.

**dividend**  Distribution of a portion of a corporation's profits to its shareholders. Most dividends are paid in cash, but they may also be paid in stock. Dividends are generally paid quarterly.

**dividend coverage ratio**  Earnings per share or cash flow per share divided by dividends per share. This ratio expresses the ability of a firm to continue paying its dividend.

**dividend payout ratio**  Dividends per share divided by earnings per share. This ratio is a measure of what portion of the EPS is paid out as a dividend.

**dividend reinvestment plan (DRIP)**  A plan offered by some corporations and some brokerage firms in which cash dividends are automatically reinvested in the issuing firm's stock. Commissions are generally low or nonexistent.

**dividend yield**  The most recent 12 months' dividend on a stock divided by its current share price.

**dollar cost averaging**  Investing an equal amount of money at regular intervals so that more shares are purchased when prices are low and fewer shares are purchased when prices are high.

**downtick**  A security transaction at a price lower than the previous transaction in the same security.

**earnings per share (EPS)** Net income divided by the number of outstanding shares. The EPS may be basic or diluted depending on the whether the basic or diluted number of shares is used in the formula.

**emerging markets** Countries in the midst of high economic growth. These countries are usually less developed than others, and they are sometimes emerging from communist rule.

**euro** The recently created currency of the European Union.

**exchange rate** The price of one country's currency in terms of another country's currency.

**ex-dividend date** The first trading day on which the seller of a security is entitled to an upcoming dividend. The opening price of the stock is generally lower by the amount of the dividend on this date.

**exercise price** The price at which a call owner has the right to buy the underlying security or the put owner has the right to sell.

**expense ratio** The ratio of a mutual fund's expenses to its assets expressed as a percent. Expenses include management fees, 12b-1 fees, and general operating expenses of the fund.

**face value** With reference to a bond, the value stated on a certificate, which is payable on maturity. A bond may be sold for more (a *premium*) or less (a *discount*) than face value during its life.

**Fannie Mae** The common name for Federal National Mortgage Association (FNMA) securities. They are backed by pools of mortgages, and the issuing institution passes through payments of principal and interest.

**Federal Deposit Insurance Corporation (FDIC)** A government agency that insures deposits at member banks. Each account that is separate by FDIC definition is insured for up to $100,000.

**federal funds rate** The rate of interest that banks charge each other on overnight loans. Also called the *fed funds rate*.

**Federal Reserve System** A system of 12 reserve banks with responsibility for overseeing the banking system. Through the Federal Open Market Committee (FOMC), the Federal Reserve establishes monetary policy and carries out open-market operations in order to reach desired policy goals. Also called the Fed.

**fixed annuity** An annuity whose returns are fixed and do not vary with the stock market or other investment returns.

**float** The number of shares of a company's stock that is held by the investing public. A low float often means higher price volatility.

**forward contract** A contract specifying that a currency, commodity, or security transaction is to take place on a specified date in the future.

**front-end load** A commission charged on the purchase of a security, usually a mutual fund.

**fundamental investing**   Investing strategies based on the viability of a company as an ongoing business and on its value relative to its stock price.

**futures contract**   A contract that binds both the buyer and the seller of a commodity or financial asset to a transaction at a later date, at an agreed-upon price. A futures contract is different from a forward contract in that the futures contract is easily marketable. The futures contract is different from an option in that only the seller is obligated.

**general obligation bond**   A municipal bond that is backed by the full faith and credit and taxing power of the municipality issuing it.

**Ginnie Mae**   Common name for the abbreviation GNMA, the initials of the Government National Mortgage Association. GNMA securities are pass-through pools of mortgages in which the issuer passes interest and principal payments through to the GNMA owner.

**going public**   The process of selling ownership of a privately held company to public investors in a stock offering.

**good 'til cancelled (GTC)**   A securities buy or sell order that remains in place until it is either executed or cancelled by the investor. Also called an *open order*.

**growth stock**   The stock of a company whose sales and earnings are growing at an exceptionally fast pace. Often growth stocks do not pay dividends because the issuing company needs to reinvest its profits in the business. Stockholders expect their returns to come from stock price appreciation.

**hedge**   A securities transaction designed to lessen the risk of an existing or planned position. For example, an investor might hedge a stock position by buying a put, which gives him or her the right to sell the stock at a specified price.

**immediate annuity**   An annuity set up to begin payments immediately after the initial deposit.

**income statement**   A financial statement that outlines a firm's revenues, expenses, and net income over a period of time. Also called a *profit and loss statement* (P&L).

**index**   A group of securities whose values, and sometimes income, are tracked in order to provide a benchmark for the performance of a particular market. Popular indices include the Dow Jones Industrial Average, the Standard & Poor's 500 Index, and the Nasdaq Composite Index.

**index fund**   A mutual fund that buys the securities listed in an index, or a representative sample of them, in order to mirror the performance of the index. Because these funds trade only when an index changes, transaction costs and turnover are very low.

**indication**   An expectation of the opening price of a stock, usually given in a range. Indications are usually given when a stock is expected to open at a price very different from its previous day's closing price, due to news announced after the close.

**Individual Retirement Account (IRA)**   A retirement account to which individuals can contribute the lesser of $3000 per year or their earned income (2003 rules). Nonworking spouses can also contribute if a working spouse's earnings exceed their combined contributions. Contributions may be tax deductible, depending on income levels and the availability of an employer-sponsored retirement plan. Investments in an IRA grow tax deferred until withdrawn, at which time they are taxable as ordinary income.

**inflation**   A general increase in the prices of goods and services. The level of inflation is often measured by changes in the Consumer Price Index.

**initial public offering (IPO)**   The first public sale of a company's stock.

**inside information**   Information about a company that is not available to the public but is known by the officers and directors of a company, who are called *insiders*. It is illegal to trade in a company's stock based on inside information.

**institutional ownership**   The percentage of a stock's outstanding shares that is owned by mutual funds, pension funds, large money managers, and the like.

**interest**   Payment for the use of borrowed money.

**interim report**   A financial statement issued by a company between annual reports. Interim reports are generally unaudited and not as comprehensive as annual reports.

**in-the-money option**   A call option whose strike price is below the market price of the underlying security, or a put option whose strike price is above the market price of the underlying security.

**intrinsic value**   (1) The value of a stock calculated using quantifiable factors such as assets, earnings, and dividends. (2) The value of an option if it were immediately exercised. For a call, the intrinsic value equals the market price minus the strike price. For a put, the intrinsic value equals the strike price minus the market price.

**inverted yield curve**   A yield curve in which short-term interest rates are higher than long-term interest rates.

**junk bond**   Any bond whose rating by an agency such as Standard & Poor's, Moody's, or Fitch is lower than BBB or Baa. Such a rating denotes high risk; accordingly, such a bond's expected yield to maturity is high.

**letter of intent (LOI)**   An agreement with a mutual fund company to invest a certain amount over a specified time period in order to qualify for a reduced sales charge.

**leverage**   (1) An investment method that increases potential returns by requiring small amounts of capital to be invested. Leverage methods include borrowing funds (*margin*) to purchase securities and buying options or futures whose cost is relatively small in relationship to the underlying investment controlled by the contract. (2) The relative amount of debt carried by a corporation. Higher leverage may be a sign of higher risk.

**limit order** A securities buy or sell order with a limit placed on the buy or sell price that the investor is willing to accept.

**liquidity** The ability to sell an investment without incurring a loss. Investments with penalties for early withdrawal are not liquid. Stocks that trade with very small volume may not be liquid because a large order to sell can cause the price to drop.

**load** The commission charged by brokers or agents when they make mutual fund or annuity transactions.

**lockup** The period of time, usually 6 months, after an initial public offering during which certain insiders may not sell their stock.

**long** When you own a security, you are said to be "long" the security.

**long bond** The 30-year U.S. Treasury bond.

**lump-sum distribution** A distribution from a retirement plan, such as a 401(k), that is paid as one lump sum rather than as a series of payments.

**margin** Borrowed money used to buy securities. The *initial margin requirement* is the minimum amount that must be deposited for a transaction. *Maintenance margin* is the minimum percentage of equity that must be maintained in the account. A *margin call* is a brokerage firm's request that a customer deposit more money or securities in order to bring the account to maintenance margin levels. You may not trade on margin in a retirement account.

**market maker** An individual or firm that makes a market in a particular security by buying from sellers and selling to buyers. Market makers profit from the *spread*, or difference between the price at which they buy and sell to the public.

**market order** An order to buy or sell a security at the best price currently available.

**market timing** An investment strategy in which investors move in and out of a security or all securities frequently, on the basis of technical, economic, or interest rate indicators.

**markup** A commission that is charged as part of the price of an investment. The dealer or broker buys a security at wholesale and sells it at retail. The difference is the commission or markup. Bonds are often sold with a markup.

**money market deposit account** An interest-bearing account at a bank, savings and loan, or credit union. There are limitations on the number of transactions that may take place in these accounts.

**money market mutual fund** A mutual fund invested in short-term interest-bearing securities. Shares are priced at $1 each, and interest rates paid fluctuate.

**municipal bond** A bond issued by a city, state, or other government body besides the U.S. government or its agencies. Interest on municipal bonds is not federally taxable, and it is generally not taxable at the state and local levels for investors who live in the municipality. Never buy municipal bonds in a retirement account that already enjoys tax advantages.

**mutual fund**   An investment company that operates a portfolio of securities and sells shares of the portfolio to investors. Advantages of investing in mutual funds include diversification, professional management, liquidity, and small minimum investments.

**National Association of Securities Dealers (NASD)**   The self-governing body of brokers and dealers of securities. Violation of NASD rules can result in an individual broker or firm being fined, censured, or expelled from the industry.

**National Association of Securities Dealers Automated Quotation System (NASDAQ or Nasdaq)**   A computerized system that displays quotes and transactions for securities traded over the counter.

**net asset value (NAV)**   The per-share value of a mutual fund computed by taking the closing market value of all securities in the portfolio and dividing it by the number of outstanding shares. The NAV of a mutual fund will change daily as the values of the securities held in its portfolio change.

**net income**   The profit of a business, computed by subtracting expenses from revenues.

**new issue**   A stock that has recently completed its initial public offering.

**New York Stock Exchange (NYSE)**   The oldest and largest organized stock exchange in the United States.

**nifty fifty**   Fifty large growth stocks that were investor favorites during the early 1970s. In a bubble that later crashed, investors seemed willing to pay almost any price for these companies. These stocks are often compared to the Internet stocks of the late 1990s.

**no-load fund**   A mutual fund that does not charge a commission for purchasing or redeeming shares. These funds still charge a management fee and may charge an additional annual fee, called a *12b-1*.

**nominal interest rate**   (1) The rate of interest stated on the face of a security. The nominal rate can differ from the actual rate of interest received due to compounding or purchasing the investment at a price other than face value. (2) The stated interest rate on an investment as opposed to the real interest rate. The nominal interest rate minus the inflation rate equals the real interest rate.

**not held**   An instruction on a purchase or sale order for the broker to use personal judgment in executing the order.

**odd lot**   A stock trade for fewer than 100 shares. Odd-lot theory says that investors who trade in odd lots are unsophisticated so odd-lot volume is a contrarian indicator. When odd-lot volume is up, you should sell, and when odd-lot volume is down, you should buy.

**odd-lot tender**   A tender offer by a company for holders of fewer than 100 shares to sell their shares back to the firm. Odd-lot tenders are designed to reduce the number of small shareholders and the accompanying cost of issuing dividend checks and annual reports. These offers are beneficial to the shareholders who do not wish to incur a commission for selling a few shares. These tenders are common after a spinoff that may result in many odd-lot shareholders.

**offer price**   The best price at which other investors or market makers are willing to sell. Also called *offer, asked price*, or *ask*.

**open-end mutual fund**   A mutual fund that sells new shares to investors daily and redeems any shares that investors want to sell. Redemptions occur at net asset value (NAV), and sales to investors occur either at NAV or NAV plus a commission. Most mutual funds are open-end. The opposite is a closed-end mutual fund that trades on the stock exchange.

**open interest**   The number of options or futures contracts in existence for a particular security. *High open interest* means there is more active trading and liquidity for a given stock.

**open order**   A securities order that is good until executed or cancelled by the investor. Also called a *good-'til-cancelled* (GTC) *order*.

**option**   A security that gives its holder the right but not the obligation to buy (*call option*) or sell (*put option*) 100 shares of an underlying security at a designated price through its expiration date.

**option premium**   The market price of an option.

**original-issue discount (OID)**   The difference between the face value of a bond and the price at which it was originally sold or issued. A common example of a bond with an OID is a zero coupon bond. Each year a portion of the OID is considered income because discounted bonds rise in value as they near maturity, which is their full face amount.

**out-of-the-money option**   A put option whose strike price is below the market price of the underlying security, or a call option whose strike price is above the market price of the underlying security. An out-of-the-money option has no intrinsic value.

**oversubscribed**   An initial public offering for which there are more orders to buy shares than shares available for sale.

**over the counter (OTC)**   Securities that are not listed on an exchange but rather are traded in the OTC market that exists over telephone lines or computer networks.

**paid in capital**   The amount of capital generated in a stock offering.

**paper gain or loss**   The amount of gain or loss that would be realized if an investor chose to sell an investment. Also called *unrealized gain* or *loss*.

**par value**   The face value of a bond; the amount it will pay on maturity and the amount on which interest is calculated. For a common stock, par value is an arbitrary amount, which is of no real significance.

**penny stock**  A low-priced stock, usually under $5 per share. Penny stocks are considered very risky because they are often issued by new unproven companies, their markets may be very illiquid, and they are easily manipulated.

**point**  A $1 change in a stock's price or a 1 percent ($10) change in a bond's price.

**positive yield curve**  A yield curve in which short-term interest rates are lower than long-term interest rates.

**preferred stock**  A stock that has preference over common stock in the payment of dividends and in liquidation of the company. Unless designated as *participating*, preferred stock dividends do not change as a firm's earnings grow. *Cumulative preferred stockholders* must be paid all missed dividends before common stockholders are paid any dividends.

**price-earnings growth ratio (PEG)**  The ratio of a stock's price-to-earnings ratio (P/E) to its earnings per share growth rate (EPS). A PEG near 1 is said to be a fair value, while much over 1 indicates an overvalued stock and much under 1, an undervalued stock.

**price-earnings ratio (P/E)**  The current market price of a stock divided by its most recent 12 months' earnings per share (EPS). The P/E ratio is a valuation ratio designed to indicate whether a stock is too richly or too cheaply priced given its EPS.

**prime rate**  The interest rate that banks charge to lend to their most creditworthy customers.

**privately held company**  A business whose stock is not traded publicly.

**program trading**  Sophisticated, computer-driven arbitrage trading strategies that involve taking simultaneous but opposite positions in stock index futures and their respective lists of stocks. Profits are made on market inefficiencies. Due to the sheer volume of transactions (an index may have 100 or 500 stocks), program trading may add to market volatility, though proponents say it increases market efficiency because trades are made only when markets are out of balance.

**proxy**  A shareholder's assignment of the right-to-vote shares at a shareholders' meeting. Proxies are mailed to shareholders before annual meetings since most shareholders are unable to attend.

**publicly held company**  A company whose stock is traded on public markets.

**put**  A contract that gives its owner the right, but not the obligation, to sell 100 shares of the underlying security for a specified price until its expiration date. The seller of the put has the obligation to buy 100 shares of the security if the put owner chooses to exercise the contract.

**quick ratio**  A liquidity measure for a firm that takes current assets less inventory and divides this by current liabilities. A higher ratio implies an ability to meet short-term obligations. Also called an *acid-test ratio*.

**quiet period**  The period of time preceding an initial public offering when the stock issue is in registration and the company may not make any promotional statements.

**real estate investment trust (REIT)**   An investment company that purchases real estate property or real estate loans. Shares of the company are sold to investors and traded as a stock.

**real interest rate**   The nominal or stated rate on an investment less the rate of inflation. The real interest rate is the return after taking into account the loss of purchasing power from inflation. In times of high inflation, the real interest rate on an investment may be negative.

**recession**   A period of declining growth in output, formally defined as 6 successive months of slowing growth in the Gross Domestic Product (GDP).

**record date**   The date on which all owners of a security are entitled to receive an upcoming dividend.

**red herring**   The name for a preliminary prospectus given to potential investors in an initial public offering before the registration has been approved by the SEC.

**registered securities**   Securities held in certificate form that are registered with the company as to their ownership.

**resistance level**   The price at which a security encounters selling pressure, causing it to repeatedly move up to, but not pass, the price level.

**return on assets (ROA)**   The ratio of a company's profit to its total assets. This is a measure of how much profit a firm makes given the amount of assets it has available.

**return on equity (ROE)**   The ratio of profit to stockholders' equity. This is a measure of the efficiency of a firm's operations. Note that high levels of debt relative to equity can inflate the ROE, making a firm appear financially strong when it is the opposite.

**revenue bond**   A municipal bond associated with a particular project, such as an airport or toll bridge, whose revenues will support payment of interest and repayment of principal. Revenue bonds are considered more risky than general obligation bonds, which are supported by the taxing authority of the municipality.

**reverse stock split**   A method of reducing the number of shares of stock a company has outstanding in order to increase the stock's price. For example, a stock undergoing a 1-for-10 reverse split would have its number of outstanding shares divided by 10 and its share price multiplied by 10.

**rollover**   The process of withdrawing funds from a qualified retirement plan, such as an IRA or 401(k), taking possession of the funds, and then depositing them into the same or another qualified retirement plan. To avoid income taxes and any applicable penalties, a rollover must be accomplished within 60 days. An employer is required to withhold 20 percent of the distribution from a qualified employer retirement plan for potential taxes and penalties.

**Roth IRA**   An individual retirement account in which contributions are never tax deductible but withdrawals are tax exempt if certain conditions are met. Income limits apply for eligibility to contribute to a Roth IRA.

**round lot**   The normal trading unit for a security. A round lot for stock is 100 shares. For bonds, it may be 10 or 100 bonds, depending on the market.

**Sallie Mae (SLMA)**   The Student Loan Marketing Association, called Sallie Mae, is a government-chartered corporation that makes a secondary market in government-guaranteed student loans. Sallie Mae bonds are sold to investors as a means to purchase student loans from financial institutions.

**savings bond**   A bond issued by the U.S. government in small denominations. Series EE savings bonds are issued at a 50 percent discount to their face value. Series HH bonds pay interest semiannually. Interest on savings bonds is not taxable at the state or local level. They can be purchased from most banks or from offices of the Federal Reserve.

**Securities and Exchange Commission (SEC)**   The federal agency that oversees securities trading and administers U.S. securities laws.

**Securities Investor Protection Corporation (SIPC)**   Similar in concept to the FDIC, the SIPC covers customers of brokerage firms in the event of fraud or insolvency. Up to $500,000 in securities is covered per account, $100,000 of which can be cash. For SIPC purposes, a money market mutual fund is considered a security.

**Separate Trading of Registered Interest and Principal on Securities (STRIPS)**   Zero coupon U.S. Treasury bonds created by separating the interest and principal portions of Treasury bonds.

**settlement date**   The date on which a buyer must present cash to pay for a security and the seller must present the security sold. The standard time frame between a stock transaction and its settlement date is 3 business days. Options trade with next-day settlement, and bonds can be settled on the next day or within the standard time frame of 3 business days.

**short interest**   The number of shares of a stock that have been sold short. High short interest can be a bullish sign because it indicates pent-up demand for the security when short sellers buy in order to replace the shares they borrowed.

**short interest ratio**   A stock's short interest divided by its average daily trading volume.

**short sale**   An investment strategy with which profits are made from falling stock prices. Short selling involves an investor's selling stock that he or she does not own. In order to sell stock, the investor must borrow shares so that the shares may be delivered to the buyer. Eventually the position must be covered because the borrowed shares must be returned to the lender. The short seller's plan is to buy the shares back at a price lower than he or she sold them for. The risk in short selling is very high since there is no limit to how far the stock's price can rise. You may not sell short in a retirement account.

**short squeeze**   Something of a self-fulfilling prophecy in which a rising stock price pressures those who have sold short to buy in order to limit their losses. The demand created by short sellers who are trying to cover their positions causes additional price increases, which in turn pressures the remaining short sellers even more.

**single premium deferred annuity (SPDA)**   A deferred annuity purchased with a lump-sum payment. The amount deposited grows tax deferred until it is withdrawn.

**spinoff**   The distribution to a company's shareholders of the stock of one of the company's subsidiaries. A spinoff reduces an investor's basis in the parent company's shares by the amount designated for the basis of the spinoff. No taxes are due until shares are sold.

**spot rate**   The cash price of a currency, metal, or other commodity.

**spread**   (1) The difference between the bid and asked prices of a security. (2) An investing strategy using options or futures contracts such that opposite put and call positions are taken with differences in expiration dates or exercise prices.

**stock power**   A form similar to the back of a stock certificate that can be completed in order to transfer the certificate. A stock power can be sent separately through the mail in order to avoid sending a signed stock certificate, which is negotiable.

**stock split**   A strategy a company uses by which it increases the number of shares of its outstanding stock and thereby decreases the price per share. A split is usually announced when a company wants to make its stock more affordable since the stock's price, earnings, dividends, and any other per-share data are decreased proportionately. For example, a 2-for-1 split would double the number of outstanding shares but cut the stock price in half. Because everything is adjusted, there is no intrinsic value to a stock split.

**stop-limit order**   Similar to a stop order, except that a limit price is set. When the designated price is reached, the order becomes a limit order rather than a market order. There is no guarantee that an order will be executed if the market price *gaps through* (trades above and below, but not at) the limit price.

**stop order**   An order that becomes a market order when the stop price is reached. A buy stop order becomes a market order when the stock trades at or above the designated price. A *sell stop order* becomes a market order when the stock trades at or below the designated price. A stop order does not guarantee execution at the stop price.

**straddle**   An options strategy in which the investor buys a put and a call on a security. The investor profits if the security is very volatile. In a short straddle, the investor sells both a put and a call and profits if the security is not volatile.

**street name**   The term for securities held at a brokerage firm in a customer's account. Holding securities *in street name* alleviates the problem of keeping them in a safe deposit box and delivering them to the broker after a sale. Dividends and interest on securities held in street name are paid into the brokerage account on the payable date.

**strike price**   The price at which an option or futures contract may be exercised.

**support level**   The price at which a security encounters considerable buying activity, resulting in the security's price falling to this point but not going below it.

**taxable equivalent yield (TEY)**   A yield calculation used to compare tax-exempt securities such as municipal bonds to taxable securities. The TEY is computed by dividing the tax-exempt yield by the investor's federal and/or state tax rates. The

TEY shows how much a taxable investment would have to yield in order to provide the same after-tax return as the tax-exempt investment.

**tax deferred**   An investment on which taxes due are paid at a later date. Examples include 401(k) plans, IRAs, and annuities. Taxes are not due on income and capital gains from the investment in a tax-deferred account until the funds are withdrawn.

**tax-efficient fund**   A mutual fund whose investment strategy is designed to minimize the investor's taxes. The strategy entails buying securities with little or no interest or dividends and trading infrequently so as to minimize the realization of capital gains.

**tax exempt**   An investment whose interest payments are not taxable at a particular level. For example, municipal bonds are not taxable by the federal government. Most states do not tax investors who reside in the state in which a bond was issued.

**technical investing**   Investing strategy that tracks changes in stock prices and volume over time, and theoretically enables investors to predict and capitalize on future stock price movements.

**tender offer**   An offer to buy some or all of a corporation's stock. The offer may be made by another company that wishes to perform a takeover, or it may be made by the company itself. See **odd-lot tender**.

**thinly traded security**   A security that is not actively traded. A small number of bids and offers means that large trades may move the market price.

**ticker symbol**   The initials that designate a stock for trading purposes. The ticker symbols for NYSE- and AMEX-listed stocks have three or fewer letters. For example, the symbol for AT&T is T. Ticker symbols for Nasdaq stocks have four or more letters. For example, the symbol for Sun Microsystems is SUNW. A stock's ticker symbol is not necessarily the same abbreviation used in the newspaper.

**time value**   The amount by which an option's price exceeds its intrinsic value. For an out-of-the-money option, the entire premium represents time value.

**trade date**   The date on which a transaction takes place.

**transfer agent**   The agent of a corporation that is responsible for keeping stock and bond ownership records, sending dividend and interest payments, and transferring stock and bond certificates. Transfer agents are usually banks.

**Treasury bills, notes, and bonds**   Debt issued by the U.S. government. Bills mature in 1 year or less and are issued at a discount. Notes have maturities between 1 and 5 years, and bonds mature in as many as 30 years.

**treasury stock**   Stock that a corporation has issued, subsequently repurchased, and now holds in its treasury. It may be eventually reissued or retired. Dividends are not paid on treasury stock, and the number of these shares is not included in the number of outstanding shares used for computing per-share data such as earnings per share.

**triple tax exempt**   The description of a municipal bond that is free of federal, state, and local income taxes for investors living within the bond-issuing municipality.

**Uniform Gift to Minors Act (UGMA); Uniform Transfers to Minors Act (UTMA)** An act whose name differs by state but that allows the establishment of investment accounts for minors. An adult, who may or may not be the donor, must act as custodian. Gifts are irrevocable and become the property of the child at the age of majority. The first $750 of income earned in a custodial account is not taxable. Depending on the age of the child and the amount of the income, additional income may be taxed at the donor's rate or the child's rate.

**unit investment trust (UIT)** A portfolio of investments sold in shares to investors. UITs differ from mutual funds in that they are not actively managed. The investments held generally do not change over the life of the trust.

**unrealized gain or loss** The amount of gain or loss that would be realized if the investor chose to sell an investment. Also called a *paper gain* or *loss*.

**uptick** A transaction whose price is greater than the one immediately preceding it.

**variable annuity** An annuity whose payments depend on the performance of securities in investment accounts.

**volume** The number of shares or face value of securities traded over a particular period, usually 1 trading day.

**warrant** A security that conveys the right to purchase a specified number of shares of stock at a particular price. Warrants are often issued with another security such as a stock or bond, but they generally trade separately after their issuance. They usually have an expiration date.

**wash sale** Selling a stock in order to take a tax loss and then purchasing the same stock or a substantially similar security (for example, a convertible bond) within 30 days before or after the sale. In this case the loss is not tax deductible.

**when issued (WI)** A security that has not yet been issued. Trading when-issued stocks often occurs between the announcement of a split and the payment date of the split.

**window dressing** The practice by a portfolio manager of selling losing stocks and buying stocks that have performed well near the end of a quarter, when portfolio reports are made public. This can create the appearance of successful management.

**yield** The return on an investment, which can be calculated in many different ways. See **current yield, dividend yield, yield to call (YTC)**, and **yield to maturity (YTM)**.

**yield curve** A graph of yields on the same security (usually U.S. Treasuries) at different maturities.

**yield to call (YTC)** The yield on a bond that is callable before it matures. This yield calculation combines interest received with any capital gain or loss on the difference between the purchase price and the first call price.

**yield to maturity (YTM)**   The yield on a bond that is held to maturity. This yield calculation combines interest received with any capital gain or loss on the difference between the purchase price and the face value received at maturity.

**zero coupon bond**   A bond that does not make interest payments to the bondholder. Zero coupon bonds are sold at a discount from their face value. The difference between the purchase price and the maturity value constitutes interest. Zero coupon bonds are a popular fixed-income investment for retirement accounts because they may be purchased with a small amount of money and their maturity value is predictable.

# INDEX

## ABOUT THE AUTHORS

**Ellie Williams** and **Diane Pearl** are popular personal finance writers and former partners in MONEYWISE, a personal finance training and education firm. They also have extensive professional experience in both the investment and banking industries.